A Devotional Journey Through Exodus

Sharon M. Wood

A Devotional Journey Through Exodus

Edited by Kathleen Tudor

First Edition

Illumina Publishing
P.O. Box 2643, Friday Harbor, WA 98250

Cover design and publishing services by W. Bruce Conway

Printed in the U.S.A. on recycled paper

ISBN: 978-1-4507-6554-1

Library of Congress Control Number available from publisher upon request

DEDICATION FOR THE DEVOTIONAL

Some may believe "It takes a village to raise a child", but I know for certain it took an island of dear sisters in Christ to finally get this book on its way—to be specific, those who fellowship with me at Orcas Island Community Church. I would name them by name, but my greatest fear is that I would leave someone's name off the list. Three people have consistently helped me and prayed for me. To anyone who knows me, one of my primary supporters would be my husband Dick. He is my greatest critic and also my dearest friend, always giving me enough rope to hang myself and yet always saving me before I do something foolish. To my surprise and great joy, when Dick finished the manuscript he said: "Sharon, this is truly wonderful. This has to be published! I know you meant it for people outside of our family, but it is a gift to our family. Through it our children and their children will know the faith of their Mother and Grandmother!" Thank you Dick.

The second person, who worked tirelessly behind the scenes, was Kathleen Tudor. This devotional is the product of her prayers for me and her artful and devoted editing. She is one of my many very talented and generous island Christian friends. Kathleen was the first to do the study in its entirety. Then tirelessly she edited it with me over a period of three years. When I got frustrated with my limited computer skills (which was so often I expected her to run for the hills at any time) she stood by me and talked me off all the buildings I had considered jumping off of. Then, she took all of her skills and formatted it for me. Most important to me, she believed in the message of this book from its very beginning and she confidently said as Dick did, "This must be published!" Thank you Kathleen.

God also gave me a very important partner in this book. She will probably have no idea how greatly she has given me confidence and courage to pursue this devotional. Her name is Rosa Montgomery and by the time this book goes to press she will be 93 years young. This year, after 27 years, she has retired from teaching her weekly Bible study because of limited eye- sight and a bout with illness that has robbed her, we pray momentarily, of her generally good health. Rosa is the sister of Ruth Graham. Everyone knows that name, but here on island and in our church Rosa is a cornerstone in the lives of everyone she has touched with the gospel of Jesus Christ. She was one of the first people to read the study as I considered publishing it. After reading the first few days of the devotional she said, "I like it and I think you should publish it. "But", she said," I want you to clearly state, with confidence, 'I believe' when you share your faith. You have been a Christian for over thirty years and you are sharing the truth of the gospel and of your faith." As is stated in the introduction I am not a theologian, but "I believe" the words of the gospel and because of Rosa I confidently published this devotional. Thank you Rosa.

A Devotional Journey through Exodus

Table of Contents

INTRODUCTION

People all over the world, everyday, open their Bibles and are blessed with God's participation in their lives. So, before you begin to read *A Devotional Journey through Exodus,* you need to know that I am not an accomplished theologian. I am a lay person. Over the years I have become thoroughly convinced that we do not need to be Bible scholars, we simply need to read His word and let Him speak to us personally each day. My experience in attending over thirty years of Bible studies is that you can expect to be blessed by the insights of other people who have simply taken the time to read their Bibles.

This is not an in depth study of Exodus, I purposely read no other commentaries or studies on the book. At this time I also want to make it perfectly clear that it isn't that what I have to say is so earthshaking and monumental-- it is God who is earthshaking and monumental in what He has to say to us. My daily devotional with God gave me His insights for my day through the book of Exodus. It is my prayer that this simple devotional will be a sharing of what God spoke to me on the day I studied the scripture. Perhaps my essay will only be a jumping off place where we can come together as sisters and brothers in Christ and reason together and then again God may take you to an altogether different place on this day as we grow in the faith through His word.

My journey through Exodus began in the summer of 1997 when my husband Dick retired and we became almost full-time RVers. I knew it would be a great adventure to travel the United States and Canada and see what we could see. The only thing which was a bit of a stumbling block for me personally was that for well over twenty years I had always been involved in a weekly women's Bible study of some kind or another. I was used to being blessed by the insights of other women as in a group we shared our own personal encounters with God that week. Perhaps I'm a little ashamed to admit it, but I needed that group accountability to make me really concentrate on the scriptures. It was clear to me that I would not have that accountability traveling nor would I have a structured study program.

I had never studied the book of Exodus from beginning to end, so I decided that it would be the book I'd study for my own personal devotional needs. It was a historical book in nature and after all, I reasoned, I wasn't taking on the book of Revelations, so I felt pretty safe venturing out on this journey. Besides, I thought, Exodus was a book about a journey and I was certainly on a journey in my new season of life. I would no longer be accountable to a group of women it was just going to be me and my accountability to God on this journey.

I became a born again Christian when I was 31, while attending Calvary Chapel of Costa Mesa in the early 70's. It was a strong foundational structure in inductive Bible study and the teaching style was most often expository and extortive in nature. Within the women's ministry I eventually became a group leader and then had the opportunity to teach at times. When the teaching times came I discovered that God always had something to impress upon my heart when I studied with the desire to share that knowledge with others. To my amazement He gave me the words and conviction to share simple and true messages with my listeners if I simply got out of His way and let Him speak through me.

To get the most out of my devotional studies I have always journaled. Writing my prayers and observations has always allowed me to stay focused and not be distracted during my prayer and study time. So, I decided while we were traveling that I would write a small essay to God each day about the verses of scripture I had read. Then, as always I would pray in writing about that insight on a personal level—in essence that became what God had shown me about my life that day.

I am not a computer person. My devotional was written over a period of months in a simple three holed lined spiral notebook. It didn't matter where I was. I was always equipped to study. I didn't set out to write a devotional for other people, but after a few weeks it became clear that God was doing a work that might—heavy on the might—be worth sharing. So, the format of reading a few verses in Exodus and then finding a few scriptures from God's Promises for Your Every Need which supported the essay that God had impressed upon my heart that day became the beginning ritual of each morning.

The essay that followed was hypothetically what I would have shared with others about what I had learned that day if I had been called on to share. When I began to transcribe my notebook onto the computer I felt impressed to add a couple of questions at the end of each essay so the reader could ask themselves privately a few questions or participate in a group discussion if the devotional was used that way.

My prayer is that we will listen for His voice as we search the scriptures together. I pray that you will not be foolish and decide only to read my essay each day. God's Word is what you want to read each day and His words are what you need. My essay will hopefully be thought provoking, but your perspective and God's personal work in your life through these scriptures will only be milk and not meat if you fail to read the scriptures each day for yourself. This is why the scripture references are not written out for you in the devotional—you will need to look them up and read them.

Prayerfully, by not transcribing the supporting scripture it will be my subtle way of making the Bible your primary reference book for responding to the circumstances in your life. Maybe you will never even read the essay. Maybe God will speak to you long before I do, but my essays are at least a beginning point. The same is true of my short prayer following each essay--it is a beginning place to personalize what God wants you to place before Him in your communication with Him. After all, we were created in His image for His pleasure and His pleasure in us is heightened like the true Father He is when we come to Him in prayer.

DAY 1

NOW A NEW KING AROSE OVER EGYPT, WHO DID NOT KNOW JOSEPH – EXODUS 1:8

READINGS FOR TODAY – EXODUS 1:1-12 AND PSALMS 18:20-24

Man has such a small view of the world, only God has the complete view. A non-believer functions primarily in the present and is completely consumed by his self-centeredness. The past is of little concern to the self-centered man, unless it might catch up to him at an inopportune time, and he is really only interested in the present and his personal plans for the future. In my opinion that is what the sin nature of the natural man really is—self-centeredness. Man, for the most part, believes the world revolves around him, that he is in charge of his life and that he can plan his future.

As Christians we are to be God-centered and we value the past because God can speak to us about the present through the past. The Bible is the tool that God uses to speak to us and through it we know God is in control of everything and that by submitting to Him and His will for our lives we will be abundantly blessed. By the time Exodus is written Joseph is not even in the memory of the Egyptians. The Hebrew slave who once saved Egypt from starvation holds no particular place in the memory of the new king over Egypt. Pharaoh sees only that the "sons of Israel are more and mightier than we in number." Pharaoh is the typical non-believer.

We would be wise to remember that all we try to say, do or master is only for a fleeting time in man's memory. Once we are gone from the face of the earth we are generally replaced or forgotten. To strive to be in God's memory is much more profitable than to be in man's memory. Giving God the glory for our accomplishments in life says to others who God is and it is an affirmation to us personally of the power of God working in us.

He created us with our talents and He has allowed us to be successful in using them. When it comes to weighing the "importance" of who we are we can hold fast to the truth that we are the blessed servants of God. We can rest in the knowledge that God is honored and blessed because we have been of righteous service to His kingdom and because of that we can dwell in peace.

God is always in control of the past and the future. He is our travel agent. The new pharaoh decided to "deal wisely with them." No matter what Egypt did to the children of God they "multiplied and spread out more." The purpose and the plan for Israelites was established with Abraham when God identified them as His people. God produced in the hearts of the Egyptians "a dread of the sons of Israel" as a key element in separating them from the Egyptians and eventually causing them to become His people and move out into their own country.

Pharaoh chose to ignore the God of the Israelites because he was self-sufficient and self-centered. He considered himself to be in charge of his life and the lives of his subjects. By being in charge of his life he underestimated the power of God and he chose his wisdom over God's. As believers, no matter what the prevailing intellectual mores are, we prefer God's wisdom over man's limited wisdom. God's perspective and God's way of doing things is often discounted by the world and in some instances it is even dreaded. God's way is irritatingly simple to the world. What is even more irritating to the world is that it is perfect wisdom and it gets equally perfect results. Man seeks the easy way out; God seeks the best way out!

Life is easier to live when we place God on the throne of our lives. He is the author and creator of life. He controls everything. We do not create anything. Our job is simply to respond by living life as He commands in His Word. Everything has a purpose in our lives and everything is used by God for specific purposes whether we give Him permission or not. Pharaoh believed he was in charge. He meddled in the order of God's providence to no avail. Everything he attempted to orchestrate produced just the opposite of what he sought to accomplish.

Like Moses and the Israelites we have no easy way to play out our place in God's plan for our lives, but we have the assurance that we are His and He is in control. Even if the world thinks the future looks bad, we know God has a perfect plan for the future. We expect a more glorious and wonderful future than any man can imagine because He has promised it to us. Our salvation is at hand every day and I believe we must seek God and allow Him to fulfill His plan of salvation in us each and every day.

A BEGINNING PLACE FOR PRAYER TODAY:

Lord, You are in charge of the future. You know what today will hold for me. Please be in the middle of all my dealings today. Let me see the people and events of this day as a wonderful gift. Help me to feel and see the opportunities open to me to serve You and help others learn to trust You. Help me not to dread the future. I want to be in Your memory, not in man's. Let the things I do and say be a blessing to You, Father.

DISCUSSION QUESTIONS FOR TODAY:

1. Can I think of a time in my life when I forced my way and the results were disastrous?

2. What are my goals today for pleasing God with my life?

DAY 2

SO THE EGYPTIANS MADE THE CHILDREN OF ISRAEL SERVE WITH RIGOR – EXODUS 1:13

READING FOR TODAY – EXODUS 1: 13-17 AND MATTHEW 6: 25-34.

When God wants our full attention He usually has to put us into the harsh places of life. These oppressive situations are not crosses; they are the "rain that falls on the just and unjust." (Matthew 5: 45) Hard as it may seem at the time, these events are part of living life. God longs to be the center of our lives.

Wonderful things can happen when we pray. The power of the Holy Spirit is unleashed in us. We no longer work in our own strength. We no longer look for our plans to solve or give comfort. In times of distress, we look to Him and see Him work. Being reminded of Who is all powerful we are renewed in our faith and in our childlike faith we marvel at how well He can take care of us if we let Him.

No matter what God allows in our lives we can be confident that it has a purpose if it is turned over to Him. Romans 8:28a is a life verse for many people: "All things work together for good to those who love God." It only takes a few events in our lives to convince us of this truth. In the middle of a trial it is easy to throw up our hands, be discouraged and see no purpose, but on the other side of the unexpected event we are saying; "Oh, yes, now I see!"

Pharaoh's harsh treatment brought the people of Israel together and made them stronger than any other events could have. They understood the hardship of their brothers, they looked closer at their own lives and they drew on the knowledge that they had a God to call upon and to follow. The midwives knew that murder was against God's commandments. Because of God's commandment they did not kill the male children of Israel as Pharaoh commanded. God's commandment was honored and the Israelites grew in number and in unity as a people. He needed these people to consider themselves "set apart" from the world they lived in. Hardship produced that separation and dependence upon God.

What struggles have I passed through or what struggle am I in the middle of today? Who is my strength and my focus? It cannot be me, for I will fail in my own strength. Thank Him for the hardship and look hopefully for its blessing. The world sees only the hardship, but the believer will see the blessings and give God His proper praise for His love and compassion in his life.

A BEGINNING PLACE FOR PRAYER TODAY:

Thank You, Father, for the troubles of today and the ones of the past, You are refining me and making me fit for service to others. Thank You for all your blessings. You are the strength of my life and the horn of my salvation and I will praise Your mighty name and step out of the way. Help me not to hinder Your will for my life. Teach me to accept everything from Your hand. Thank You, Father.

DISCUSSION QUESTIONS FOR TODAY:

1. What are the difficulties I face today?

2. What problems have become blessings because I was forced to let God work them through?

DAY 3

AND SO IT WAS BECAUSE THE MIDWIVES FEARED GOD THAT HE PROVIDED HOUSEHOLDS FOR THEM. – EXODUS 1: 21

READING FOR TODAY – EXODUS 1:18-22, PSALM 1:3 AND I CORINTHIANS 1:18-20

One of God's greatest strengths is that He constantly "confounds the wise." (I Corinthians 1: 18-20) We think we know how things will work out. We plan, we orchestrate, we worry and we fuss about the decisions concerning our lives. But ….God already knows the outcome if we'll just commit the whole dilemma to Him.

When the midwives decided to disobey Pharaoh, we would automatically expect them to suffer the consequences of that choice. But, God, as usual, is in control, not Pharaoh. The midwives prosper and are provided for by God; simply because they feared and obeyed His commandments. Psalm 1 is the promise of God: If you will honor me I (God) will prosper you.

There is no way to have lasting spiritual prosperity unless God is honored. Sin can give us pleasure for a moment, treachery or misdeeds can gain us wealth and position, but these cannot give us peace or eternal life. When the Lord uses the descriptive words: "He provided households for them", we get a complete picture of safety and security. It is similar to the third verse of Psalm 1:

He shall be like a tree planted by the rivers of water,

that brings forth its fruit in season, His leaf also shall not

wither, and whatsoever He doeth shall prosper.

Our delight is in the law of the Lord. We do not find comfortable fellowship with the world. We can return to our solidly planted household and serve the Lord in the security of that household. There is no peace in pleasing the world. It is too hard, we cannot please everyone and because we cannot, we are always striving for unattainable standards of success. God is simply saying that He wants us to love Him, keep His commandments and He will provide the frame work so we can use our talents and produce good fruit for our labors.

The basics for producing fruit are good soil and water. Searching the scriptures daily we are watered, but when we begin to act on those scriptures we become confident and are planted firmly in the soil of those scriptures. We can grow confident because we have confidence in the wisdom of the God we serve, not man or his government. But it takes discipline, i.e. work, to be in the Word, to stay planted and secure and to not experience panic when life hits us.

When things get confusing we need to meditate on God's Word day and night in the security of our homes before we go out into the world. The peacefulness of our spirit can only be achieved when we know what God says we should do. I think that anything less than obeying God's commandments shakes our confidence, we lose our productivity and our sense of purpose, not to mention the joy of living.

A beginning place for prayer today:

Hold me secure in Your Word, Father. Keep me ever mindful of Your commandments. Let my household, even if I'm the only one in it, serve You. Please let me know your Word so well that I will not stumble or if I do that I only lose my way for a little while. Keep me alert to the lies of the world. Help me to speak your truth when I am called upon to answer for my actions or the actions of those in my charge. Keep me firmly rooted in Your household Lord.

Discussion Questions for today:

1. When I am confused about the best course of action to take in your life, what do I do?

2. What is the best way that I know to be confident that my life is pleasing to God?

DAY 4

SO THE WOMAN TOOK THE CHILD AND NURSED HIM, AND THE CHILD GREW AND SHE BROUGHT HIM TO PHARAOH'S DAUGHTER AND HE BECAME HER SON. —*EXODUS 2:9B TO 10A*

READING FOR TODAY: EXODUS 2: 1-10 AND PROVERBS 31: 30 AND 31

Moses' mother, Jochebed, was a remarkable woman of God. She kept God's commandment at great risk to herself. Never did she contemplate allowing Pharaoh to rule over her God given right to protect her child. What fear she must have experienced, as she sought to protect her son, she placed his life over her own.

Again, we see the divine hand of God at work orchestrating the daughter of the Pharaoh to be the recipient of the child. God softened her heart to show compassion on Moses. Using the wit of Moses' sister God was able to propose to the daughter of Pharaoh that a Hebrew nurse be hired for the child. Jochebed was hired to take care of her own son. Is God not capable? Is He not complete in all He does?

God had a plan for Moses' life. He knew to whom he was entrusting the care of Moses when he gave him to Jochebed. He knew she would be worthy of the task. When God gave us our children He knew we could be worthy of that trust if we would learn to trust Him. Into our care He has given us children we are entrusted with to raise as faithful servants of God. Why is it we discount the importance of being a mother? There is no bigger honor or blessing that God can bestow upon us.

Motherhood can be at times a heart ache, but it is our personal responsibility to direct that child's path in the honorable ways of God. I can remember when our youngest son was in jeopardy of losing his college football scholarship. He had gotten too full of himself and was having a great time, but he wasn't studying hard enough. He was being dishonorable to God by not earning his scholarship.

Passing through on vacation that year I observed he wasn't making a big effort to get those grades up. He was still dazzled by the college scene. I continued on vacation for about a week and then announced to my husband that I needed a plane ticket back to Utah. My heart clearly knew that our youngest was in jeopardy of losing all that he had worked for in high school—he was momentarily under the spell of the enemy!

Much to his surprise, I arrived at the college, settled into the local 6 Motel for the last three weeks of his summer school and took over his life. Even though he respected me, he resented me--big time! I pushed and challenged him unmercifully. We worked side by side on projects that were required and even extra credit projects he hated doing. By the time I left the grade point average was back where it should have been and he had saved his scholarship. His dislike for my "interference" was something you could almost taste in the air.

My dislike for his attitude toward me was truly tearful and painful for me, but I knew for this season he needed a top sergeant. When we parted it was stiff and uncomfortable to say the least. I went home disheartened that I had raised such a foolish and ungrateful son.

Jochebed received an unexpected blessing for giving up Moses to be adopted as the son of Pharoah's daughter—she was allowed to be the nurse for Moses. I also received an unexpected blessing, mine arrived in the mail in the form of a thank you note about two weeks after my return home. In that note he told me what a jerk he'd been, how he knew he'd only made it through because I loved him enough not to let him slide. He said in the note that he'd take responsibility for that scholarship from now on and this event in his life would never happen again. He lived up to his word and today he is a police officer with a college degree.

God sees the hearts of the Mom's who sacrifice and give of themselves daily. He uses our children to perfect us and at the same time He uses us to train them up in the way that they should go (Proverbs 22:6). I am convinced that great blessings come to the one who loves God and is obedient to His Word. Unfortunately great sorrow and pain usually follow the one who does not honor Him either by bearing the child of her womb or standing up to the damaging ways of the enemy as he tries to destroy that child.

Into Jochebed's hands was placed the deliverer of God's people. As a nation we need to repent and take responsibility for the abortions we have allowed. Who have we allowed to be killed? Have we slaughtered the genius who could have produced moving literature or music, preached transforming sermons, invented revolutionary devices, or even the genius who could have long ago cured cancer or any other number of terrible diseases? We will never know the depth of our foolishness. Only God knows the potential for greatness in each child that has been destroyed by abortion.

Jochebed was the woman for her day. She did not consider her own pain or loss. She freely gave Moses up and God freely gave him back! The giving up of a child to God is probably the best thing we can do in life. They are only ours for a season. Each child of God has a destiny which we have the distinct honor of facilitating. We are not the beginning nor the end of that destiny, because we are allowing God to work that out. Jochebed was given the privilege of nurturing Moses and of sharing with him his heritage as a Jew. Quietly, she undertook her responsibility with great thankfulness and dedication. She had been allowed to serve God as the nurse of Moses. Unselfishly she never really knew if she would ever hear him call her "Mother" – her rightful title and honor, but she persisted in her care of him without immediate reward.

A BEGINNING PLACE FOR PRAYER TODAY:

What kind of a heart do I have? Lord is it a trusting heart; a responsible heart? Father, You alone know the beginning from the end. You alone know how I need to serve. Show me daily my responsibilities. Let me be the woman for my day that You need. Help me to put aside selfish and petty things. Please help me to focus on Your Word. How can I be the Mom you need me to be, if that is my role? Give me a willing heart and take away my fear of letting You have Your way in my life.

DISCUSSION QUESTIONS FOR TODAY:

1. How am I facilitating the training of my children in the ways of the Lord? Do I go before God each day and then respond to the prompting of the His leading, even when I know it will be tough going?

2. If God took away all the potential failures for our children, would that really be what we would want for our children? What would they lack if those trials and tribulations were not allowed to come their way?

DAY 5

"FOR I KNOW THE THOUGHTS THAT I THINK TOWARD YOU, SAYS THE LORD; THOUGHTS OF PEACE AND NOT OF EVIL, TO GIVE YOU A FUTURE AND A HOPE." JEREMIAH 29:11

READING FOR TODAY – EXODUS 2:11 – 15, JEREMIAH 29: 11-14; PSALM 20:6-8

Moses had to make a mistake in life in order to be the person God needed him to be. He knew what injustice was, but he wasn't mature enough to deal with it. God needed to refine him. Moses needed to be instructed by God in many things before he could really be used for God's divine purposes.

We are easily discouraged by failure. God uses all the events of our lives to refine us. We do not know what God's purpose for our life is, but we do know we are to love Him and to serve Him in everything we do. Failure is a hard thing to deal with; unless we learn to see it from God's perspective. God's perspective is the opposite of the world's perspective. In God's economy you are not a loser. With every failure we have lessons to grow by. I think running from the truth of what we can learn from a mistake is the worst mistake. Choosing to grow from a mistake makes us winners and active participants in God's plan for our lives.

Moses took justice into his own hands. He knew violence was wrong. He looked both ways to see if anyone would see his sin and when he saw no one "he killed the Egyptian and hid him in the sand." Strange, isn't it, even when we know the consequences we are still ready to disregard those consequences. We want to take our own course of action. Once sin is committed, the consequences are not far behind. The consequences become God's tool for our growth. It has been my experience that lessons learned by this means are never forgotten.

When sin rears its ugly head our first response is to hope no one will notice. Running away from truth is usually the first thought of a believer or a non-believer, but with maturity we learn to seek forgiveness from God and then from those we may have harmed--taking responsibility for our actions. Moses was not a mature man of God yet-- he ran away. God had a plan for him and God used this event to mature Moses.

The events of our lives are seldom as we had planned them to be. So....it seems to me that it is wise to operate under God's rules so that when we do, even by our own choice , experience failure, we can have the hope of growth. The expectation of "all things working for good for those who love God" is a high note to live life on! In Jeremiah 29 He promises us that He has a plan for us "to give (us) a future and a hope." Failure is not the biggest problem in our lives, it's how we handle failure that can become the real problem.

A BEGINNING PLACE FOR PRAYER TODAY:

Lord I fail You every day. Help me quickly to seek Your forgiveness and give me the boldness to be responsible doing what is right in Your sight. Even when no one else is looking, let me always remember that my deeds are done in Your sight. Keep me close to Your Word so I cannot deceive myself but always walk in Your truth. Father, I want to be a wise servant. Help me to accept my failures and hope expectantly to see their fruit when You are in charge of my life. Thank You Lord.

DISCUSSION QUESTIONS FOR TODAY:

1. In the Christian economy we "fail forward"; what does that mean to me?

2. How we handle failure can become a real problem in our lives. What does that statement mean to me?

DAY 6

In the day when I cried out, You answered me, and made me bold with strength in my soul. – Psalm 138:3

Reading for today – Exodus 16-22 and Psalm 138

The Lord is always our provider. So often we are like Moses, caught adrift and not knowing what will happen next, but God provides. A job is lost, a promotion is denied, a marriage fails or flounders, a child disappoints or goes astray, but when we least expect it God provides. We can't say: "Oh, I did that!" for the provision is too perfect and the timing too right. We need to look daily for those provisions and rehearse to ourselves that "God has blessed me today." Counting our blessings will give us hope, joy and confidence in our God.

Moses fled Egypt, but with him he took his desire to serve the needy. Seeing the women shoved aside by the shepherds at the well, he helps them water their flock. Notice, he did not help them because he needed something from them. He selflessly helped them. Their father was the person who rewarded Moses for his good deeds. He knew a good man when he met one and thus welcomed him into his family through the gift of his daughter. It was a great reward for a simple act of kindness. Moses was alone and wandering, but God provided for him.

Verse 8 of Psalm 138 says:

THE LORD WILL PERFECT THAT WHICH CONCERNS ME;

YOUR MERCY, O LORD, ENDURES FOREVER;

We see the mercy of the Lord everyday in our lives as He seeks to perfect us into the image of His Son. God is not in the business of forsaking us! He is in the business of being that potter who faithfully molds and shapes us. Our job is to submit to Him and give Him the circumstances of our lives. Moses must have been confounded by his circumstances, but he kept putting one foot in front of the other. He didn't give up on life, he just adjusted.

When we submit to our circumstances, instead of fighting them or feeling sorry for ourselves, God can work with us. All of us, at one time or another, have had the experience of having a dream dashed.   Sometimes the worst days of our lives become the most rewarding and the most surprising. Moses now has a new life!

A beginning place for prayer today:

Thank you, Father, for this day. You have provided for my needs and most of the time You even supply my wants. Make me grateful for everything and give me joy to pass on to others. Help me to take my eyes off of myself and to see those around me who are in need. Life is so much easier because You provide. Help me to remember that you have put the order in my day for a purpose. It is my job to respond graciously to all circumstances. Thank You for being in my life. I love You, Lord.

Discussion Questions for today:

1. Are things in my life not quite as I thought they would be? How submissive to God have I been in the past? What blessings has God given me that were totally out of my realm of control or even comprehension?

2. As I think back on the really important decisions I have made in my life, such as the college I attended, career I pursued, job accepted, and my consideration of a life-long mate, could I say that these pivotal decisions involved God or was it me entirely who evaluated and made the decision? If it was me without God's counsel, could I now say that perhaps the outcome might have been better had I sought God for wisdom and guidance?

DAY 7

SO GOD HEARD THEIR GROANINGS AND GOD REMEMBERED HIS COVENANT WITH ABRAHAM, WITH ISAAC, AND WITH JACOB. – EXODUS 2:24

READING FOR TODAY – EXODUS 2:23-25, PSALM 25:1-6, PSALM 34:1-10

Does it ever feel like: "*God just isn't hearing* my prayers?" Well, what we've just read in scripture tells us differently. God not only hears the prayers of a righteous man, but He desires to answer those prayers. The result, however, of those prayers will be His choice and in His timing and perfect will.

Because of God's love for us He doesn't say yes to all our requests. Some of our prayers wouldn't really prosper us or be in our best interest. When a single man or woman prays for a mate he doesn't want just any mate, he wants the best and so does God. When job opportunities or school experiences are the pits, He wants us to have the best job or the best education. It will take time for most things to develop. Illness is often the hardest to deal with. "Why me Lord?" "Cure me." "Spare me." "Spare my child, my Mom or Dad, my husband, my wife." It is often hard for us to wait until the illness runs its course, but in God's economy it must, because only then is a perfect work done in everyone who is involved.

Hind sight always gives us wisdom, but when the immediate events of today converge upon us it can take a mighty step of faith to say, "Show me Your ways, O Lord; teach me your paths. For You are the God of my salvation. On You I wait all the day." We must believe that He has our best interest at heart and look carefully at all the sides of a pressing issue. After we have prayed about the problem and done everything that is logical (not emotional) in a way that God would be honored it is then time to commit it to God! One of my favorite pastors used to say, "You've done your best, it's time to commit the rest!"

The Israelites were groaning and they were suffering, but God was using it to strengthen their resolve to accept God's help. Sometimes we go only as far as the "done our best" part and we don't really "commit the rest." We do destructive things like worry or feel really frustrated every waking minute of the day. We moan about because we don't have what we need and that becomes the focus of our lives. God's focus is on our obedience. He's looking for obedient servants who will trust Him with everything. Without that obedience, there is no peace in our lives. I have come to believe that we can never have perfection in our lives, but we can have peace and peace is the source of all joy. Without peace, there can never be joy.

God had made a covenant with Abraham, Isaac and Jacob to bring them into the Promised Land. That promise land is ultimately heaven, but in the mean time He's got to keep us moving on this journey through life, so we'll be able to be in the "promised land". Our groanings may seem to be bouncing off the walls, but God hears. He's working; we just need to commit whatever is troubling us to Him. We don't have the answers –that's okay, God does!

A BEGINNING PLACE FOR PRAYER TODAY:

Lord I wish I understood the anxieties of my life. You do Lord, so help me to lay them at Your feet and trust You for Your perfect plan. I can't solve these things in my life because I know that I am only responsible for myself. You are responsible for everything else and everyone else in my life.

Help me to just let go for I am so comfortable holding on for dear life! I want your perfect peace in my life. Thank You, Father, that You wait patiently for me to move forward and learn Your ways. The more I learn about You, the more I learn to trust You, for I know You acknowledge my requests whenever I place them before You. Please give me patience to wait. Thank You, Father.

DISCUSSION QUESTIONS FOR TODAY:

1. Is there a prayer in my life right now that God doesn't seem to be hearing? Could it be that perhaps there is something else going on in my life unbeknownst to me, and that God is perfecting that first?

2. Once I have prayed something through am I content to wait for God's decisions and His timing? What are the alternatives to waiting on the Lord?

DAY 8

AND GOD SAID TO MOSES "I AM WHO I AM." AND HE SAID, "THUS YOU SHALL SAY TO THE CHILDREN OF ISRAEL, I AM HAS SENT ME TO YOU!" – EXODUS 3:14

READING FOR TODAY – EXODUS 3:1-14, PSALM 139

"I AM WHO I AM." What a marvelous statement! That is who God is—not "I was," I will be" or "I might be". I AM WHO I AM. He is full of the present that consumes my life. He stands near me and never afar and no matter who or what He allows in my path He can take care of it. This is really a significant truth about Christianity. It is a personal relationship with the living, great and wonderful "I AM".

When I know within my heart that "I AM" is in the presence of all my today's I can meet the challenges of those days. God sent Moses to His children, Israel. Where has He sent me and to whom? I AM has a purpose for my life and He will never leave me or forsake me and He will always be my guide.

We are all like Moses when it comes to the unexpected events and requests of God where our lives are concerned. Who are we to be in this situation or faced with that person? Out of fear, out of laziness, out of selfishness we don't want to move out of our comfort zones. We say, "Why me Lord? Couldn't You send someone else on this journey?" And there is a stillness following our lament and we know…."No, I must go!" It is God's desire that I serve, that I do, that I be on the front lines of this day. I must be ready to fight for God's best in my life and for the best He has to offer others in my life.

No situation is "a happening" in my life. Psalm 139 makes it clear that He has designed me, He has set my life in motion and all my days are of His full knowledge. So wherever I find myself, in the middle of whatever, He is there too. I have choices to make each day. I will listen to the voice of God and accept His sovereignty or I will run away and not take up the challenge of this day. But whatever I choose, God will be in the middle of this day with me. My day will be victorious in His strength or I can chose to be in a battle on a front which I have chosen and God will have to allow it, even if it isn't a victorious battle. He is the great "I Am" and He will be there with me.

Is there a Pharaoh for me to face today? What is it? Maybe I should ask God to reveal it to me. I must not be afraid or even a little anxious. It is His perfect will and He will make me victorious. He is the great I AM and He sends me into this day and He will bless me for my faithfulness. (Re-read Psalm 139: 16-18)

A BEGINNING PLACE FOR PRAYER TODAY:

Open my eyes Father. Let me see this day as you see it Father. There are people and events in this day I know about and some I either embrace or dread, but You are the author of this day. Help me to accept each moment as a journey we take together. Let me speak to You all day. Please share the joys and the challenges of this day with me and give me Your wisdom in all my dealings so that I might glorify You to all I encounter. Thank You, Father.

DISCUSSION QUESTIONS FOR TODAY:

1. What circumstances in my life have made me question if God was still standing with me? How did those circumstances eventually workout; despite my doubt?

2. Do I ask God into every circumstance of my life? Why or why not?

DAY 9

AND I WILL GIVE THIS PEOPLE FAVOR IN THE SIGHT OF THE EGYPTIANS AND IT SHALL BE, WHEN YOU GO THAT YOU SHALL NOT GO EMPTY HANDED. – EXODUS: 3:21

READING FOR TODAY – EXODUS 3:15-22, JEREMIAH 29: 11-14, PSALM 149:4 AND MATTHEW 7:7

God had a plan for Moses and for all His people, Israel. As surely as God spoke of His plans for the people of Israel He speaks to us in Jeremiah 29: ll-14. The great I AM wants to give us favor in the sight of our personal Egypt which translated for us means our world today, the majority of which are non-Christian. He is glorified by our faithfulness to trust Him and openly obey Him before man. How else will others want to know Him unless they see fruit in our lives?

God gives us promises in His Word that He fully intends to keep. He is, in fact, the only one who makes promises that are always kept. Unfortunately, we are limited by our human natures. One part of us wants to trust and wants to obey, but the other side of our frail human nature wants the "time table" for how long it will take for God's plan to be completed. If we knew the length of time it would take for completion—then it wouldn't be trust!

Obeying would be easy if we were guaranteed the favor we sought in the "time table" we knew God had spelled out. Our job is to obey His word, without the guarantee of a time table. If it were not so, it would only be obeying to serve ourselves and not God. It is the "Lord who has made us and we are His". (Psalm l00) When we do not trust Him we are in essence saying we are making ourselves into what is acceptable to us. We begin to handle life as if we are capable of making decisions without Him.

We ignore the fact that God has a total picture of our life as it says in Psalm 139. He alone knows the beginning from the end and the in between! He alone knows what and when the finished product of me will be as it says in Philippians 1:6. I have only a small piece of a very large picture when I am making my decisions. What a shame it is that I sometimes choose to limit the size of the finished picture, and the completeness and the clarity of that picture because I won't trust and obey God.

Trusting God requires that I get to know His character. The more I obey Him, the more of my life I give, and the more I see Him work in my life, the more I will know and experience Him. But…obey what? Jeremiah 29:11-14 says that I must seek Him. Reading a portion of His word each day gives me His directions for my life. When I don't read His word I follow my own "natural instincts" and in that there will be limited good and a great possibility for sin and unhappiness. When I pray to understand and put into practice what He tells me to do I gain His favor and His covering. In His favor "is a hope and a future."

When no one else listens, God does! He hears and He answers our needs because we ask and call upon His name. Once He hears us, He will bring us out of captivity (the captivity of the world's view). He can work with us and mold us because we trust and obey Him. That molding is what the world sees.

That new creature in Christ is what the world needs and wants. Our growth will be evidence to all of Egypt that we have peace and safety in the plans of our God. As the Egyptians saw the favor of God on the Israelites, so we can expect the world to see the favor of God in our lives and I believe they are watching us!

A BEGINNING PLACE FOR PRAYER TODAY:

Lord, I am so small and insignificant in this world. Help me to see that you are great and mighty and that Your plan for my life is all I need for peace and safety. I want to grow into your likeness, not the picture I think I should be. Help me to let go of these plans and let You take over. Give me Your comfort and Your confidence so that I will represent You well to this world. Thank You Father, in Jesus Name.

DISCUSSION QUESTIONS FOR TODAY:

1. How can I get to know the character of God and why should I desire this knowledge?

2. What state of mind does God require of me before He can work in me?

DAY 10

WHO GAVE MAN HIS MOUTH? WHO MAKES HIM DEAF OR MUTE? WHO GIVES HIM SIGHT OR MAKES HIM BLIND? IS IT NOT I, THE LORD? NOW GO, I WILL HELP YOU SPEAK AND WILL TEACH YOU WHAT TO SAY. –EXODUS 4: 11-12

READING FOR TODAY – EXODUS 4: 1-18 AND PSALM 91

When we are afraid we make excuses to the Lord. We are no different than Moses, who said: "I can't, You know my weaknesses. You know how uncomfortable that makes me Lord." The answer is "Yes, I know," He says. "But if I keep you in a comfortable place you will never grow or change or be a vessel for My use."

It is so easy to forget how powerful and complete God is in all things. He has made our physical being and allowed our circumstances. He knows our weaknesses, our strengths and our capabilities. Everything that comes our way is to prosper us spiritually and to mold and change us. His changes in our being are permanent--never a band aid, but a complete healing if we allow Him to do His work.

It is hard to let go and move out in a new direction. Like Moses, we are comfortable, even sometimes with sin and bad circumstances. We know those circumstances and we're comfortable in them. But….those circumstances are not God's best for us. We know they are not God's best because we lack joy and hope and a vision for the future. God wants us to have all three.

We are not put on earth to just be a bump on a log gathering moss. He has created bumps for that purpose—but we are not those bumps, we are His children. Our inheritance is rich, but we have work to do here on earth. To let others know who He is we must get outside of ourselves and move into the unfamiliar, the sometimes uncomfortable and definitely into the unknown. But, with Christ as our covering and the Holy Spirit as our guide He will protect us, guide us and cause us to grow spiritually and emotionally. We have nothing to fear. This is the God who made everything and He loves us.

Our names are written on the palms of His hands.(Isaiah 49:16) Every time He looks down He sees us, He hears us, as He heard Moses, and yet He moves us out and on down the road for our own good. If we give up, it is a sign we have not talked to Him about it. I have noticed that when I'm ready to make excuses and throw in the towel, He says, "No, you can't do it, but now that you've given up control, I can do it and I'll give you the strength to see this through."

He might supply a person like Aaron to come alongside, or He may just give you incredible peace. But, when we ask, He accomplishes the day for us. We make it through the day sometimes even with great wisdom, understanding and compassion. Is that not a miracle? And we take these days for granted all the time!

PRAYER FOR TODAY

Dear, Father, whatever comes my way today, let me say "Yes" to it. For these circumstances and people are your people and your circumstances. Let me not make excuses, but let me move on down the road and keep on going. For the place I am going is your perfection and molding of me and of my Life and I don't want to let You down. Thank You that You love me as You do. I need your help in all the things I do. Please be with me, Father, strengthen me and let me count my blessings today. Thank You Father.

DISCUSSION QUESTIONS FOR TODAY:

1. Is there sin in my life that I need to be rid of, but I am so afraid of the changes that I stay in the comfort of the familiar sin? How can I get on the right track? Do I need someone's help?

2. Can comfortable sin keep me from being the very best, or enjoying the very best life that God has to offer me?

DAY 11

I WILL LIFT UP MY EYES TO THE HILLS – FROM WHENCE COME MY HELP? MY HELP COMES FROM THE LORD, WHO MADE HEAVEN AND EARTH. – PSALM 121: 1-2

READING FOR TODAY – EXODUS 4: 19-23 AND PSALM 121

How many times do we look "to the hills" for help when things get complicated? Unfortunately, we're still looking at ground level and we need to be at "heaven level" when we look for help. We pray: "Surely, somewhere about me there must be an answer." Even Moses said, "Can't you send someone to help me?" He had God and yet he wanted earthly help. Aren't we the same way? We discount the power of God and turn to man—a professional, a friend or a pastor.

When we look at things from ground level we still see only the earthly and physical view of life. Our limited perception of life's circumstances will always be the same—Limited—because we are human. The Holy Spirit calls us to a higher place. When we look completely up we see only the clear blue sky…a place of one view, God's view. There is a peace in just looking up. It takes all that surrounds us and makes it disappear; we no longer see the confusion. When I can't see the confusion, peace comes.

Looking up gives us peace and confidence that He is the road up and out of this valley, the only road! He is capable of great things. The psalmist reminds us: "He made heaven and earth." Surely, He can help me sort out daily issues. I need to focus on who I belong to and who sets a guard over my life here on earth:

He will not allow your foot to be moved; He who keeps you will

not slumber. – Psalm 121:

If I look up He is wide awake and focused on me so that I can walk up and out of the valley on steady feet. God is specific in His promises, but He is also specific in His directions. Our firm footing for the journey out depends on our readiness to look up and then look into His word. He gave Moses exact directions as he left the valley of Midian and He gives us specific directions today.

The simplicity of His word is often too straight forward. We've grown comfortable with compromise in our lives, because we look at the ground level instead of looking up for the perfect truth. Even when the choice of no compromise is difficult, the peace and directness of it gives us strength. Looking up we can stand straight and tall and go forth with confidence, not man's help nor man's reasoning, but with GOD CONFIDENCE! When I look up I confidently know:

The Lord shall preserve your going out and your coming in

from this time forth, and forevermore. – Psalm 121:8

What an incredible promise: "Forevermore". How long will He preserve me? FOREVER + MORE! That is all the way to eternity. Can I ask for more? I don't think so!

A BEGINNING PLACE FOR PRAYER TODAY:

Thank You Lord, that You are above all of life's circumstances and that when I look up You cut to the real priorities of my life and confusion goes away. Help me to be thankful for all You have done for me and for all you have given me. I cannot begin to count your blessings. Let me not look at ground level. Let me look into your sweet loving face and smile because You are wide awake guarding my every move this day. You can even keep a guard over my mouth so that I can only praise YOU and share YOU with others. Thank You Father. I love You.

DISCUSSION QUESTIONS FOR TODAY:

1. Where am I looking for answers today? When I go to professionals how do I evaluate their counsel?

2. Why is our view of a problem limited sometimes?

DAY 12

THE LORD IS IN HIS HOLY TEMPLE, THE LORD'S THRONE IS IN HEAVEN; HIS EYES BEHOLD, HIS EYELIDS TEST THE SONS OF MEN. THE LORD TESTS THE RIGHTEOUS. – PSALM 11: 4 – 5A

READING FOR TODAY– EXODUS 4: 24-26 AND PSALM 11

Often when we set out to do God's service we are not quite equipped. Things and people and even circumstances take us by surprise. When we are taken by surprise it is usually sin that sets us up for it. Sometimes the sin is our own and sometimes we are a ripple in the pond of someone else's sin. Our own disobedience, self-centeredness, ambition, bitterness and unforgiveness can go unnoticed by us, but God notices.

God needs to have His servants fit for the battle of winning souls to Him. He cannot allow us to be disobedient. Some sins in our lives we are comfortable with and God has to put us through a trial to eliminate them or even call our attention to them. He needs to make us aware that there is sin in our life. Moses had a sin of disobedience in his camp. He had not circumcised his sons.

His wife Zipporah must have known of the tradition and wondered in her heart why her sons were not circumcised. In Genesis 17:13-14, God said His covenant would be with the children of Abraham if they were circumcised. But, it says that the "male child who is not circumcised shall be cut off from my people, he has broken my covenant." Moses was disobedient. He had not kept the commandments of God in his own household. We cannot serve God if our own lives are not in order because we choose to overlook our sins.

When the Lord challenged Moses, Zipporah circumcised her son and threw the foreskin at Moses feet and said, "Surely you are a husband of blood to me." The Lord let Moses off the hook. Her act of obedience for God's commandments showed three things: Moses had been neglectful in his duties and she was a wife who loved and honored her husband and would honor God's commandments, even though she was a Midionite. How could Moses go to the Israelites and expect them to follow him if he did not adhere to their traditions which were the very commandments of God?

Sometimes we just don't see the sin in our own lives. It is important to ask God to show it to us. We also need Zipporahs in our lives, people who will speak the truth to us and come along side of us to challenge us and to help us change.

Have I been and am I obedient to God? Is there sin in my life or in the lives of the people I love. I cannot dismiss it because it could destroy them or me. He does not cause me to sin, but He lets the sin I commit convict me to either obey Him or suffer the consequences of living in that sin. He sees it all just as it says in Psalm 11.

It seems it would be much easier on us if we would just talk to God each day and ask Him to show us our hearts and also to keep us vigilant for those we love. Are things going smoothly or if not smoothly then do I have a peace about what is going on about me? If not, then I need to question God, "Why not?" "What am I missing?" These need to be the constant questions of our hearts. A constant dialogue with the Lord keeps us in tune with what is going on in our lives. When we stop dialoguing with God we begin to work in our own wisdom. We always want God's wisdom, not our own, because our own wisdom just isn't good enough and that's a real understatement!

A BEGINNING PLACE FOR PRAYER TODAY:

Lord God, show me my heart today. Leave no stone unturned. I do not want to lose Your fellowship or Your blessings. Help me to be wise in all the things I do and say. Please help me to always check my motives and deliver me from pride. All my accomplishments are Yours and I want them to glorify You. Make me your worthy servant and vessel. Place on my heart those I have offended. Let me begin to make things right with them. Thank You Father.

DISCUSSION QUESTIONS FOR TODAY:

1. Do I ask God to search my heart for sins that I may be overlooking? What can I expect Him to do in my life if I give Him freedom to take up residence in my heart?

2. Do I have a friend and confidence in my life that I really trust to tell me the truth and pray with me when I need God's guidance?

DAY 13

IN MY DISTRESS I CRIED TO THE LORD, AND HE HEARD ME. – PSALM 120:1

READING FOR TODAY– EXODUS 4:27- 31 AND PSALM 120

I am never alone. All I have to do is call His name and He joins my spirit to His through His indwelling Holy Spirit. When Jesus went away He said He did so that the Comforter might come along side us and be our guide to all truth and teach us and remind us of what we already know about God. (John 14:26) Yet some days we forget. But, God doesn't forget us.

The people of Israel who were captive began to call out and God answered them. He sent Moses to be their guide and He sent him armed with miracles to help His people. He never leaves us or forsakes us, we just need to ask. He says we have not because we ask not. Simple?

I think so! God is incredibly complicated in all His ways and we cannot even begin to understand Him, but….when He deals with us He is incredibly simple. He loves us and He wants us to prosper and all that is required of us is to obey His commandments.

Man has eternally sought to be happy. He has used his intellect to devise pleasure, escape pain and solve the world's problems. And…he has been a complete failure. Why does man fail? He fails because he centers all his energies on himself. But when God becomes the center of his energies, he learns to let go of his earthly concerns and his priorities are lined up and truth becomes easier to see. Confusion, pain, frustration and failure all end at the feet of Jesus.

When we reach out to Him He reaches down and puts His hand of peace upon our shoulder and all is well. In these moments we have an opportunity to be still and quiet to enter into His peace and His rest. Clouds disappear and the clear vision of who He is and how much He desires to speak with us becomes the peace that surpasses all understanding. It is the peace that only He can give and only we who believe can experience because the world does not know Him and cannot know His peace.

The psalmist laments how long he stayed in his pain, but it ended when he cried out to God and God was able to show him where he had chosen to stay. Perhaps today is the day we need to come out of our choices and see God for who He is. We need to believe His promises even though the enemy would have us keep our eyes only on what we see through clouded vision. It is time to believe and rejoice in Him, for He hears our prayers and loves us. He died that we might have life and that more abundantly— TODAY! His promises are not just promises reserved until heaven, TODAY is when He desires to be a part of my life.

A BEGINNING PLACE FOR PRAYER TODAY:

Thank You Father for this day. I will rejoice and be glad in it because You have made it for me. You speak to me in a thousand ways throughout the day with all your blessings. Let me count them; let me rejoice in just how much You love me. I do not desire to dwell in the camp of the enemy. Let me come up out of this valley of frustration, pain, jealousy, envy and strife and see Your face and behold life as you see it for me. Thank you Lord for Your Holy Spirit and Your ever present presence in my life. Thank You Father, I commit this day to you.

DISCUSSION QUESTIONS FOR TODAY:

1. When was the last time I spent too much time in a place of needless pain? What did it take for me to finally to surrender it to God?

2. Why and how does man fail at being happy? Is being happy what Christianity is all about?

DAY 14

SO MOSES RETURNED TO THE LORD AND SAID "LORD, WHY HAVE YOU BROUGHT TROUBLE ON THIS PEOPLE? WHY IS IT YOU HAVE SENT ME? FOR SINCE I CAME TO SPEAK TO PHARAOH TO SPEAK YOUR NAME, HE HAS DONE EVIL TO THIS PEOPLE; NEITHER HAVE YOU DELIVERED YOUR PEOPLE AT ALL. – EXODUS 5:22-23

READING FOR TODAY – EXODUS 5 AND PSALM 22

If we do not think God is a forgiving God then we need to re-read Psalm 22 and look at the challenge Moses delivers to God in Exodus 5:22-23. In Psalm 22 we see the suffering, misunderstood Jesus, crucified on the cross. There was no easy way for God to accomplish His work for us.

He could not spare Jesus the suffering of the cross. He could not make the hearts of the people around the cross understand His plan for salvation. He had to let them feel abandoned and betrayed. Jesus suffered the cross and He felt all the emotions we would ever feel. Then He was equipped to represent us before the Father. He was acquainted with our sorrows and our grief.

How it must hurt the heart of God when we say He has abandoned us. That He doesn't understand that there must be a better way for us. It is calling God a liar and saying that all His love and care and safety doesn't exist! It is saying He doesn't have a plan for our lives.

Our relationship with Him is to be based on faith. So when we experience these things our faith is being tested. God graciously overlooks these detours in our lives. He waits patiently for us to get back on track. But we must not allow ourselves too much time in self-pity. Self-pity is self-centeredness. When we are self-centered we are not God centered. Trouble needs to be turned over to God immediately. When we feel faint of heart or overwhelmed we must confess it to Him immediately.

The longer we carry worry, doubt and pain, the heavier the burden gets. It says in the Word to cast all your cares upon Him , for He cares for you.(Psalm 55:22) He will take those burdens and make them lighter; maybe they won't go away, but they will get lighter because He will give me His peace. Our impatience and our natural instinct to take the easy way out are not Jesus' characteristics.

Remember scripture says we are being conformed into His image (Romans 8:29). That means that like Jesus on the cross I will trust God that He knows what He is doing. I will suffer so I can identify with Christ and also with my brothers and sisters who experience life's terrible trials. I will never feel above someone else's pain, I will understand what it is to suffer so I can come alongside of the poor and weary of spirit.

The message of faith is that nothing comes to me, but that it first must pass by the throne of God. He allows it and I must not challenge it. My job is to accept this challenge of life. How will I become more like Christ through this experience? The challenges I face are the conforming tools of God. Searching scripture and prayerfully seeking God to help me uncover my sins or the part I have played through disobedience is my responsibility. If I am in a place of someone else's making I must try to see what part I have in it and bring that before God.

God tells me to flee sin. He does not want me to operate in sinful situations which I can eliminate out of my life with His help. But…He does not give me a time table, because His works are perfect and complete. No matter how much time it takes, He will work it out for my good. Though He allows challenges in my life, I will be conformed into the image of Christ. I will know peace in the process only if I can surrender the process to Him.

A BEGINNING PLACE FOR PRAYER TODAY:

Lord I thank You for the challenges of this day. My strength and my joy are a gift from You and no matter what the challenges are I am equipped because I belong to You. Open my eyes and ears wide to see and hear from You today. You have made this day for me so that I might thrive spiritually; don't let me miss my opportunities to grow into Your image because I choose to be less than the best. Thank You for Your Word, speak to me all day as I reflect upon Your glory and grace in my life.

DISCUSSION QUESTIONS FOR TODAY:

1. How well am I doing at accepting the challenges of life? Do I complain or do I praise His name when I discuss the difficulties of my life?

2. What do I think God intends for us to learn from trials?

DAY 15

TEACH ME YOUR WAY, O LORD, I WILL WALK IN YOUR TRUTH; UNITE MY HEART TO FEAR YOUR NAME. I WILL PRAISE YOU, O LORD MY GOD, WITH ALL MY HEART, AND I WILL GLORIFY YOUR NAME FOREVERMORE. – PSALM 86: 11-12

READING FOR TODAY– EXODUS 6; 1-9, PSALM 86

Is the Lord my Lord or is He the God of Abraham and Isaac? If I am a Sunday Christian, then He is probably the God of Abraham and Isaac, but if I have a personal and every day of the week relationship with Him, then He is more than likely the Lord of my life.

I can have as much of Him in my life as I choose. He only comes along side when He's invited. The world and all its business, its concerns and worries, seem to keep Him out of my daily life. The enemy likes it that way! It is easy to forget who gave us life, and so we pursue life instead of pursuing the Creator. If we are not pursuing life, it is pursuing us. The only real peace in life is when our life is lined up with Christ our Savior, for that is what He is: Our Savior.

He has saved us from Hell, but He has saved us from even more than we can comprehend. He has saved us from this world. Only the world limits man from being what God has intended him to be. If we can allow Him to be Lord over us—every moment, every hour of the day, He can give us joy and peace because we will have pleasure in the simple blessings of life. Those blessings are health of mind, health of spirit and health of soul.

When I picture Him as Lord, I picture Him as the Lord of the castle for whom I work and serve. I picture Him as kind and loving, wanting me to understand and to be mature in spiritual things. I picture Him giving me tasks to do that are designed to help me become all I can be by serving others in His name. The Lord of the castle walks about quietly observing all the work of His servants and He's there to give instruction, and even His physical strength, to assist us in our job today. But, there is a hitch, I must ask for His help. He stands waiting, ever so close at my right hand, but I must ask.

My mind is at peace when it is decided. Decided means that I know what I am to do today. It does not mean I know what the outcome will be, but I know how to approach it. When I don't know what to do, I wait on the Lord of the Castle to show me. I ask Him to show me. I want to walk with Him over the grounds of the castle and see His perspective of the day. My spirit is not crushed down, it walks upright, looking about with expectation because the Lord of the castle has things for me to see and enjoy as well as ways to make me a wise and a good steward of this day.

Lastly, my soul, the very being of who I am and who He has created, will be healthy because it is exercising itself to be what my Lord has planned for it. When I walk within the bounds of His Word I have nothing to fear, not even failure. Through Him I will be redeemed because "He is good and ready to forgive, and abundant in Mercy to all those who call upon Him." Psalm 86:5

A BEGINNING PLACE FOR PRAYER TODAY:

Lord, please let me be a servant in Your castle. Keep me from desiring to be King of the castle. I want You sending me out each day on assignments I know that will prosper me and those I love. The world always has an agenda for me and for the practical part of life I must often follow that agenda, but my attitude and my ultimate judgments are all in Your hands.

The success of this day is not measured in the terms of the world, it is measured by the value of my service to You. Help me to be ever aware that because I claim to be a Christian people are looking at me. They want to see Your handiwork in my life or gladly standby to point out my inconsistencies as I try to serve You.

This is my day to experience the pleasure of Your company and I do not want to waste this day. Thank You Father for the gentle touch You use to guide me. I want the best that You have for me. Close the doors you do not want open for me and open the doors I need to walk through so that I will be a blessing to You. Thank You for this new day.

DISCUSSION QUESTIONS FOR TODAY:

1. Who puts the order in my day?

2. Am I lacking in some spiritual area of my life simply because I have forgotten to ask for help from God? Is it time to take an inventory of my spiritual needs?

DAY 16

THE LAW OF THE LORD IS PERFECT, CONVERTING THE SOUL; THE TESTIMONY OF THE LORD IS SURE, MAKING WISE THE SIMPLE. THE STATUTES OF THE LORD ARE RIGHT REJOICING THE HEART; THE COMMANDMENT OF THE LORD IS PURE, ENLIGHTENING THE EYES. – PSALM 19:8-9.

READING FOR TODAY– EXODUS 6:10-30 AND PSALM 19

It is easy to get off track and be out of God's will for our lives. We can look about us and see the world and our part in it through our own eyes. But, God says to search My scriptures and seek Me. He who has made the heavens and the earth has testified to us of His power and in His Word is the strength we need to meet every situation we encounter. He wants to make us wise so we will stay in His protective circle.

Things are only complicated because we make them so. To God all things are simple. No matter what the issue His truths are always there. We can be like Moses and question Him every step of the way, but it all comes back to the simple: DO AS I SAY!

Truth is always simple, but following it is the difficult part. We do not want pain or suffering when we stand on His principles, but sometimes it is the first fruit of standing on His principles. Then, after a season, while others rush about in their wisdom, you have experienced your pain and you are not rushing around in your own wisdom, but you are experiencing the peace of God's wisdom.

God loves to see us have peace and order in our lives. He can work with us when we are at peace. Our humanness often demands the tangible from God before we'll step out in faith. God allows the psalmist in Psalm 19 to show us His power and accomplishments. He reaffirms through the psalmist that the "heavens declare the glory of God"; that "each day unto day utters speech" or the testimony of the sureness of God's being in charge. We can look back and see His handiwork. How it must sadden Him that we cannot look forward and expect more of the same.

Fear of the unknown is our greatest fear. Moses keeps saying, "What if?" to God; just like we do today. But God does not give him any more than one commandment. One commandment at a time is all God wants us to accomplish or begin to comprehend. It says "the commandment", singular, of the Lord "is pure; enlightening the eyes." We see clearly when we focus on one commandment at a time. Each of us is looking at a different commandment for our lives today.

When we see it, we begin to approach wisdom on it. When He has completed that commandment in our lives He will move to another one. He will use a commandment and its' lesson to add strength and surety to the next commandment we need to learn. He has such order and love for us if we will but obey and not be caught up in a "spirit of anguish and cruel bondage", to the "What ifs?" we use as excuses as did the Israelites in Exodus 6:9.

Lord, please help me to put aside "What if?" It is not necessary. There is no painless way to go into the unknown except with You. You offer me peace and confidence. Lord let me accept your peace and confidence so I can learn all I need to be Your servant. I long to dwell in Your house forever and never to be out of the shelter of Your arms. Thank You Father for seeking to shelter and protect me. Thank You that You want me to move forward one step each day closer to Your presence in my life and in my eventual eternity with You.

DISCUSSION QUESTIONS FOR TODAY:

1. How does fear or anxiety creep into our lives?

2. Why is peace and order a sign that God has taken up residence in our hearts?

DAY 17

> *THE LORD IS MY LIGHT AND MY SALVATION; WHAT SHALL I FEAR? THE LORD IS THE STRENGTH OF MY LIFE; OF WHOM SHALL I BE AFRAID? THOUGH AN ARMY MAY ENCAMP AGAINST ME, MY HEART SHALL NOT FEAR; THOUGH WAR MAY RISE AGAINST ME, IN THIS I WILL BE CONFIDENT. – PSALM 27: 1 AND 3*

READING FOR TODAY– EXODUS 7: 1-13 AND PSALM 27

Pharaoh is very much like modern man. He hardens his heart against the power and majesty of God and then he tries to prove that he can do the things God can do. Through science and medicine, their own intellect and philosophy men try to ignore God. Each time they solve their problems they pat themselves on the back and walk away from God a few more steps.

With each step of self-reliance man hardens his heart and moves away from what God has planned for him. Eventually a man can step so far away that eternal darkness and separation from God is his only inheritance. Moses and Aaron finally let go and let God. They go to Pharaoh and they know, because God has told them that Pharaoh will refuse them. Finally, they realize that they have nothing to fear for God is on their side; we need to stand confidently on the principles of God before modern man. No one wins against God.

Defeat, heartache, failure…these represent the legacy of not heeding God. Strength, courage and triumph are the blessings of God. Calling on our mates, our children, our friends and relatives to accept the moral standards of God is not always easy. In fact, not compromising is sometimes the hardest and loneliest thing we can do, but it must be done.

To save a child, a friend, or a relative from Hell, is what Christianity is all about. They can be mad, upset, even feel we've not been supportive, but we have given them our best gift, our knowledge of scripture and the hope of Christ who lives in us.

The confidence of a life hid in Christ is worth more than all the earthly temporary pleasures we can attain. We are making an investment in our future and the future of others which cannot rust or perish, but will stand forever. It is important for our well-being that we go confidently about doing that which we know is right. We must answer the "Whys" of others with "because God said so!"

We must ask ourselves each day if others are looking at us, will they see that confidence in God within us? Just as God told Moses; "I want the Egyptians to know that I am Lord." He says the same thing it to us today. Some harden their hearts like Pharaoh, but some may come to know Him as Lord if we persist in showing Him as the Lord of our lives by standing firm in our confidence in His Word.

Lord give me Your confidence. Let me speak joyfully of all Your gifts to me. Let me speak Your name with reverence and awe before the believer and the unbeliever, even in my own home. Help me to live out your commandments of love fully in the presence of all the people who need Your touch, but let me first start at home. I want to serve you first at home and be confident that those I love the most know You best through me. Use me Lord and don't let me disappoint You.

DISCUSSION QUESTIONS FOR TODAY:

1. When do I become uncomfortable standing on the principles of God before man? What is the only thing that can really give me confidence when speaking of God's principles to others?

2. Why is it so important that I personally stand on the principles of God before my fellow man?

DAY 18

WHO CAN UNDERSTAND HIS ERRORS? CLEANSE ME FROM SECRET FAULTS. KEEP BACK YOUR SERVANT ALSO FROM PRESUMPTUOUS SINS; LET THEM NOT HAVE DOMINION OVER ME.
– PSALM 19: 12-13B

READING FOR TODAY– EXODUS 7; 14-25 AND PSALM 19: 12-14

We can be like Pharaoh when we close our hearts off to God's leading and even His pleadings for us to repent. Hopefully, we only turn Him off for a short season. It is easy to be stubborn and not see our part in a situation. Sometimes a simple "Yes" to God's bidding can save us from great pain and sorrow. Presumptuous sins are so terribly damaging to us.

We presume we know best, we presume we can handle it or we presume it's not that bad and then we suffer. God is the one who holds the standards we need to seek; it is not we who hold them. A heart can be hardened in part to God's leadings and even though we are Christians we will suffer. When we are chastened by God we look at the results and we are saddened, but how much we could have avoided the mess if we had only done what we knew He would have wanted in the first place.

Because we are free-will beings God has dignity and majesty. If we serve Him it is not because we are robots He has programmed, it is because we truly trust, love and respect Him. When we think about it, this relationship gives us dignity too! We have dignity before our brothers and sisters in Christ, as well as, a good witness before the world. When our witness is strong through action, then our witness through words can be accepted as truth

Each day we must ask God to show us those "presumptuous sins" so we can be blameless and innocent of "great transgressions." Great transgressions can be "simple" ones in our minds. But…if we withhold love, mercy, grace, forgiveness, peace, understanding, patience, acceptance (the list is endless) we sin with great transgression because the results are inflicted on the people who need these things and we need to see our disobedience as the murder of their spirit and ours.

Yes, it's shocking – but it's true. Murder of someone's spirit is exactly what we are guilty of before the Lord. Each of us is the child of someone we can let down, the friend of someone we can let down or the mate of someone, the boss of someone, the parent of someone or the employee of someone and the possibilities of harm are endless. Will we murder the spirit of someone today, even the Holy Spirit, because we will not search our hearts and turn from presumptuous sin? Will we just harden our hearts, go in our house and let the fish stink outside as Pharaoh did and take no responsibility? We must daily fervently seek His face to see if we are reflecting God's love or our sin.

A beginning place for prayer today:

Lord please help me to take responsibility for my life today. Help me to look into my heart as You would look at my heart. I desire a soft heart, a willing heart and only You can keep this heart clean and free from great transgressions. Forgive me Father, for my complacency in the comfortableness of who I think I am in life overtakes me all too often.

Discussion Questions for today:

1. Why do I think presumptuous sins are so damaging to us and others?

2. Why didn't God just program us to be His servants to begin with; why must we choose to be believers?

DAY 19

BUT WHEN PHARAOH SAW THAT THERE WAS RELIEF, HE HARDENED HIS HEART AND DID NOT LISTEN TO THEM AS THE LORD HAD SAID. – EXODUS 8:15

READING FOR TODAY– EXODUS 8: 1-15 AND PSALM 31: 14-24

Are we like Pharaoh, guilty of half-hearted obedience? When all else fails we turn to God? He has our attention now! We can no longer ignore or walk away from the foul smell of our sin and the problems we have created. We must do something and God is it.

In sorrow we see clearly what our problems are and we repent. Now the choice comes, which course will we choose? For the most part, everyone one wants a simple, painless path through life, but that is not what we are always called to, especially when we have to clean up a mess.

All too often, when the pressure is off and God's peace stills our hearts we sort of let our fervor die and let the uncomfortable needs slip from our view. Surely, He doesn't mean for me to cause more strife by standing firm? Well, yes, He does if that is what it will take to make the wrong right. "I'm sorry" is more than a phrase, its actions. It isn't a matter of saying I forgive or I'll become more patient or more tolerant, it's BEING forgiving, more patient and more tolerant.

Like Pharaoh's frogs our sin may cease, but the stench of it will take time to clean-up and be eliminated. Just because we become believers doesn't mean we won't suffer the consequences of our past sins. No one escapes the consequences of sin. The Lord becomes our refuge in the storms of personal change. Steps toward growth and change are ours to choose and God's desire is to help us through those steps. Half-hearted obedience only stacks the dead frogs higher.

It has the appearance of progress, but unless the shovel is put to the pile every day until it's gone…the pile stays, attracting more problems. Unless we take our weaknesses before God every day He cannot help us clean-up the mess of our sinful behavior. Ignoring or being tolerant of sin doesn't eliminate it either.

Abortion and homosexuality are two blatantly obvious examples of what happens in a Christian nation when we decide to be tolerant or ignore sin. Yes, there is turmoil and anger, even among friends, but God is not to be compromised. We have evidence of the pile of frogs caused by these sins growing higher and higher and the stench is now unbearable. This evidence brings us back to the truth of verse 19 of Psalm 31:

How great is Thy goodness, which Thou hast stored up for those

who fear Thee, which though hast wrought for those who take

refuge in Thee before the sons of men!

We are before the sons of men, but more importantly we are before and answer to the righteous and holy God of the universe. Half-hearted obedience or the willful choice of desiring to be called a child of God but staying politically correct to the world's tolerance of sin will only cause our sin to be unrepentant before God. What choice will we make today? What path will we put our feet to—the world's path or God's path?

A BEGINNING PLACE FOR PRAYER TODAY:

Lord, You alone know my disobediences. I may look like I'm making progress, but I want real change in my life. Make me like you Father. Give me a sharper, clearer view of where my sins are stacking up. Direct me toward the piles with a shovel to get these messes cleaned up. Help me Father, because I want to be for You the best servant I can be. Let verse 23 and 24 of Psalm 31 minister to my disobedient heart and let me place my hope in full obedience to Your Word.

DISCUSSION QUESTIONS FOR TODAY:

1. Why do I not want to have a proud spirit before God?

2. What are some of my past disobediences? What have I learned about the character of God as a result of repenting and putting actions to my prayers for forgiveness?

DAY 20

How blessed is the man who does not walk in the counsel of the wicked, nor stand in the path of sinners, nor sit in the seat of scoffers, but his delight is in the law of the Lord, and in His law he meditates day and night. And he will be like a tree firmly planted by the streams of water, which yields its fruit in its seasons, and its leaf does not wither and whatever he does, he prospers. – Psalm 1: 1-3

Reading for today– Exodus 8: 16-23, Psalm 1

The power and the majesty of our God is shown when we choose to stand apart from the world. There should be strong evidence that we as believers are different and blessed with the peace and righteousness found only in adhering to God's law. God wants to nourish us as the tree planted by the river so the world will seek Him and know His power.

God drew a protective line around the Israelites in Egypt and this separation saved them from the plague. Often our homes and families aren't separated from the plagues of this age because day and night we do not meditate on His law. Frequently, we plan our lives around the professional people of the world whom we have decided might be better at or more up-to-date in prospering us.

We squander our personal gifts seeking fame and fortune for ourselves. Why can't we understand that we lose everything when we gain the whole world? Doctors, lawyers, accountants and even professional counselors all have gifts that God has given them for our wise use; the key is "wise use". God meets our needs through His Word first and then He directs and He allows the right professionals to come into our lives.

If we follow the precepts of the Bible we will have very little use and certainly not life time dependencies on the professionals of this world. When the Holy Spirit is given full reign in our lives, He gives us insight and direction not even the world can comprehend. And, when we seek professional help we can evaluate their advice with the Word of God as the measuring stick of what is truly God's perspective in their advice.

We are God's light and salt in the world. We were saved not to just go to heaven, but to be productive here on earth. To be the most valuable we can be for God we must be seen as something special, really different; not just pious, judgmental, unearthly good separatists, but as people with the answer for joyful life—JESUS!

In this world, but not of this world—this is how we want to be seen, always approachable and most importantly as seekers and those who meditate upon God's Word. Whatever He says we do and then we use those principles to choose the professionals of this world to accomplish those principles only.

A BEGINNING PLACE FOR PRAYER TODAY:

Lord let me be truly different in the world's eyes. Put me in Your Word seeking You daily so the plagues of this world cannot affect me and those I hold most dear. Keep my heart and my motives pure. Let me a have a heart to serve and to listen, not only to those around me but to You as You prompt me throughout this day with Your Holy Spirit. Please give me that line of separation around my home and in the actions of my daily life that lets everyone know who I serve. The fruit I yield in season will then be Your wisdom and I will not wither under the pressures and temptations of this life. Thank You Father.

DISCUSSION QUESTIONS FOR TODAY:

1. Is it easy to fall into the philosophies of the world and be comfortable in compromise?

2. Why is it important to know the character of God? How do we become acquainted with the character of God?

DAY 21

THE LORD IS THEIR STRENGTH, AND HE IS A SAVING DEFENSE TO HIS ANOINTED. SAVE THY PEOPLE, AND BLESS THINE INHERITANCE, BE THEIR SHEPHERD ALSO AND CARRY THEM FOREVER – (PARAPHRASED) PSALM 28:7-9

READING FOR TODAY– EXODUS 8: 24-32 AND PSALM 28

The world tries to make compromises with God, but God deals justly with believers and non- believers alike. There can be no compromise with God's Word, because there is neither gray nor shades of white or black, there is only black and white, good and evil. Why does man seek to compromise with God?

We seek to compromise with God because we have a basic sin nature called self-centeredness. We want what we want, when we want it. This is not a pretty picture of man. For our own well being, God knows He must require obedience from us to His desires for our lives or we will bear the burden of our own sin nature.

As Christians, we are forgiven if we seek His forgiveness. God honors our desire to serve Him and wants to keep working with our honest desire to do His will, His way. "His way" is the most important operative of obedience to God.

His way requires us, like Moses, to go into the wilderness and seek His way through prayer. Prayer is the offer of our heart to God. We sacrifice a blemished heart before God to get it purified at His altar through prayer. When our heart is sacrificed and then replaced with His heart we have His vision and His desires working in us.

We can't fool God or man with lip service. God knows our hearts and man hears the words of our hearts and sees the ultimate actions our hearts play out daily. God is the only person we can never surprise. Going to church on Sundays can either become an honor to God or a token sacrifice to God for the bad behavior of the past week. We tell our children not to pursue ungodly things and yet we pursue "just a few minor ones"— compromise! God is not fooled, man is not fooled, we have altered God's desires to suit ourselves.

There is no reward for compromise. It may prolong the inevitable results of sin, but the results will come just as God predicts. He is either our shepherd or He is not. We will either be dragged away by the wolves or be among those who speak God's truth and live it before the world.

Man is foolish to try and compromise with God. Like Pharaoh we will postpone the inevitable plagues of our lives, but we will ultimately suffer for our disobedience and experience those plagues if we choose to compromise God's commands in our lives.

A beginning place for prayer today:

Lord, I know what is right. I have read Your Word. I fear my own failures, but with You I cannot fail. I know what You require of me is not easy nor maybe even pleasant, but I want your blessings and not the consequences of my actions. Father, I commit this day to serve You, using your strength and allowing You to carry me, because I am weak and if left to my own strength I will compromise and sin. Go before me and be my shield, that I may glorify You even in the little things of this day! Thank You Father that You are as interested in the little things as You are in the big things of my life.

Discussion Questions for today:

1. Why can we not fool God with deceptive words?

2. Why are the words "His way" the operative words for true obedience?

DAY 22

BUT THE HEART OF PHARAOH WAS HARDENED, AND HE DID NOT LET THE PEOPLE GO. –
EXODUS 9: 7B

READING FOR TODAY– EXODUS 9: 1-12 AND PSALM 8

How could Pharaoh harden his heart against his own people? And…just as Pharaoh's heart hardened; what was happening to the hearts of the Israelites? Man can hold out against God as long as he is above the tragedies of life. Perhaps that is why it is easier for a camel to go through the eye of a needle than for a rich man to get into heaven. (Matt. 19:24) The wealthier we are: physically, intellectually or monetarily, the more self-confident we are and the less God confident we will become.

Pharaoh just looked upon the plagues; he stayed aloof, except when the frogs and insects swarmed into his house. He is compromised and offered Moses three days distance to go and sacrifice, but as soon as the frogs and insects were dead he turned his back on the power of God. Meanwhile, the Israelites were seeing new and afresh the God of Abraham. He is in the middle of their suffering and He going before them to bring down the mighty Pharaoh of Egypt.

Even today God goes before us because we are His people. He gives us the gift of His presence, His care and He meets all of our needs. As it says in Psalm 8:"His fingers have made the heavens" and yet even the psalmist marvels: "What is man that Thou dost take thought of him?" He sets his children above all the creatures of the earth. It is all too marvelous to comprehend, but God loves His people. Pharaoh valued nothing, but himself. He was even willing to gamble with the livestock of Egypt. God knew Pharaoh and He knew his stubbornness, haughty pride and complete detachment from other people's suffering. His sin-nature allowed God to impress upon the Egyptians and the Israelites the complete power and thoroughness of Israel's God.

The needs of God's people come first in His economy. He kept their livestock safe because they would need them soon to depart Egypt and eventually establish the Promised Land. Whenever God makes a plan for us it is perfect, He covers all the bases; things we never even consider, God provides.

If we are wise we will daily apprise ourselves of what God has done for us. A thankful heart will not easily become self-centered, bitter, frustrated, anxious or angry with God. A thankful heart looks at everything around it and sees the love of God in every day life. It is such a breath of fresh air to look up and say as the psalmist says in verse 9 of Psalm 8: "Oh Lord, our Lord, How majestic is thy name in all the earth!"

A BEGINNING PLACE FOR PRAYER TODAY:

Father, how do I begin to thank You? Your provision for me is so complete from birth to death and then even into eternal life. I am so loved. Keep me mindful of all my blessings today and let me share generously my life with others. All that I am and all that

I have is Yours. Let me not be selfish with either small or large kindnesses. I have so much to give. Help me to remember that even a smile and kinds words can mean more to your children than sometimes all the wealth of a Pharaoh. Thank you Father for this day.

DISCUSSION QUESTIONS FOR TODAY:

1. Can I think of something that God has done for me in the past and when I look back on it I cannot believe how complete His provision was under the circumstances of that event?

2. What does a thankful heart achieve in our lives each day? What is the alternative to a thankful heart?

DAY 23

FOR THE RIGHTEOUS GOD TESTS THE HEARTS AND MINDS. PSALM 7:9B

READING FOR TODAY– EXODUS 9:13-24 AND PSALM 7

God desires that all should come to know Him. In Pharaoh's case He allowed Pharaoh's hard heart to save His people from certain destruction. God cannot be mocked without serious consequences occurring, but when God is honored then He honors and upholds. In verse 14, 15 and 16 of chapter 9 in Exodus God says, "I will send all my plagues to your very heart…that you may know that there is none like me in all the earth…If I had stretched out my hand and struck you and your people you would have been cut off from the earth, but indeed for this purpose I have raised you up, that I may show My Power in you." He has given even Pharaoh his position, earthly power gone astray, so that He can show the Israelites and even the Egyptians that it would be wise to heed the warnings of the Lord.

Whenever we think we are in charge of life God comes along and reminds us, even abruptly if necessary, that we are powerless unless we are in His will and not our own. He continually upholds the righteous by strengthening His character in their hearts and minds. He dwells in our hearts. He sets His deepest desires for each of us in our hearts so that our minds can reason the value of His desires for our lives. We cannot over-rule or disregard the wisdom of the Lord indefinitely. Evidence will eventually show He is right if we make wrong decisions—that's what the conviction of the Holy Spirit accomplishes.

He could easily strike us off the face of the earth for our evil, foolish ways, but he chooses not to do so. He chooses to strive with us to get our attention and to save us from our sinful nature, just as He did with the Egyptians. Verse 20 says, "He who feared the word of the Lord (respected and honored, put value to His words) among the servants of Pharaoh made his servants and his livestock flee to the houses." Obviously, Pharaoh stayed inside because he survived but he did not command his subjects to do so. He stayed stubbornly in his own power and self-reliance and blatantly refused to bow his knee to the Lord.

"God will not always strive with man."(Genesis 6:3) There will come a day when it is too late even to get into heaven. But, for today there is time to stand for God and to be made spiritually alive by God if we will but turn our hearts toward Him. Perhaps we foolishly disregard His commands today because we want our own way, but as surely as God caused destruction all about the self-reliant Pharaoh of Egypt, He will allow the same to happen to us. Conviction of wrong doing, wrong motives, selfish behavior or even outright evil behavior should never be ignored, "for the wages of sin is death". Death can come to our eternal souls long before it comes to our physical body if we continue to be disobedient to His commands.

A BEGINNING PLACE FOR PRAYER TODAY:

Lord, please make me wise and let me see quickly when I am striving in my own will and strength. Show me your wisdom and train me up in your principles so I will not be cut down by the hail stones of this life. Add lighting and thunder to even my simplest faults so I will see them and repent and be grieved by them as if they were as obvious as murder. Help me Lord to not be satisfied to live in my own strength, keep me from behaving like the Pharaoh of Egypt. Soften this heart of mine and keep it pure before you Father. Father I thank You for Your loving care.

DISCUSSION QUESTIONS FOR TODAY:

1. Have I ever been convicted by the Holy Spirit that I was too much in charge of my life?

2. Have I ever hardened my heart toward God and done what I wanted? Were there consequences?

DAY 24

FOR YOU HAVE ARMED ME WITH STRENGTH FOR THE BATTLE; YOU HAVE SUBDUED UNDER ME THOSE WHO ROSE UP AGAINST ME. PSALM 18:39

READING FOR TODAY– EXODUS 9: 25-35 AND PSALM 18:39, 46-50.

In Exodus 9:30 Moses lets Pharaoh know that he does not believe him. He knows the evil and vain nature of Pharaoh. Once Pharaoh thinks he has fooled God, he will return to his old ways. So why stop the hail? It was a further reminder to the Israelites and to the Egyptians that God was still in charge.

Each time God is glorified by our standing with Him against evil we are strengthened by His presence in our lives. Our worst days of trial are probably our best because we have been the most reliant on His strength. Evil will be with us until the Lord returns. It is important to remember that He has equipped us to fight the battle. The fact that we know what evil is and what sin looks like puts us way ahead of the world in wisdom. The world compromises with evil and is overcome by it and is always surprised by its magnitude and strength, while we are not.

God calls us to be as gentle as doves and as wise as serpents. We can always hope for the best, but we must always be aware of evil in ourselves and in others. Evil is the outcome of sin. When the works of man produce evil they are the result of sin. We have a responsibility to evaluate all our efforts here on earth with the standard question: Will this produce good or evil?" The simplicity of God's Word tells us what is good: Peace, patience, love, joy, longsuffering, kindness, goodness, faithfulness, gentleness, and self-control. Against such there is no law." (Gal. 5:22-23).

The whole counsel of God—the Bible—is designed to lead us into the abundant life of Christ. God produces that abundance in our lives, but He requires honest work and effort on our part to stay in obedience. Sin is often compromise so we can avoid pain for a season in our lives. When we seek a temporary peace with compromise we are prolonging the inevitable of having to deal with sin at a later date and possibly in a more complicated and convoluted way than we ever could have imagined.

As parents we dislike conflict and sometimes for the sake of peace we compromise in our discipline. We know what evil looks like, we know what the consequences of sin will be in the lives of our children, but we fool ourselves with compromise. The reality of using a firm voice and a steady hand on an evil situation until the course of that child's life is firmly set back on track is often painful for everyone involved. Personal experience has taught me that a child usually doesn't rise up and call you blessed until he becomes an adult and sees the results of your steadfastness on his behalf. But…whether praise or understanding ever comes from that child, God will honor your obedience, for you have seen evil and have wisely allowed God to turn it around for good. You have held a course equipped by God which is acceptable in His sight and even fruitful before the world.

We should never be surprised by sin in ourselves or other Christians. The old sin nature can always surface. We will never be perfect until we see Him face to face—so with imperfection comes sin. We must take heart that we are growing each day as we earnestly seek Him. When we see sin in our lives or in others we need to rejoice even in the confidence that we see it. We cannot be overcome or destroyed because we see sin and are armed to protect ourselves with the blood of Jesus. Pharaoh never fooled God, he only fooled himself.

True wisdom is found in the Word of God. Man's intellect always produces something that has loop holes and cracks into which he can fall. God's path is straight, narrow and well lit. The whole counsel of God needs to be sought in all the decisions we make. God's good is never temporary. It is the stuff of the eternal and the unchangeable character we will take to heaven with us.

A BEGINNING PLACE FOR PRAYER TODAY:

Evil is all about me in this world Lord. Make me wise and keep my eyes open to my own compromise with it. Just a little sin in any area of my life is an open door to more sin. I desire to know the good qualities of Your abundant life and be better acquainted with them in my life, more than I prefer to understand the qualities of evil.

Help me to separate myself from the world where I know the temptations are too great. Watch over all my business dealings and give me a heart that always checks my motives. Help me to exhort others to their highest standards by praising those who go out on a limb to be on the righteous side of an issue. Thank You Father that Your Word so clearly tells me about the fruit of good in my life. Let me strive after the good only.

DISCUSSION QUESTIONS FOR TODAY:

1. Why do we sometimes fall into the trap of compromise when we should solve a problem immediately with God's standards? Can we think of a time when we compromised for what we thought would be peace, and instead, complicated a situation into something that was anything but peaceful?

2. Why is it so important that I stand up for God's perspective on good and evil?

DAY 25

GOD SETS THE SOLITARY IN FAMILIES; HE BRINGS OUT THOSE WHO ARE BOUND INTO PROSPERITY; BUT THE REBELLIOUS DWELL IN A DRY LAND. PSALM 68:6

READING FOR TODAY– EXODUS 10: 1-11, PSALM 68: 1-6; 19 AND 20, 32-35

Fear is always the enemies' tool. If he can frighten us enough, maybe we'll change our course of obedience to God and go his way. Pharaoh has everything to lose, his work force is trying to leave town so he tries the old fear tactic. Satan uses this tactic all the time to try and keep us in bondage.

If we serve our God in a manner that is outlined in His scriptures we have nothing to fear. No where in the scriptures does it say: "Serve me and I will abandon you!" Quite the contrary, it says: "I will never leave you or forsake you." His blessings are His promises to us. It is only when we decide to take short cuts in our Christian walk that we need to be fearful.

Shortcuts can be harmful because they aren't the course of action that keeps us working for the Lord. They start us on a path of working for ourselves. We find ourselves in a dry land and our prosperity of spirit is gone. We lose temporarily the solitude or peace of being a member of God's family. Our joy and gladness disappears into worry and even anxiety because we know we are making our own way. God-confident and God- centered lifestyles are not the experience of the individual who alters God's commandments. Even putting God's law on hold for a better time or later will produce fear.

It's really pretty simple: What God says is right is right; what God says is wrong is wrong. There are no shades of gray and there is not always an easy way to accomplish that which is pleasing to the Lord. But…there are always blessings to God's way and destruction of something or someone in Satan's order of doing things. Keeping our eyes looking up and counting our blessings always eliminates fear from our lives. When fear and all its emotions are under control then God is the one governing our lives; not the enemy.

A BEGINNING PLACE FOR PRAYER TODAY:

Father, make my path straight forwardly Your pathway for my life. Let me stop planning so hard and let me experience the joy of my life one day at a time. Focus my heart on the blessings of this day and on the memories I can create by simple acts of love to those who are around me. Apprehend my heart and give it the wings of peace it can have if I am obedient to Your Word. Lord, you have blessed me so abundantly. Help me to be the person you desire me to be, living the life you desire me to live. Thank You Father, for this day. In Jesus name, I seek and want to find Your presence.

DISCUSSION QUESTIONS FOR TODAY:

1. If a situation in my life is producing worry or anxiety, what should I do about that situation before the Lord?

2. When we choose to conduct our lives in a manner that is pleasing to God, can we always expect things go smoothly right away? Do we even have a time guarantee on when a problem will come to an end? Why should we then be so faithful to pursue evil with good?

DAY 26

OUR SOUL WAITS FOR THE LORD; HE IS OUR HELP AND OUR SHIELD. FOR OUR HEART SHALL REJOICE IN HIM, BECAUSE WE HAVE TRUSTED IN HIS HOLY NAME. PSALM 33: 20 & 21

READING FOR TODAY– EXODUS 10: 12-21; PSALM 33 AND II CORINTHIANS 4: 7-10

Then the Lord said to Moses, "Stretch out your hand toward heaven, that there may be darkness over the land of Egypt, darkness which may even be felt."(Exodus 10:21) DARKNESS WHICH MAY EVEN BE FELT. Can we imagine such a feeling of darkness? We as Christians will never know the depth of the kind of loneliness or despair the world experiences. Without Christ as our personal Savior there is no one to turn to; no one to trust; a complete aloneness.

What a complete blessing Christ is to us, for when he left us He left with us the indwelling of His Holy Spirit. As it says in II Corinthians 4:6-10:

FOR IT IS GOD WHO COMMANDED LIGHT TO SHINE OUT OF DARKNESS, WHO HAS SHOWN IN OUR HEARTS TO GIVE THE LIGHT OF THE KNOWLEDGE OF THE GLORY OF GOD IN THE FACE OF JESUS CHRIST. BUT, WE HAVE THIS TREASURE IN EARTHEN VESSELS THAT THE EXCELLENCE OF THE POWER MAY BE OF GOD AND NOT OF US. WE ARE HARD PRESSED ON EVERY SIDE, YET NOT CRUSHED, WE ARE PERPLEXED, BUT NOT IN DESPAIR; PERSECUTED, BUT NOT FORSAKEN, STRUCK DOWN, BUT NOT DESTROYED—ALWAYS CARRYING ABOUT IN THE BODY THE DYING OF THE LORD JESUS THAT THE LIFE OF JESUS ALSO MAY BE MANIFESTED IN OUR BODY.

If we feel alone it is a trick of the enemy because God is always with us. A simple prayer, just one word: "Jesus", brings Him into the very darkest or the very brightest of our moments. He desires that fellowship with us. He promises us His strength as our help and our shield from all that the world would try to destroy in our lives. Each time we think that darkness has overwhelmed us we need only to call His name and light will descend upon our souls. In His light there is clear vision and warmth. Christ's words are His vision or view of life's circumstances and there is comfort and warmth in His constant fellowship. "Nothing can separate us from the love of Christ." (Romans 8: 39)

What a remarkable thing that His light is in us. What a terrible thing that anyone should have to function without it. This is why it is so important that we share the joy of the Lord as expressed in Psalm 33. "The earth is full of His goodness", but if we know someone who doesn't know Him then we know someone who could be experiencing the darkness of Exodus 10: 21. Who needs God's light that I know? Remember: Darkness is of the enemy!

A BEGINNING PLACE FOR PRAYER TODAY:

Please renew my heart, Father. Keep Your light shinning in my heart so that I may shine for You. I want others to see Your light in me. Let them want to know my peace and my strength because You are present in my life. Dispel the darkness in all the corners of my heart this day. I desire to shine for You, Father. Help me this day to share Your nearness and the hope I have in You as the one in charge of my life. Thank You

Father for all Your love toward me. Go before me this day and shine Your light upon my path that I may be a servant worthy of Your loving presence.

DISCUSSION QUESTIONS FOR TODAY:

1. Can I imagine what darkness "you can feel" would be like?

2. Am I experiencing the fullness of His light in my life today? If not, then what can I do to get the light shining in my life again?

DAY 27

For with you is the fountain of life; in your light we see light. Psalm 36:9

Reading for today— Exodus 10: 22-29 and Psalm 36

When man is without light in his life according to Psalm 36:"he is without the fear of God before his eyes (vs. 1a), he flatters himself in his own eyes (vs. 2a), the words of his mouth are wickedness and deceit; he ceases to be wise and to do good (vs. 3), he devises wickedness on his bed, he sets himself in a way that is not good; he does not abhor evil."(vs. 4) Pharaoh was without light and these were the traits of Pharaoh's character and these are the characteristics of sin as we know it today.

Those who choose not to serve God choose to function in darkness. But, those who choose God choose to have His light function in their own homes and personal lives. The blessings of God's light according to Psalm 36 are: the mercy and faithfulness of the Lord (vs.5), His righteousness, His judgments and His preservation (vs.6), the loving kindness and trust in the shadow of his wings (vs.7), we can drink from the river of His pleasures and in Him is the fountain of life because in Him we see light (or righteousness), (vs. 8 and 9).

Why is it some of us lack these blessings? It is painfully simple. Some of the darkness just creeps in when we are weak or not vigilant to ask God to keep us in His light. It usually starts with flattering ourselves—pride—and then ends at its most terrible point when we have gone so far that we no longer abhor evil and can settle for "the means justifying the end" even when that end is evil. We fool ourselves, then we try to fool others and with words we cover our tracks and make excuses. When we are deep in sin we do stupid and harmful things to ourselves and others. It can even get so bad that we must scheme and think how we will cover up or stay ahead of those who could expose us. We even lay awake at night to scheme.

Verses 10 and 11 tell us how we can stay out of darkness. The Psalmist says: "Oh, continue Your loving kindness to those who know You and Your righteousness to the upright in heart." If I seek to know God, I seek to know His commandments and I learn what righteousness is in God's sight. My heart cannot be upright unless it knows what that looks, sounds and feels like in my own behavior. Verse 11 says "let not the foot of pride come against me." From the smallest to the biggest of my actions and motives, if I look to myself I am prideful. When I become self-centered and not God-centered—I make all my judgments by my own standards.

If verse 10 and 11 are not heeded and pursued; then we become that worker of iniquity who has fallen, is cast down and is not able to rise up. Pride, "the foot of pride", is upon our necks and we are cast down even as verse 12 states. Pharaoh has worked his way into that very position. His own pride will eventually lead to his destruction. Addictions, unhealthy relationships and basically taking what appears to be the easy way around complete obedience to God's word all find their root in pride. They are all forms of self first, not God first. The more I know about God, the more I see my sin nature for what it really is and the quicker I want to have that "upright heart." When I stop seeking that upright heart, I stop seeking God. He cannot work in me until I repent and I am restored by His forgiveness and unmerited mercy and grace. All of this is possible only if I will reach out to God for these gifts. And when He reaches out to me I will have His ever present light just as the Israelites had even in the darkness of Egypt.

A BEGINNING PLACE FOR PRAYER TODAY:

Lord, it is just too easy to serve myself. My prideful ways are ever before me. Forgive my sinful nature in this area of my life. Keep me open to service "for You and not "for myself." Whatever it is that comes my way, please let it be approached with an upright heart. May I not be too good to be subordinate to You or Your children. Make me a valuable servant in Your sight today so I can work in Your light not in unproductive darkness.

DISCUSSION QUESTIONS FOR TODAY:

1. Has darkness tried to creep into my life lately? What areas of my life am I manipulating and having to scheme about in order to have my way?

2. Can I flatter myself into taking shortcuts? How? Have I been fooling myself or others by making excuses or covering up my errors in judgment?

DAY 28

Let Your Light So Shine Before Men, That They May See Your Good Works, And Glorify Your Father Which Is In Heaven. Matthew 5: 16

Reading for today– Exodus 11: 1-3; Matthew 5: 14-16, Psalm 16

Because God showed His favor to the Israelites and Moses they are given "favor in the sight of the Egyptians." They become "the light of the world. A city that is set on a hill (and) cannot be hidden." God was glorified through Moses and Aaron's faithfulness. God's power, strength and preservation of His people were evident through all the miracles that were performed. These miracles were not under the commands of Moses; he was simply the mouth piece for God. All that was done was done with the preface: "Thus saith the Lord ..."

Today, as in the days of Moses and Aaron, we must be light to the world. As it has often been said, "Your life may be the only Bible some people will ever read." For God's sake there must be a difference between us and the non-believer. I have found that we preach the Gospel much stronger by our deeds than by our words. The person with the quiet confidence of a life hid in Christ goes about living in such a way that others want what they have. Our bait for being fishers of men is that quiet confidence and because it is so subtle it is often more compelling than any street corner witnessing or confrontational debates that we might pursue.

Likewise, our children are better persuaded by our lifestyles, than by empty words. If each of us can affect our children for Christ, we will have done quite a wonderful service even if we never set foot in the formal missionary field or preach from a pulpit. What a ripple affect we can create for Christ if each of our children in turn influence their children for Christ and so on through the generations.

When it comes to evidence of success, a Christian marriage is quite an appealing thing to share with our non-believing friends. God's partnership of mutual submission to one another under God's authority makes quite a statement as to how He values men and women. It keeps gender identity from becoming a problem and it certainly keeps our society healthy both physically and emotionally. God's order for His children is stable and peaceful not to mention loving and caring. How could the world not be impressed?

Taking a stand for God's morality in this day and age will certainly set us apart. If we gain unpopularity, it will be to our heavenly account. And...we certainly know what the sin of this age has already produced in harm and in some instances has already been down right devastating to the family unit. We have nothing to lose and everything to gain by standing firm and not compromising God's moral principles.

Yes, we should look and be different. Now the question for today is: Do we? Can I say as the psalmist says in Psalm 16: 2, 5 and 6: YOU ARE MY LORD, MY GOODNESS IS NOTHING APART FROM YOU. O LORD YOU ARE THE PORTION OF MY INHERITANCE AND MY CUP; YOU MAINTAIN MY LOT THE

LINES HAVE FALLEN TO ME IN PLEASANT PLACES; YES I HAVE A GOOD INHERITANCE.

A BEGINNING PLACE FOR PRAYER TODAY:

Lord when people see me, let them say there goes a person after God's own heart. Let anyone who knows me know who I serve and why I am so blessed. Forgive me if I let you down and don't give You the credit for all my so called accomplishments. Without You Father there is nothing of value and with You, Father, all things, people and circumstances have great joy for they are all your gifts to me. Thank You for this day. Help me to make the most of it for You Father.

DISCUSSION QUESTIONS FOR TODAY:

1. What qualities of God attract people to Christians and what attributes of God attract me to other Christians?

2. What qualities of God am I displaying for my family at home? What's the most important place for my qualities to be evident—in the world or in the home?

DAY 29

NEVERTHELESS THE FOUNDATIONS OF GOD STANDETH SURE, HAVING THIS SEAL, THE LORD KNOWETH THEM THAT ARE HIS, AND LET EVERYONE THAT NAMETH THE NAME OF CHRIST DEPART FROM INIQUITY. II TIMOTHY 2:19

READING FOR TODAY– EXODUS 11: 4-10 AND PSALM 21

The blessings of God toward David in Psalm 21 are our blessings if we trust in the Lord as David did in verse 7. When we are His He shows us love, mercy, goodness and blessings. But, for those who oppose Him He will "swallow them up in His wrath and the fire shall devour them."

In this mornings Bible study, Pharaoh and Egypt have opposed God and they are about to feel His wrath as their first born will be swallowed up by death. When God and His commandments are ignored, man is swallowed up and devoured by his own sin. No matter what God has done in the past, some men still reject Him today. Evidence of God's power does not always bring man to his knees before the true and living God. We must accept the fact that all the miracles of Christ when He walked upon the earth and even His resurrection from the cross still escapes many.

Years ago, while standing at the Wailing Wall in Jerusalem, on a once in a lifetime trip, I experienced sadness watching Jews perform their religious rituals at the wall just a few yards away from where Moslems were positioned on their prayer rugs, performing their rituals. They were surrounded by the tangible history of Israel and the historical witness of Christ's life and resurrection and yet they did not believe nor would they accept Christ as the Son of God. It dawned on me later that if I were at that moment so sad and discouraged, how much more Jesus must have felt and the Father who sent Him?

God's wrath is a fact. He does and He will defend those who are His. The harshness of His wrath upon Pharaoh is no less than that which will be played out upon man today because he continues to dismiss the commandments of God and the gift of His Son's shed blood upon the cross.

The scriptures are the historical fact that God protects us if we trust Him. Faith in Christ is a demonstration of our trust in Him and our avoidance of everything that He says will harm us. In II Timothy 2:19 we are reminded to depart from iniquity so we can be known by Him. We want Him to make a difference in us so that we can stand out to the world as being His. He showed the Egyptians the difference between the power of their gods and the power of the true and living God of Israel, but Pharaoh and his people would not depart from their iniquity and God did not know them.

God desires to know each one of us, but if we are not to perish we must seek to know Him. He will bless us with His intimate fellowship if we seek Him. The active part of faith is doing what God commands. Our works cannot save us, but they are proof we believe His commandments and we want Him to know us. Even the devil believes in

God. Believing is not the issue for a Christian—it is in the simple act of walking by faith that we accept Christ as the Lord of our lives. Because we are constantly seeking to know God's will we will allow God to set us apart from the world. The wrath of God cannot be denied and our pursuing of iniquity could one day be the dividing line between us and God. I do not know about you, but for me the worst possible phrase I could ever hear the Father say to me would be: "I never knew you."

A BEGINNING PLACE FOR PRAYER TODAY:

Lord if there is iniquity in my life today let me seek diligently to depart from it. I may not be a murderer but with evil words I can kill. Let me see sin as sin, not greater or lesser sins; sin for what it does to me and to my relationship with You. Don't let the enemy fool me into thinking that it's just a "character flaw". Keep me mindful of all my shortcomings so I can call upon Your power to put them under Your control and allow You to eliminate them from my life. Thank You Father that you desire to make me different from the world. Thank You that you set me apart from Your wrath and choose only to bless me if I will but trust You.

DISCUSSION QUESTIONS FOR TODAY:

1. What does it mean to walk in faith with God?

2. Do we want an intimate relationship with God or are we satisfied with a superficial one? How do we maintain the intimate relationship?

DAY 30

THE LORD WILL GIVE STRENGTH TO HIS PEOPLE; THE LORD WILL BLESS HIS PEOPLE WITH PEACE. PSALM 29:11

READING FOR TODAY– EXODUS 12: 1-7 AND PSALM 29

Psalm 29 reminds us of the glory and majesty of God in all that He has done and is capable of doing. The key phrase to me throughout the Psalm is "the voice of the Lord". Moses and Aaron heard and believed the voice of the Lord. They took His words as instructions and commandments.

We do not have the audible voice of God in our lives today, but we have His written word. It is our instruction for living in this world. Like Moses and Aaron we need to consider it a commandment. I think we all need to be constantly reminded that a commandment is an order not a suggestion. Moses and Aaron were in a war with Pharaoh and they knew God was their only hope to defeat him. So as soldiers in a war they took each command from God seriously and tried to follow it to the letter.

In the Old Testament sacrifices were a part of their lives and God's request for a lamb was quite acceptable and reasonable. God's requests are not always reasonable or even acceptable to us at times. Sometimes they seem impossible and even hurtful to our pride and our personal desires so we choose to receive them as suggestions and not commands. To be a good soldier for Christ today, we have to receive all of God's Word as a commandment for our lives. Unfortunately, it is not uncommon to see the church being politically correct today and making the smorgasbord method of faith acceptable – it says to the world I'll take only off the Lord's table what appeals to me and I'll ignore the rest.

When we accept the power of His voice in our lives, we begin to realize the strength He can give us and ultimately the peace we have doing the commands of that voice. He gives us order and even boundaries as to how far we will strive with the enemy. In the optimum life of a Christians, He can set the priorities of our lives. When we are drawn into enemy territory, we can stand on high ground and see sin for what it really is and we can choose wisely to serve only God because we have chosen to study His Word and obey His commandments.

When we desire to serve only God I have found that we stop associating with frustration because in its place is the acceptance of God's will in our lives. We accept that sin exists and we draw away from it. We replace anxiety and fear with peace because we know there is only one road to travel and to choose any other route will put us in danger. If we accept our responsibility and pursue to the best of our abilities all the avenues at our disposal and then commit what we cannot handle to God then we can take comfort that God is in charge. Little by little He will reveal the truth of every situation if we are faithful to follow his voice to the letter.

The blood of the sacrifice was placed on the door posts of the Israelites. Prayer is the blood we place at the door posts of our homes. God accepts those prayers as we have accepted the blood of Jesus in our lives. Jesus becomes the strength and power which stands between us and the destruction of the enemy and this world.

How strange the Israelites must have appeared before the Egyptians: blood sacrifices, blood on the door posts of their homes. No matter how commitment and responsibility look to man, we must always seek to have God's approval on our lives. I think it is important that we value the responsibility to be a peculiar people in the world's eyes. Everyone who opposes God's commandments is of the world and your mate, your children, your parents and even your friends can at times be a part of the world. Opposing evil can often make you appear unreasonable even to those you love.

Try standing your ground with a teenager when you say no to allowing them to do what they want when you know it will cause them harm and see for yourself how reasonable you appear to them! Or, have an open discussion on homosexuality or abortion or even sin and see how reasonable you will be judged by friends and neighbors who do not know the Lord. I think it is unwise to assume that the battle for your soul and those you love exists outside your own inner circle. The full armor of God as spoken of in Ephesians 6: 11-18 must be worn at all times in your home and outside of it. Moses and Aaron desired to serve God's voice in every minute detail; should we not also desire the same thing?

A BEGINNING PLACE FOR PRAYER TODAY:

Father, do not let me take the easy route and get in trouble. Help me to remain in Your word so I can hear your voice and be armed for all that would destroy my peace. Peace is joy and in obedience only will I find peace and experience joy. Keep me ever mindful of Your peace and put my pride aside so I can be responsible and honest with people I deal with each day. Let me serve you with a pure heart which has been cleansed by Your blood as the door posts of my dwelling place are also protected by Your blood.

DISCUSSION QUESTIONS FOR TODAY:

1. Commitment and responsibility are key words in describing a relationship with Christ. Why are they such important attributes of a Christian?

2. Is it wise to think that only outside of my home I can run into opposition to the principles of my faith? Can strong opposition show itself right under my own roof?

DAY 31

The Lord also will be a refuge for the oppressed, a refuge in times of trouble. And those who know your name will put their trust in you; for you, Lord have not forsaken those who seek you. Psalm 9: 9

Readings for today: Exodus 12: 5-12 and Psalm 9

The perfect lamb was sacrificed for the sins of Israel and for their protection as God instructed them and prepared them for the next leg of their adventure with the Pharaoh of Egypt. Each family that knew the Lord received His protection with obedience. God's specific instructions were followed and Egypt was to face the judgment of God. The children of the wicked would be destroyed, but God's families would find refuge and the wicked would sink into the pit which they had created.

Sin is always a pit we make for ourselves. God does not intend anyone to perish or to be miserable, but we can choose it. Even in sin we are not forsaken because of the sacrificial gift of Jesus' blood upon the cross. If we seek Him, He is faithful to be our refuge and He will lift us up from the very gates of death. He hears and does not forget the cries of the humble. When sin seeks to ruin us we need only to cry out and He will hear our cries.

His answers are not always what we expect, but they are always merciful and complete. Each step of the harm that Egypt would seek to perform upon the Israelites God had a ready and complete plan for its defeat. Our plans are only complete by our own understandings, but God's are complete and perfect by His infinite and all knowing comprehension of our future and for all those we love and will be affected. When things are not going our way we can take comfort that we have asked for His will to be accomplished in our lives and He will perfect it and complete it for our good.

God is always in the business of protecting us. He has been since He created man and remains so even unto this very hour of our existence. He can step into the gap and hold anxiety and fear at bay with the hand of His protection if we ask for that protection. With those requests, the Holy Spirit is unleashed upon an unsuspecting world and He sets his protection about us because He loves us. The all powerful creator of the universe loves me. I am little and insignificant in the sight of the world, but in the sight of my God I am of awesome value. His Son's blood protects me, just as it protected the Israelites of the very first Passover. Sin cannot harm me if I am covered by His blood; I am saved from all harm because of my choice to be obedient to Him.

A beginning place for prayer today:

Lord, let me not be fearful of this day nor of the future. You are my protection, even from myself if I will but call on You. Keep me ever aware of the safety of pursuing righteousness in my daily life. As you extend love and forgiveness to me let me also do the same for those I love or meet. Help me to not create pits of destruction for myself or others.

Keep me ever mindful of all You have done for me. Help me to focus on how very much You love me and will protect me if I will cast all my cares upon You. Let me trust in Your love and mercy. Please, Lord, be ever in the forefront of my mind today. Thank You Father for your constant and unchanging love.

DISCUSSION QUESTIONS FOR TODAY:

1. Has there been a situation in my life that seemed so dire and complex that I knew I needed explicit directions in how to respond? Where did I find my answers?

2. What have I learned or been reminded of today about God's intimate care for my times of trouble and need?

DAY 32

AND THE BLOOD SHALL BE A SIGN FOR YOU ON THE HOUSES WHERE YOU LIVE; AND WHEN I SEE THE BLOOD I WILL PASS OVER YOU AND NO PLAGUE WILL BEFALL YOU TO DESTROY YOU WHEN I STRIKE THE LAND OF EGYPT. EXODUS 12:13

READING FOR TODAY– EXODUS 12:13 AND PSALM 19: 7-14

How precious is the blood of the lamb that was slain! To the Israelites it was a sweet, precious, innocent lamb whose blood protected them simply because it was put at the doorposts of their home on that fatal night of the plague. We know today that that blood represented the future blood of Jesus upon the cross for us.

There was then and there is now no way that man's sins can be passed over except by the acceptance of the blood of our Savior, Jesus. Because of that blood we have the assurance that the plagues of this world will pass over us just as the plagues of Egypt passed over the Israelites. Our hope of being saved and set apart does not rest on our own righteousness, it rests on the mercies of God toward us. No good deeds, no vows will save us, only the acceptance of that sacrifice will set us apart for eternity.

This world holds many plagues: anger, bitterness, unforgiveness, strife, divorce, sickness, financial disaster; the list goes on like this as steady as the beat of a drum. Just when we think we cannot go on, God's strength moves in, the power of the Holy Spirit is activated in us and the plague passes over us. We are not destroyed, but we are refined. We are made stronger by the knowledge that we cannot be destroyed by plague because we are His for now and for eternity.

That blood allows us to have confidence in all areas of our lives because we see and understand that God does what He says He will do. His "law is perfect restoring the soul; the testimony of the Lord is sure."(Psalm 19:7) When we have that personal, intimate relationship with God we become wiser, our hearts can rejoice at simple things and the plague can rage about us and not destroy us.

The more familiar we are with God, the more we realize the commandments of the Lord are "pure and enlightening". He keeps things simple and uncluttered if we rely on His law. We are not shaken or tossed about too long by a plague because His blood is our anchor in times of storms. Sometimes trouble can even be spotted long before it arrives and takes hold of our lives, because we are warned by His Word.

Best of all, I am righteous before Him because my heart is simply convicted that Jesus loves me. He wants to protect me. The surer this reality is in my life, the more I desire to have His blood cover me and the more precious His judgments are to me. I will cease from my own desires, my own judgments and I will desire His judgments on my life. According to John 14: 26, I do not have to rely on my own understandings, the Holy Spirit is my constant guide and companion. He will speak to me and tell me the things I need to know and hold dear if I am faithful to pray and stay in His Word.

A beginning place for prayer today:

Father, Let the words of my mouth and the meditations of my heart be acceptable in Thy sight. I truly desire to hide myself in the blood of Your Son Jesus. The plagues of this world will come and go, but I will be acceptable in your sight because I believe in You. Keep my eyes on Your blood and pull me away from the plagues of this day. Set me apart for Your service. Thank You Father, In Jesus name I pray.

Discussion Questions for today:

1. Have I begun to commit more of myself and what I desire and plan to do to God or am I still operating in my own strength?

2. Have I ever noticed that the more I commit to God, because I have to spend time in His presence, the more I feel His presence throughout the day?

DAY 33

HOW PRECIOUS IS YOUR LOVING KINDNESS, O GOD! THEREFORE THE CHILDREN OF MEN PUT THEIR TRUST UNDER THE SHADOW OF YOUR WINGS. PSALM 36:7

READING FOR TODAY– EXODUS 12:14-27 AND PSALM 36:6-9

The Lord's instructions to the Israelites were very detailed. They followed His instructions word for word as they worshipped the Lord. We don't always follow the Lord's instruction to the letter, instead human nature sometimes allows us to smorgasbord — pick and choose — the letter and the law—but the Israelites did not. Seldom are we in life and death struggles as they were, but nonetheless we need to observe closely why they were successful in their petitions for help from the Lord.

Also, make note that they worshipped the Lord after receiving His instructions. Sometimes we even forget to say "thank you", let alone worship Him for all He has done. Much prayer and supplication can be our pattern while a problem or a request hangs in the balance. Then if the accomplishment of our request is not too noteworthy we can even forget how serious we considered the problem in the first place. What a disappointment we must be to the Lord at these times!

Worship means we give ardent, humble love and devotion to something or someone. It is a high form of respect that we are to give God if we are to be successful Christians. Unfortunately, even Sunday services can be left out of a Christian's life very easily. The golf game, sleeping in or the protestations of mates and children who don't want to give up their day of rest can persuade us to not even attend church, except of course on holidays.

Sunday worship is extremely important. It goes beyond feeding our souls and giving us fellowship with other believers, it should be our day to devotedly pay our respects to the Lord for all He has done in our lives the past week. It sets us apart as "His peculiar people" and it says to the world: My life is governed by God, I need to say thank You to Him and honor Him.

Note also that the Israelites are to explain this Passover celebration to their children because God says they will ask: "What do you mean by this service?" Going to church is just one small way to teach our children of our devotion to God. We can tell our children many good things about honoring the laws of God, but our strongest statements are made without words. When we do what we tell them to do, we underscore the value of it in our lives for them.

Worship is also praise. It is good to worship on Sunday with songs of praise, but it is even of more value to praise Him not only on Sunday, but everyday and share the goodness of the Lord on a daily basis. Letting our children see us in the Word daily, letting our children hear our prayers and for us to mark for them verbally all the blessings and the strengths of the Lord which have been bestowed on us by Him is really our best worship of the Lord.

A BEGINNING PLACE FOR PRAYER TODAY:

Lord, thank You for all Your blessings in my life. Help me to see what it is that You desire me to do today. Help me to praise You out loud today, to proclaim You to family and friends and even to strangers. Make me your best possible ambassador and keep Your righteousness before me in all that I do. Help me Lord. Please help me. I ask these things in Jesus precious name.

DISCUSSION QUESTIONS FOR TODAY:

1. The Christian song "What A Friend We Have In Jesus" is a testament to the theme of this mornings study. Is Jesus my friend or is He somewhere far off and hardly ever involved in my daily living?

2. How verbal am I about my relationship with Jesus in the presence of others? Do people know He is my source of life?

DAY 34

NOW I KNOW THAT THE LORD SAVES HIS ANNOINTED; HE WILL ANSWER HIM FROM HIS HOLY HEAVEN WITH THE SAVING STRENGTH OF HIS RIGHT HAND. PSALM 20: 6

READING FOR TODAY – EXODUS 12: 28-41 AND PSALM 20

God's ways are the only ways in which our lives can prosper and escape death. Each of us faces new challenges daily, some more dramatic than others, but each of us has the same saving grace of God at our disposal if we will but look up and keep our eyes on Him. He is our only source of constant wisdom and strength.

Unleavened bread is flat and not necessarily pleasing to the eye, but it meets the nutritional needs of the people who eat it. God knew they needed the nutrition of the basic bread so he allowed them to have the basics. Because they did not stop to leaven it or make it appear better looking but just moved out as they were directed, they were blessed with even more. The Egyptians gave them livestock and gold and silver and urged them to leave. They left in grand style--leaving Egypt as victors rather than the mere slaves they had been for 430 years.

When God does a work it is complete. All our needs are met and usually far better than we could ever imagine. His stamp of approval says "Well done good and faithful servant." When He goes against evil that too is a complete work. It took 430 years for God to prepare the Israelites to be given their own land of milk and honey. Man trusts so often in his own strength or wisdom and his desires are often met, but in such difficult and often incomplete ways. Man can manipulate and speculate, but only God knows the end from the beginning. He alone can bring something of value to completion and that thing to perfect completion.

"Trusting in horses and chariots" is comforting because we can see the power of that. Trusting in God is often scary because we can't always see how God will complete something. God was very wise once again as He requested the Israelites to celebrate the Passover for continued generations enabling each generation to become a participant in one of His greatest miracles. But we as Christians now have hind-sight and we can see the Passover as God's description of the future sacrifice of Christ upon the cross for us. The Blood of Christ is our covering today and it gives us eternal life. God makes no requests of us that are not in our best interest. How foolish we are to ignore His commandments to us.

Nothing has changed. God is still out there trying to give us freedom and trying to make life here on earth simpler for us. The enemy is alive and well like Pharaoh, but he can be defeated and God can deliver us from our chains, but we must trust Him. If we want more faith in our lives, we need to trust more. If we want more change in our lives we must let Him do it, in His way and in His timing. God can make "all things beautiful in His time." We just have to trust Him with everything.

A BEGINNING PLACE FOR PRAYER TODAY:

Lord, please let me trust You today. You can use all the "stuff" of this day to Your glory if I'll just get out of the way. Please help me to sort through this day with Your wisdom. Defeat the enemy today as he tries to confuse me and scare me. Let me keep my eyes on You. I don't need leavened bread, I just need the basics, all else is just the "stuff" of life. I want purpose and service in my life that will please You. Thank You for this day, equip me with trust and let the horses and chariots of my life vanish as you do Your perfect will in my life.

DISCUSSION QUESTIONS FOR TODAY:

1. Are there things in my life today that I am not trusting God with and are hanging on to for dear life? Why?

2. How can I learn to trust God more? What role does faith play in my ability to trust?

DAY 35

As a deer pants for the water brooks, so pants my soul for You, o God. Psalm 42: 1

READING FOR TODAY– EXODUS 12: 42-49 AND JOHN 17: 4-26

When a person comes to a true knowledge of God's saving grace he begins to long for the things of God. The fellowship of God in his life becomes of prime importance. He becomes insignificant; the things of life become insignificant, Christ become all. A believer's heart should question each day for the answers to: "What would You have me do today Lord?" and "How can I be used for Your purposes:"

And when God responds, as He does in each new day, the believer begins to look closer at the people and situations that surround him knowing that he is truly God's child. God has set us apart and called us to a joy and a peace that the world cannot know because they do not know Him. Communion is the sacrament of the Christian that Passover represents. No man is to partake of it unless he is a believer. God set Passover aside for only the Jew and the converted believer. We are a part of that special fellowship because we have the circumcised heart of a Christian.

God makes room for all of us under the blood of the cross, but it is really just a symbol, a religious act if the one who takes communion does not accept the headship of Christ in his life. As Passover could not be celebrated by a foreigner or hired servant so the true full relationship of fellowship with Christ also cannot be experienced. We must believe that He is Lord of our lives and then give Him authority over us before we can experience the power of God in our lives and make communion real and not just another religious act done before man.

He calls us His children if we seek after Him as a child seeks after a parent. What child would wake up each morning not wanting to check his parent's bedroom to see if they were there? What child would expect to provide for his own needs? The parent provides those needs. When a child needs help he goes to the parent. He expects that parent to have answers and to have provision for his needs. When we are a child of God, whether we are eight or eighty, He responds to us as a loving parent.

Perhaps, being a Christian is too simple and that is the biggest stumbling block to people who think there must be more to it than letting God be our heavenly Father. Becoming a Christian is really answering the question: "Who do I serve?" and "Can I put my life under the leadership of God?" God says we cannot serve two masters. We must either be a child of God or a child of the enemy.

We can seek light or we can seek darkness. Cognitively speaking, Christianity represents what some would call black and white thinking whereas the world operates in shades of gray. They live in constant confusion because they are so limited by their own sin natures. We can pant after our needs in the world or we can go to the throne room of

God and pant after His righteousness. To be a Christian is to make the decision on: "Whom will I serve?" and "Can I allow Him to be Lord of my life"?

A BEGINNING PLACE FOR PRAYER TODAY:

Thank You Lord that You are my heavenly Father. Awaken my heart to seek after You. Let Your ways be my first desire as I make decisions today. I want a full relationship with You. I want all Your wisdom and power in my life. Nothing else do I want on Your throne, only You. Let me put aside the foolishness of this world's values and let me pant after Your fellowship and Your Word so I can be filled with Your peace and love today. Thank You for this day. In Jesus name I ask all these things.

DISCUSSION QUESTIONS FOR TODAY:

1. Have I found that Christianity is often too simple for the intellectual to accept? Why do I think this is?

2. Why do I think the world prefers shades of gray when it comes to sin as opposed to the black and white thinking process of a Christian?

DAY 36

The law of Your mouth is better for me than thousands of coins of gold and silver. Psalm 119: 72

READING FOR TODAY— EXODUS 12: 50-51 AND PSALM 119: 71–80

"Thus all the children of Israel did as the Lord commanded…" (Exodus 12:50) The children of Israel were delivered from the worst plague God could deliver on Egypt because they all did what the Lord commanded. Doing the Lord's will in the middle of our personal Egypt will also produce a release from our bondages today.

He always stands ready to revive us if we will call upon His name and then do as He says. Fear can work to produce mighty miracles in our lives when the fear in us is only a fear of God. Fear should be a healthy respect for the power and control that only God possesses because He alone possesses our lives. When we see Him as the author and creator of us, we have a healthy fear of Him. It is wonderful to know He is always in control and to understand that if we let Him take over our lives we will be released from the fear of making mistakes. Fear is also a healthy emotion when it alerts us to physical and emotional danger. The Israelites were afraid for their physical being in Egypt and only God could save them.

Nothing has changed in this world since the events of Exodus. We are still afraid today for our personal safety and emotional well-being. And…God is still in the business of giving commands which protect us. Fear can only rule over us when we don't have a right perspective of God's law. The right perspective is "do what God says and don't do what He tells you not to do." Is that too simple? Well, it may be, but it's true! Try to think of one of His thou shalt nots or thou shalt admonitions that does not save us from some kind of potential disaster.

Following God's commands are not always easy. There is often personal pride and selfish desire that has to be set aside. Disciplining children is a good example of tough, consistent work, but a disciplined child is a delight and an unruly child is a constant heartache. Forgiving those who hurt us deeply is difficult, prayerful work, but the benefits of a peaceful soul greatly outweighs the alternative of a life filled with bitterness, anger and unrelenting pain.

Gambling or addictions to drugs, alcohol or even food are painful in their reward. The cost they tally up in ruined lives and relationships seems like just too high a price for the sin of indulging ourselves and then becoming enslaved to something we thought we could control. When the addictions and problems of life are handed over to God there is the promise of peace and joy as He works them out of our lives.

However, success in getting out of Egypt will always come under the heading of "do all God commands you to do." Personal growth comes when you have to fail first in order to get success. God wants us strengthened and perfected in character. An easy life does not produce anything, but complacency and laziness. And there are armies today still against us like the armies of Egypt. They are called "politically correct" behaviors and attitudes, enlightened "new age" philosophies and "man's intellectual accomplishments", but they still have to be fought against. We lose the blessings of God's abundant life when we just don't do all He commands us to do and worst if all we fail in getting out of our own personal Egypt.

A BEGINNING PLACE FOR PRAYER TODAY:

Lord, fear can keep me frozen in my personal Egypt. Help me to fear the things you have told me to hate. Keep all other irrational fears away from my heart. You alone have the answers to life. When I am tempted, help me to ask for Your help and Your protection from all the things I am too weak to handle. You have set this day before me and You know its purposes. I have nothing to fear if my heart is clean before you. Give me a clean heart as you search me. I desire to serve only You. Make me wise Father, so I will serve You and not myself. Keep me in Your ways O Lord!

DISCUSSION QUESTIONS FOR TODAY:

1. What is healthy fear and what is fear that is of the devil? Have I ever been frozen by fear and then through prayer found it to be baseless?

2. How much growth in my spiritual life could I expect if life always went my way? Do trials have a purpose?

DAY 37

COMMIT YOUR WAY TO THE LORD, TRUST ALSO IN HIM AND HE WILL DO IT. PSALM 37: 5

READING FOR TODAY– EXODUS 13: 1-8 AND PSALM 37

AND YOU SHALL TELL YOUR SON ON THAT DAY SAYING IT IS BECAUSE OF WHAT THE LORD DID FOR ME WHEN I CAME OUT OF EGYPT. When was the last time I shared with my children what the Lord has done for me? As Christian parents we often take too much credit for our successes. Our children are not always acquainted with our failures.

They also don't know how God has blessed and used those failures to His glory and our credit for real growth. We get discouraged when we look at our young people. They have everything and they expect everything. Perhaps the failure lies in part that we have failed to communicate that God is why we have what we have. They probably don't even know that God doesn't have grandchildren.

As I read Psalm 37 I see God's provision for his children. It is clear "righteous living brings righteous reward" and selfish behavior produces evil. TRUST IN THE LORD AND DO GOOD; DELIGHT YOURSELF IN THE LORD AND COMMIT YOUR WAY TO THE LORD, REST AND WAIT PATIENTLY ON THE LORD, CEASE FROM ANGER AND FORSAKE WRATH; simple commandments for life. Do my children know these are the principles by which I seek to live? Do they understand where my success, strength and even power come from in time of trouble?

Unfortunately, we try to spare our children the cold hard facts of how hard life can be; we limit their knowledge of how wonderfully God can bring forth righteousness and prosperity in spite of the world's abuses to us. Do my children know that THE STEPS OF A RIGHTEOUS MAN ARE ESTABLISHED BY THE LORD AND HE (THE LORD) DELIGHTS IN HIS WAY?

Moses is commanded by the Lord through the celebration of the Passover to tell each new generation once a year, at least, about God's hand in their deliverance. Unless they did this the future generations would forget. God had a purpose when He gave this commandment to the Israelites. We have forgotten that purpose today if we do not honor our children with the gift of who God is and has been in our lives. Do your children know how I came to know Him as my personal Savior: Do I share with them all He has done for me?

Perhaps this day should mark the beginning of a new and fresh commitment to sharing Christ with our children. It really needs to begin with a personal awareness of Christ in our every day lives. "Thank You Lord for this day" is a good place to start with them. He made it just for me and it has a purpose in it. "Thank You Lord for my job." Our children should know that God has put us in this place as a place of ministry and we should talk about how we are using it for ministry. Simple things, things we need to remind ourselves of so we don't take credit for God's gifts. Our children need to hear us say it and remark openly and frequently of His love, His mercy and His laws and judgments for our everyday successes. Read Psalm 37 again and take it all in!

A BEGINNING PLACE FOR PRAYER TODAY:

God You are so good, so perfect, so loving and I am so forgetful. Forgive me for going on about yesterdays problems and today's fears before I even thank You for bringing me through where I've been and blessing me with what you've already given and entrusted to me. Help me to speak openly of all the things You have done in my life, especially in front of my children. They need to know my strengths and my weaknesses, but most of all they need to know You in my life. Thank You Father for who You are in my life. Let me be an honor and a blessing to you this day. I ask these things in Jesus name, Thank You Father.

DISCUSSION QUESTIONS FOR TODAY:

1. What have I learned from reading Psalm 37?

2. Do we do a disservice to our children when we fail to praise God in front of them for the things He has done for us today?

DAY 38

SO IT SHALL BE, WHEN YOUR SON ASKS YOU IN TIME TO COME SAYING, "WHAT IS THIS?" THAT YOU SHALL SAY TO HIM, THE STRENGTH OF HAND THE LORD BROUGHT US OUT OF EGYPT, OUT OF THE HOUSE OF BONDAGE. EXODUS 13:14

READING FOR TODAY– EXODUS 13: 9-14, PSALM 40 AND JOHN 14:10-27

Strange isn't it? The world thinks of Jesus as a wimp: the "meek Savior, the turn the other cheek weeping Savior." Yet quite the opposite is true. He is really the most powerful force of the universe and according to scripture sets all of His power toward His children. His followers are to be meek, but what meek really means is power under control. We can turn the other cheek because we pray that someone who wrongs us will find the love of Christ and become a new creature.

We can never understand Him more fully than when we need His strength. When adversity hits we say:"Oh, God", believer and nonbeliever alike utter this phrase. The difference is that when a believer begins his prayer that way he begins to commit the fear, the frustration, the loss, the despair to God; it is not an expletive without power. The strength of our God comes alongside of us and we begin to experience the Helper within us. (John 14:16) The strength of God instantly dwells within us and we are transformed and put at peace through His strength.

As His followers, we are weak, but He is strong. God guards us, God keeps us and because of His Spirit we become amazingly strong. Letting go of a problem is not a sign of weakness; it's a sign of wisdom. Letting go is also the hardest thing man can do. God respects that letting go as a sign that we love and honor Him. He gets His rightful place when we give Him the throne and call Him King. Our meekness becomes our power under His complete control. The shaking hand steadies, the tears cease and the problem becomes a steady one foot in front of the other action until the journey of the problem has run its full course.

Moving away from emotion, God focuses our attention away from a problem onto Him. We no longer have the problem, God has it. His acceptance of the problem allows us to be free to move on with the business of living, even if it is only living moment by moment at first. With each new day God allows us to move further away from our fear and move closer to letting Him rule the day.

Turning the other cheek is the simple (yet difficult) act of acceptance. Christ accepted the cross. We need to accept the good and the bad of each day because this is just another place we are passing through. The places of today are our journey's points of learning and they represent the ultimate perfection of our souls. Yes, there are tears. Tears are not just a sign of weakness. They are a sign of understanding for with them we demonstrate our sorrow or even our joy. The great commission of the Lord is for us to share His gospel with others and that can't be done until we understand the strength He is in our lives. We are strong when we understand our weaknesses and accept His strength.

The world doesn't even begin to understand the meaning of power and strength because it does not know Him (John 14: 17).

God is still in the business of bringing us all out of bondage. He has done it in the past, He will do it today and He will do it tomorrow. We need to remind ourselves daily of His strength and stop missing the blessing of His strength by trying to operate in our own strength.

A BEGINNING PLACE FOR PRAYER TODAY:

Lord, You are the strength of my life. Let me rest in your arms. Let me cast all my cares upon You and let me feel strong because I am secure in Your love, Your hope and my future in You. Help me to share my conviction of Your strength with others. Put people in my path who need Your strength and help me to come alongside to help direct them back to the place of real strength—You!

DISCUSSION QUESTIONS FOR TODAY:

1. How affective would we be as Disciples of Christ if we had never known trial and temptation?

2. How effective is the short prayer "Jesus" when we do not have words for the despair or the sorrow of a situation?

DAY 39

MY FLESH AND MY HEART FAIL; BUT GOD IS THE STRENGTH OF MY HEART AND MY PORTION FOREVER. PSALM 73: 26

READING FOR TODAY– EXODUS 13:15-18, PSALM 73: 22-28 AND JOHN 14:27

I firmly believe that God knows we are easily discouraged and so He decides for us the best way to travel through life. He knows under what circumstances we would become discouraged so He takes us on journeys of His will to protect us.

It is also true that we are by nature impatient and stubborn. Our generation is probably the worst in history for wanting "instant everything". We are not real crazy about not getting our own way; especially when we have been praying for specific answers to our prayers. We're often sure that a short cut would be best, but God knows that we would reap great harm from those short cuts. He often takes us where we least expect to be and there He blesses us for no other reason than the fact that He loves us.

We see here in Exodus 12:17 that there was a shorter way of getting to the Promised Land, but God couldn't take them that way. They would have had to do battle to cross through the land of the Philistines and He knew they would be frightened and turn back. So He took them around the potential problems and led them "out of Egypt in orderly ranks".

A sure sign we're in the wrong place is when our life lacks "orderly ranks". External turmoil can exist, but internal turmoil is not God's lifestyle for us. God's way always has order even if that order is only the peaceful acceptance of lost dreams, lost finances, lost jobs, divorce, terminal illness or even death. Knowing when to let go and let God refocus us on the things we can work at puts our lives into "orderly ranks".

Even when we don't like or are fearful of the order of things we find ourselves in we can gain strength and courage because God is working out the events we have no control over. God does not test us with evil (James 1: 13, 17), but He proves Himself daily as He redirects that which was meant to harm us. We can expect miracles and maturity in our relationship with Jesus as we let Him provide the orderly ranks of our days. Drawing close to God is accomplished as we allow Him into our lives not only in the big decisions of life, but in the everyday simple decisions too.

A BEGINNING PLACE FOR PRAYER TODAY:

Thank You Father that You have already chosen the day for me and what it will hold. It may not be a particularly productive day by my standards, but it is by Your standards because You know what it is I am to learn today. Keep me open to Your way of living this life. Help me to not be caught up with my schedule. Let me look around and see others as you see them. Let me see needs as you see them. In Jesus name let me be a blessing to You Father.

DISCUSSION QUESTIONS FOR TODAY:

1. Do I sometimes forget that God is concerned even with the little things in my life? Why is it important that I talk everything over with Him on daily basis?

2. Do we really know the priority of things in our lives? Is it wise to let God set the priorities? What am I to do when a door closes and I had wanted that door to be open?

DAY 40

WHOEVER OFFERS PRAISE GLORIFIES ME; AND TO HIM WHO ORDERS HIS ARIGHT I WILL SHOW THE SALVATION OF GOD. PSALM 50: 23

READING FOR TODAY– EXODUS 13: 19 AND PSALM 50

"And Moses took the bones of Joseph with him…" Joseph had a complete sense of who he served. He had honored God with his life and he wanted to always be with his family Israel. "God will surely visit you and you shall carry my bones from here with you." Joseph had complete confidence in God.

Confidence is easy when you can look back on the things that turned out well. But…Joseph even had confidence that God wasn't finished with Israel. He expected more for his people Israel at the hands of a merciful God. Joseph expected complete salvation for himself and his people. He had evidence of a faithful God. But he saw God as more than faithful, he saw His plans as perfect for Israel if they would order their "conduct aright."

Joseph's conduct was extraordinarily "aright" for a mere mortal. He suffered greatly at the hands of his brothers and under the false charges of Potiphar's wife. Yet, He expected goodness because God was good. How easy it would have been to have given up in the pit or later in the jail. Joseph rose above his circumstances and was satisfied wherever he was because of his steadfast faith. The constant expectancy of good at the hands of the Lord seems to be his constant source of strength.

Joseph was content "in what state I am" as Paul shares in Philippians 4:11. The grateful spirit of Joseph allowed him to be content and to have confidence in the future even to the point of being confident that God would free his people and his bones would make it to the promised land. When we are thankful we praise God and our confidence soars. Some days we get so bogged down in the concerns of the day we forget to be thankful. We discount where we've been and what God has brought us to and from.

When God is not glorified daily by us we cannot consider our conduct aright. Our lives quite simply become conduct unbecoming of a child of God. We become self-centered and not God-centered. Our lives become of such importance that God takes the back seat to "the Mighty Needs of Me". If we ask each day how we can serve, we take the focus off our expectations and put them back on the expectations of God.

God has expectations of us—but His expectations are accomplished by Him and not us. We are simply to be the vessel which He fills with His Spirit each day. It is not our job to strive. It is our job to allow the Holy Spirit freedom to work in our lives. Accepting the circumstances God has set us in and praising Him keeps our communication with Him active. Submission also allows God the freedom to take our lives in new directions. It is incredibly important that we remain the children of God, not the advisor to God.

HOW GREAT IS THE LOVE THAT THE FATHER HAS LAVISHED ON US, THAT WE SHOULD BE CALLED CHILDREN OF GOD! I John 3:1

A BEGINNING PLACE FOR PRAYER TODAY:

Lord, please re-direct my conduct. Let me focus on You. Let me praise You and be grateful. I get so caught up in me. Forgive me Father. You have work to be done in me and if I keep holding on to my requests and my decisions for my life, You will never be able to work and I will never experience Your peace. Forgive me that I think I can advise You on what is best for me—how presumptuous of me and how foolish. I release this day to You. Thank You for Your active presence in my life.

DISCUSSION QUESTIONS FOR TODAY:

1. Have I ever considered the value of getting in the back seat and then letting God do the driving, as well, as selecting the direction I am going? If I already do this, what have I learned from the experience?

2. Why is submission such an important word for the Christian?

DAY 41

HE DID NOT TAKE AWAY THE PILLAR OF CLOUD BY DAY OR THE PILLAR OF FIRE BY NIGHT BEFORE THE PEOPLE. EXODUS 13:20

READING FOR TODAY– EXODUS 13: 20-22, PSALM 73: 1-3, 16-17,26 AND PSALM 77: 10-20

The enemy can do his best work if he can get us to take our eyes off of God and look around at the circumstances of our lives. As the verse states: "He did not take away the pillar from before the people." But we can take Him from before us and place Him somewhere in the background. We can even stand on past victories and lose the battle of the present because we don't read His word every day and we get too busy for prayer and quiet time with Him. Our desires start going before us, God is not leading, we have assumed His position of authority in our lives.

I have found that we become the most vulnerable when we think we are the strongest. We operate on the old knowledge of His presence in our lives, using Him like some kind of lucky charm and we start walking ahead of Him. Checking in everyday keeps us in tune with the Holy Spirit whose job it is to keep us looking up for directions. Even though we think we know pretty much what each day holds, the attitudes with which we face it may be more important than the events of the day. Every day holds surprises; some days bigger surprises than others!

Simple jealousies, simple disappointments or delays can become completely out of hand if we fail to get a "heart check" before we start the day. Each day requires a time of cleansing for our hearts. Yesterday has a way of hanging on and keeping our hearts unclean before the Lord. We are in a different place emotionally and spiritually each day and it is usually the residue of the day before that dictates how we feel about today. Scripture is new to us every day because we are in a different place each day of our lives and what was old yesterday becomes new to our needs today. We are surprised that we never saw that scripture before and yet there it is new and fresh, ready to meet our need for today. Keeping our eyes on yesterdays' triumphs can easily cause us to stumble into the troubles of today completely unprepared if we don't check in with God.

BEFORE ME is the best place for God's presence to be in my life: BEHIND ME God isn't leading; BELOW ME God is just bearing me up; ABOVE ME God feels out of reach. When God goes BEFORE ME He leads me. In Psalm 73: 1-3 we see someone who has put his eyes on the world. He thinks the evil ones and the non-believers are being prospered and he gets himself all worked up and fearful. We do that if we allow ourselves to watch too much TV; especially the nightly news and their special spots on the rich and famous.

But when he takes himself to the sanctuary of God, he then says: "I understood." Verse 26 says; "My flesh and my heart fail; but God is the strength of my heart and my portion forever." No where can we get our attitude and path made clear except in the presence of God through His Word and then in prayer. God has answers, God has the pathway and when He is before us all else can drift from view.

I cannot change the people in my life or the circumstances of things in the world. But I can expect God to change me and teach my old sin nature to step aside. Accepting simple beliefs: "Jesus loves me, Jesus protects me, He first loved me"—these are the pillars I need to look to and these are the pillars that keep me on the right path. My portion in life from God is always there and my heart is pure in the acceptance of that portion if God is always before me—it's my choice for the day!

A BEGINNING PLACE FOR PRAYER TODAY:

Lord, help me to keep my eyes on You. Keep my eyes from jealousy and fear. Let me forget and forgive the past and look at You as You go before me. You alone can put aside the unimportant baggage of this day's journey and let me walk with a lighter load. Lord I want a hopeful expectant heart for today—with my eyes on You there is great hope for today!

DISCUSSION QUESTIONS FOR TODAY:

1. Who is leading my parade? Have I checked in with God and sought His permission to start down the paths I have chosen? Could that be why some things aren't going so well?

2. Do I have a tendency to get too envious of the non-believer's successes? What have I lost sight of when I think they are better off than I am?

DAY 42

BUT GOD HAS CHOSEN THE FOOLISH THINGS OF THE WORLD TO PUT TO SHAME THE WISE, AND GOD HAS CHOSEN THE WEAK THINGS OF THE WORLD TO PUT TO SHAME THE THINGS WHICH ARE MIGHTY. I CORINTHIANS 1: 27

READING FOR TODAY– EXODUS 14: 1-4, I CORINTHIANS 1: 27-31 AND GALATIANS 5:22-23

God tells Moses He is putting the children of Israel in a position that will make them look lost and weak. His reason for doing this is to teach Pharaoh and Egypt they are dealing with God. He wants them to see the foolishness of man and his intellect and the power and strength of the Lord.

It is not always easy in the middle of our great turmoil to camp in the peaceful arms of God. Man's intellect tells him he needs to protect himself, make plans and mount counter attacks when those plans fail. I think God is saying: "No, rest in Me, put your burdens down, you will not be swallowed up. I will make the world look foolish in all its' answers to your needs." In order and peace and with great reason He puts the turmoil at rest in our lives and works through the problem. Through His wise eyes we can make decisions that keep us righteous before Him and at the same time victorious.

God is glorified by us before non-believers when He gets the glory for the way we survive life's disasters and everyday upsets. If we were always successful through our own strengths we wouldn't need God. God sometimes has to allow potential harm to impress upon us and others that He is the one who is in charge of our lives.

There is strength in each of us provided by the Holy Spirit that does not resemble the world's strengths. It comes in the form of love, joy, peace, long suffering, goodness, faithfulness, gentleness and self-control. These are weak tools of defense by the world's standards, but they are undeniably strong, firm holds on who we represent and how He honors the execution of those gifts in our lives.

Nothing can shake us or destroy us because we have and use these gifts to rise above the problems of this world. Upon occasion we can even drive our opponents completely nuts because they really think we just don't understand the gravity of something. On the contrary, we do know the enemy, but we also happen to know the Savior on a personal basis. He is our refuge, He is our strength and we just have to keep asking for the fruits of the Spirit to manifest themselves in us and then we can be assured that nothing will defeat us!

A BEGINNING PLACE FOR PRAYER TODAY:

Some days I just don't understand life, but I seek to understand You. You will give me wisdom and You alone will provide a way in the midst of all my turmoil. Please help me Lord to accept that Your plan for my life is there just waiting to be fulfilled if I'll just camp in Your arms. Thank You Father for not giving me all the answers, let me glorify You by trusting You.

DISCUSSION QUESTIONS FOR TODAY:

1. Why does God allow potential harm in our lives?

2. Why is it not easy sometimes to camp in God's arms and let the turmoil rage about us?

3. What has scripture taught us today about God's protection for us?

DAY 43

The Lord shall fight for you and you shall hold your peace. Exodus 14: 14

Reading for today– Exodus 14, 5-14 and Matthew 6:34

"Then they said to Moses, "Because there were no graves in Egypt, have you taken us away to die in the wilderness?" This is an alarming charge that the Israelites are making of Moses, but…if the truth be known, when we get into bad places in our lives our faith can waiver too. We are like the Israelites, we have moved into the future with all the negative possibilities and we're sure things are going to get worse!

Our view of the problem is always faulty because we can't see the whole picture. We are finite in our ability to understand the ways of God. We will always have a serious eye problem in our lives until we learn to let go and let God be in charge. The enemy loves internal conversations between the power of evil and our faith in God. He can move on us with simple questions and statements: "Are you sure God cares about you? If God loves you why are you suffering? If this is the best God has for you; boy you better hope he doesn't get mad at you!" When we aren't firmly established in the Word we have no defenses and are susceptible to lies from the enemy.

Now the Israelites are new to trusting God—they're still trusting Moses so they're speaking to him. We know, or at least we should know, we can't trust man, but sometimes we do. It's okay to challenge God. I truly believe He wants the dialogue. However, discussions with the enemy only produce confusion. It is okay to ask: "Why?" as long as you are prepared not to get an answer right away or even ever for that matter.

Patience and strength are usually the answer to that request when no earthly answer is forthcoming. Sometimes we get a heavenly glimpse into the divine hand of God in a situation orchestrated by the devil and we see the good that God can make out of evil. Sometimes the end of a life comes long before we are prepared for it, but trust says: "Nothing comes to me or those I love unless it first passes before the throne of God, I do not know what the future holds, but I know who holds the future!"

What a blessing it is not to know everything. We're not responsible for what we don't know or understand about life. Turning that responsibility over to God makes my burden lighter. Worries can be like a bag of rocks. I can carry a bag of rocks around for as long as I choose, I can even add to the load, but …I can also just leave it behind and carry the food of the Word and the water of the Spirit and life's journey will be a lot easier on me.

A beginning place for prayer today:

Thank You Lord, thank You for the circumstances of my life. Keep my eyes open only to Your possibilities. Help me to let go of fear and anxiety. When I worry I am sinning against You. You are in charge and that is all I need to focus on. It's time to let go of the bag of rocks in my life and keep my load light for traveling. Help me to forgive others and accept Your complete forgiveness in my life. I want today's journey to be easy!

DISCUSSION QUESTIONS FOR TODAY:

1. Some days it is the enemy talking to me and making me frightened. When I am fearful, what do I need to do with that fear?

2. Am I carrying around a bag of rocks I need to hand over to God? Why do we carry around those bags to begin with? What do I need to do with those rocks?

DAY 44

YEA, THOUGH I WALK THROUGH THE VALLEY OF THE SHADOW OF DEATH; I WILL FEAR NO EVIL; FOR YOU ARE WITH ME; YOUR ROD AND YOUR STAFF, THEY COMFORT ME. PSALM 23:4

READING FOR TODAY– EXODUS 14: 15-22 AND PSALM 23

Our faith becomes firmly cemented when we are faced with problems knowing that only God can protect us. Faith grows in adversity because it has been tested. We become the recipients of evidence as to just how powerful God is and how much we are loved by Him.

Evidence is extremely important to mortal man. Our fear diminishes when we know certain things will happen. We know for instance that we can throw on a light switch in the dark, we know anesthetic holds pain away from us; we thrive on what we know. We are confident when we have seen something work. It is truly exciting to hear other Christians tell us what God has done for them.

For the most part, He does little things at first. Like making us want to be better marriage partners or looking at life in a whole new way—appreciating the weather or finding happiness in the smiles of our children. But, the bad news, or the good news, depending on your own spiritual maturity, is that God will at some point in our Christian walk begin to do works in us that will be painful at times.

Walking with God will make us wise, but His wisdom often comes best through negative experiences. The Israelites have seen God work for them through the plagues. They have gathered evidence of His goodness. Moses has been affirmed to them as the man to follow. So far they have experienced everything from comfortable places. They were in their own homes, granted in Egypt, but they were comfortable in their own understanding of life in Egypt. Sometimes we get comfortable with terrible things, but God has something better to offer. That step out of the familiar and into the new uncharted areas of life can truly be a frightening experience.

When the pillar moved between them and the army of Pharaoh they experienced His protection, but the first step into the sea that was truly a step of faith. Life threatening illness, the devastation of a career or financial disaster are just a few of the places in our lives where we are fearful to take the next step and we are just not so sure the sea will part. Only in scary new places does God become real to us when we let Him give us His strength because the fear is so great that only He can do it for us.

Our natural instinct is to question and just as natural as the questioning is our need to then pray for His guidance. With prayer we are steadied and then when we weaken we need to check in again with prayer. Everyday, sometimes moment by moment, we need to check in while the battle rages. Our prayers don't even have to be formal prayers; one word prayers of just "Jesus" is often all we need to keep going.

When God is all powerful in our lives then we can truly be at rest in Him. The best place in life is often in the middle of those parted walls of the sea we are presently experiencing. God stands the walls of the sea high on either side of us and we are protected when by everything we know to be familiar this protection is a miracle. What am I to learn here on the floor of the parted sea? God has our full attention and we have no strength of our own to claim. When we look at Psalm 23 we realize we don't need anything—we have the Lord. Maybe this place on the bottom of the parted sea is the worst best place of my life!

A BEGINNING PLACE FOR PRAYER TODAY:

I have no great terror in my life today, but Father I know others who do. Protect them Father. Prepare their hearts to receive Your peace and let them walk steadily through this time in their lives. Lord, let me be well studied, let me call upon You to be able to share with those in need. Help me Father to be the person You desire. I give you permission to be in charge of my life. Thank You that You love me and don't ever give up on me.

DISCUSSION QUESTIONS FOR TODAY:

1. Have I ever experienced the miracle of having the walls of the sea being parted in the middle of a trial and for no earthly reason could you explain your peace other than "Jesus?"

2. How can something bad be "the worst best time" in my life?

DAY 45

ALL THE HORNS OF THE WICKED I WILL CUT OFF, BUT THE HORNS OF THE RIGHTEOUS SHALL BE EXALTED. PSALM 75:10

READING FOR TODAY– EXODUS 14: 23-31, PSALM 75 AND ISAIAH 31: 1-5

Are you in the business of defending yourself? Too bad, what an incredible waste of energy! Getting even or carrying hatred for someone or some institution is devastating to the soul. God will be the rewarder of good and evil and we don't need to be overly concerned about evil doers, unless we become the evil doer.

I know it can happen. We can become the evil doer under the guise of being the defender of good. We use terrible words to describe our foes and we anxiously await their demise. When they prosper we can develop ulcers and headaches. Many a man has let a boss get to him. Women are notorious for jealous cutting words which fall between the cracks of the categories of helpful and destructive. We become depressed by the success of others and their public acclaim because we know the truth about them.

What does it matter? It is really time to move on for us. What have I learned from the bad experience? How have I grown? It's really a matter of heart attitude. The poorest people in the world can be the richest and the simplest can be the wisest in God's economy of things. If I give bad situations time I will see God work them through. He goaded the Egyptians into following the Israelites, and then He took care of them. God will provide trouble for those who persecute His children even if it's just to "take the wheels off their chariots so they drive with difficulty."

Jeff Johnson, a pastor friend of mine, is always reminding people that "God keeps good books" so you and I don't have to tend those books. We don't have to have any dealings in the evil dealt out to our enemies our responsibility is to keep moving and get on the other side of the parted waters. God is concerned about our character and He directs us throughout Proverbs about our character requirements and no where does it say: "We are to get even." It is a waste of our time and our energy to be consumed by the sins of others who constantly war against us.

Some sins against us are real and some are just imagined. We need to be careful we know the difference. The sin of pride is usually ours if we value someone else's opinion of us too much. And, the sin of envy is ours if we always want what someone else has, even if it was gotten at our expense.

My portion and my cup are provided by God so I need to find out what He has for me today and stop worrying about what the other guy will get. If I keep looking back I lose time while trying to move forward with my life. God took care of the Egyptians, God took care of the Israelites and He'll take care of me. That's all I need to know about life. Amen? Amen!

A BEGINNING PLACE FOR PRAYER TODAY:

Dear Father, please help me to forget the sins of others against me. Help me to pray for my enemies when the enemy drags them before me. Let me think less on them and more on You. You hold the future. I don't want to be stuck in the disappointments of the past. You have a plan for my life and I need to get on with it. Thank You for this day and please help me to use it wisely.

DISCUSSION QUESTIONS FOR TODAY:

1. Lord, have I been negatively living in the past by waiting for someone to be punished? What does this do to my disposition?

2. What do I need to be about? How do I experience an abundant life in Christ if my heart remains full of unforgiveness?

DAY 46

THE LORD IS MY STRENGTH AND MY SONG; HE HAS BECOME MY SALVATION. HE IS MY GOD AND I WILL PRAISE HIM. EXODUS 15:2

READING FOR TODAY– EXODUS 15: 1-13 AND I CHRONICLES 16: 8-12

What a glorious song of praise the Israelites sing in these verses. When was the last time I praised Him? We get so busy we forget to look up and just say THANK YOU. Did you know that when we count our blessings it's impossible to be depressed? There are a lot of sour faced, hard working Christians around today and they often look like they've been baptized in lemon juice! Where is my spirit of thankfulness today?

Praising Him makes us feel good, now is that not crazy? It's true and it is an affirmation of who He is and what He is capable of doing when we take our eyes off our petty day to day problems and just focus on how much we are loved. We have a roof over our heads, food on our plates and clothes on our backs. Can the majority of the rest of the world say that?

Where have I placed my priorities today? God always has me as His priority. He is always there for me, but am I there for Him? Am I caught up in today's worries and so I have forgotten to thank Him for yesterday's worries which He has already turned to my good? A thankless spirit is an easy trap to fall into. Think back on your prayers of the past. How many has He answered? I would venture to say so many that I cannot even count them. I just keep praying, but I don't take time to say THANK YOU and feel genuinely loved. When I praise Him for who He is in my life I feel His love.

Many words are used by us to express our negative thoughts and experiences, but too few are used for praise. It should be the reverse. We should give praise generously to God and others. Christ affirms us by our praise of Him and we can make others feel worthwhile if we give them praise, especially our children. THANK YOU is such a magnificent phrase for the one who gives it and the one who receives it, both feel loved. An easy example of this is when we write thank you notes. We feel good because we let someone know how much they have pleased us with their kindness or their words and the person who receives the note feels the warmth of being appreciated. I want God to know I love Him, and what better way than to say thank you than to tell others about him and what he has done for me?

I believe that really is our job. "Go out into the world and be disciples of men by teaching the gospel to every creature." Praise is a great evangelical tool. Unfortunately, the sharing of the suffering Christ just isn't as well received as the sharing of His overwhelming, completely selfless love and giving to us. Once we get it into our heads that He does these things for us for no other reason than He loves us, we really have something to share and praise Him about. He gives us His best every day. I bet your song of praise could even be longer than the Israelites in this chapter. Maybe today should be the day we start rehearsing that list OUTLOUD!

A BEGINNING PLACE FOR PRAYER FOR TODAY:

Thank You Lord for who You are in my life. Thank You that You really love me that much. I cannot comprehend that! Help me to count my blessings and put all the other nonsense aside. You are the Great I AM and miracle of miracles I am of Your concern. This is all too wonderful for me to comprehend. What a fool I am to fuss and stew. Help me to have a thankful heart and a constant spirit of praise to share.

DISCUSSION QUESTIONS FOR TODAY:

1. What kind of a face am I presenting to the world today? Am I baptized in lemon juice? What can I do about my attitude and appearance for the Lord?

2. Can I make a list of my prayers that He has already answered and perhaps I haven't properly thanked Him for because I have moved on to other needs?

DAY 47

The Lord shall reign forever and ever Exodus 15:18

Reading for today– Exodus 15: 14-18, Psalm 2 and I Peter 2: 4-9

Man is truly foolish to think that he rules the earth. The Israelites saw the power of the Lord and were blessed. The Egyptians saw the same power and were defeated. Our nation unfortunately once knew the power of God, but now celebrates it own intelligence over the wisdom of God. Will we go as the Egyptians into defeat? It is quite likely because we have forgotten who we serve. To be politically correct today is to be morally bankrupt.

Psalm 2 says: HE WHO SITS IN THE HEAVENS SHALL LAUGH; THE LORD SHALL HOLD THEM IN DERISION, because THE KINGS OF THE EARTH SET THEMSELVES AGAINST THE ANOINTED ONE and PLOT VAIN THINGS. Our government, and the people who are foolish enough to be duped by it, really believe that they can BREAK THEIR BONDS (or their responsibilities) to God and legislate new morality.

They have intellectualized themselves into accepting corruption as something to overlook as long as the economy is doing well. Truth has lost its' way in America. It has been replaced with "doing what seems right in our own eyes" or by going down the avenue that will make us least responsible. We quote scripture backwards if need be. "Who shall cast the first stone?" is the cry of the morally bankrupt. We have moved away from the judgment of right and wrong and into the false covering of "love covers a multitude of sin".

As a nation we are spiraling downward with each new generation. So as extreme as it may sound unless we wish to join in the reward of the Egyptians we Christians need to get a firm grip on scripture. We need to become those peculiar people, who are described in I Peter 2: 9. Everyday is a battle to keep yourself separate from the foolishness of this world. Everyday needs to be a new day to speak the truth to ourselves, our mates, our children and our grandchildren and to those friends we hold dear. It is just too easy not to offend. God is offended by America, why shouldn't we be?

No, Christians are not perfect, but God is and we represent Him or at least we say we do. He has called us to high standards simply because He knows the complete destruction of sin. His model for the family cannot be changed. His value of every man regardless of race or social position cannot be changed. His view of sin is clear. We need to think of ourselves as works under construction and be warned each day that if we choose we can become works for destruction by choosing the ways of the world over God's ways.

The world hates to hear that there is black and white. We've grown accustomed to shades of gray. The responsibility for our actions must always be pursued by how God would judge those actions. We've moved into the places of looking at motives that justify sin and people to blame our actions on. Foolishly, we seek to qualify our sin as something to be overlooked. God does not overlook sin! He forgives it, but there are consequences to sin and those consequences will always be there. In heaven it will be judgment for those who loved themselves more than God, but for the Christian there will be forgiveness.

It has often been said that we may be surprised who we don't see in heaven. Unfortunately, according to scripture God will look at some and say: I NEVER KNEW YOU. (Matthew 7: 22-23) Our job is to make sure He knows us! Focusing on our sins keeps us responsible to God every day. Letting Him view us as we pursue life through the eyes of His scripture will keep us out of the camp of the Egyptians and in the family of God. Man can have a high view of you today, but only God's view of you will matter in eternity.

A BEGINNING PLACE FOR PRAYER TODAY:

Please let me represent You well. Help me Father to speak Your perspective on right and wrong boldly. I need to be in Your Word daily so I will not be compromised by what is happening around me. I don't want to be assimilated into the world's view. Lord I desire You to reign over my life in every though spoken and unspoken. Help me to glorify You today.

DISCUSSION QUESTIONS FOR TODAY:

1. Are there moral questions I should take a clearer stand on before man?

2. What moral standards specifically have I seen compromised in this day and age?

DAY 48

SING TO THE LORD, FOR HE HAS TRIUMPHED GLORIOUSLY! THE HORSE AND ITS RIDER HE HAS THROWN INTO THE SEA! EXODUS 15:21

READING FOR TODAY– EXODUS 15: 19-21 AND DEUTERONOMY 10: 12-21

HE HAS TRIUMPHED GLORIOUSLY! That is exactly how God works. He triumphs gloriously; no half-hearted victories and He does it beyond anything we can ever imagine and in a manner no man could duplicate. He is worthy of our praise. His statutes are perfect, their outcome will always be worthy of awe and praise by us.

Do we sing to the Lord often? Sad to say most of the time we hand off a few thank yous and then grumble about the rest of the day. Miriam brought out instruments and danced to celebrate the victory. We need to keep those Christian CDs and tapes on as much as possible. Somehow music puts our hearts and our minds where they should be and that is in a place where the noise and the confusion of this world is overpowered.

I must confess the old hymns have beautiful words, but melodies which are often not too haunting. I love it when I can sit in a worship service and sing beautiful simple praise songs to Him and then upon leaving have that same song stay with me all day. When my heart sings it clears out my soul and allows me to focus on His wonderful love for me.

It feels wonderful to have phrases of those praise songs rise to my lips in the middle of the day or to wake up with one on my heart. When we are traveling we often say: "Let's have church!" We put on our Christian tapes and we worship Him as we go down the road. The atmosphere of my home for my family and friends can be altered into an atmosphere of joy and peace when Christian music has it's way of being the backdrop for my day.

Deuteronomy 10:21 says: HE IS YOUR PRAISE. When we praise Him regularly we stay out of two common traps of the enemy. One, we let people know who is the author of all our successes and we keep a proper perspective on WHO really gives us the good life. Number two, we keep His greatness ever before us and we don't take Him for granted. Probably the worst thing we do as Christians is to take credit for His gifts to us and then forget how great and awesome He is to us.

Practicing praise is important. The more we discipline ourselves to praise the sooner praise will become second nature to us. Praise should be like breathing. We can't really enjoy life until we praise Him everyday. Joy is knowing Him, not knowing about Him. Praise is my acknowledgment of His position in my life and of His supreme power over me.

A BEGINNING PLACE FOR PRAYER TODAY:

Lord, help me to praise You with music today. Keep me tuned into a good Christian radio station as I drive or work about my day. Let me want to sing to You and be a part of telling you everyday how much I love you. You have set your charge over me and it is an awesome, wonderful thing. I cannot fathom why You love me so much, but Lord I thank You that You do.

DISCUSSION QUESTIONS FOR TODAY:

1. How can I begin to praise God as naturally as I breath?

2. Does praising God make a difference in my attitude for the day?

DAY 49

SO HE CRIED OUT TO THE LORD, AND THE LORD SHOWED HIM A TREE. WHEN HE CAST IT INTO THE WATER, THE WATERS WERE MADE SWEET. EXODUS 15: 25

READING FOR TODAY— EXODUS 15: 22-27 AND II CHRONICLES 7: 14

There's a lot of bitter water surrounding us today. Even when we think we are serving Him, we can still be missing something and life just becomes bitter water. Sometimes the tree we need to throw into the water is called: "humble myself." Working in our own strength keeps the water (our problem) bitter in our lives.

Calling out to the Lord over specific problems in our lives puts us in the right place—on our knees. Unless we take time to listen to God we just don't hear His voice and we keep throwing in the wrong tree. Sometimes we don't even know what tree we're looking for. Humbling myself is giving up my request and saying "Thy will be done," because we just aren't getting what we really need done on our own.

Have I ever thought I was being misunderstood, but in reality I was the misunderstanding one? We work so often from our own perspective, seeking to support our perspective with scripture and our perspective isn't really God's perspective. The motive for our perspective can be all wrong. It can stem from selfishness, unforgiveness, a lack of self-control and a hundred other things, but when God's commandments are looked into deeply there comes a place when we can throw in the right tree and then we are able to drink the water in our cup.

Until we're ready to humble ourselves we can never be set free from the burdens of our life. We will always struggle and feel bound up by things concerning other people. Our land is US! I know it is often given the broader meaning of the world or a country or the church, but God needs to deal with US first. It's really time to check the trees about us and see what needs to be thrown in. Surprisingly, the tree might just be "letting go" and trusting God so the bitterness of our water will leave us. Perhaps our heart is right, our scriptures are sound, but we, in our own strength, are standing in the way.

Sometimes the tree thrown in must soak for a while before the water lessens its bitterness. Time is a wonderful healer of things, but it can also be our greatest problem in letting go. There are very few instant healings. Too much work has to be done to clean-up the wound before it can be healed and we grow impatient or we don't want to give God the time to make it a complete healing. But when the wound starts healing and it begins to ache less then we must take heart and praise God that we have thrown in the right tree.

A BEGINNING PLACE FOR PRAYER TODAY:

Lord, help me to find the right trees in my life. Check my heart's attitude Lord. I pray for things with all the wrong motives way too often. Let me search and search and search your scriptures until I have a clear picture of myself before I attack a problem. I'm tired of bitter water in my life.

DISCUSSION QUESTIONS FOR TODAY:

1. Are there any prayers in my life that aren't getting answered? Could it be I've chosen the wrong tree to throw in?

2. Have I ever been the misunderstanding one and thought it was someone else's problem to deal with and I was the problem? Am I a problem to someone right now?

DAY 50

OH, THAT WE HAD DIED BY THE HAND OF THE LORD IN THE LAND OF EGYPT. EXODUS 16: 3A

READING FOR TODAY– EXODUS 16: 1-5 AND II CORINTHIANS 10: 3-6

We look at this scripture passage and we think to ourselves: "What completely thankless people these Israelites are!" But if we are honest we can look at them and see ourselves. Often when we are frightened, we want peace and safety in our lives so we challenge God's wisdom and direction in our lives. Just as foolish as the Israelites sound we too often sound foolish and unthankful and we do it more often than we would like to admit. How honest are we with God?

Do we fool ourselves into thinking that God doesn't know we are being rebellious and disobedient because we don't like His choices for us? Have we set our own agendas to over-ride God's agenda by manipulating our desires over God's perfect plan for us? Rebellion is usually what we exhibit when we know things aren't going our way.

We stand up and shout in disobedience: "This isn't fair!" or "I hate this!" It is out right disobedience in accepting the will of God in our lives. We are jumping off the potter's wheel and demanding to mold ourselves! Yes, it is sinful, natural behavior that God can forgive, but none the less it is rebellious behavior and it is causing us unnecessary pain.

The molding of our personality and character to be Christ like takes complete submission on our part. God can work with a submitted heart, but He has to work over time on the rebellious heart. The rebellious heart will lose its' peace and joy and finally even manage to quench the Spirit of God from working in it. Because we are free-will beings God will allow us to be rebellious and disobedient. But…when we do that, move out on our own, we are out in the world working in our own experience and unprotected by God's wisdom, that quite frankly to me is a scary place to be!

II Corinthians 10:4-5 reminds us that we must pull down the strongholds of fear by not letting worldly knowledge EXALT ITSELF AGAINST THE KNOWLEDGE OF GOD. That knowledge lies in a firm understanding of who Jesus is and what power He exhibits in our lives. When we study His Word and execute only behavior that brings every one of our thoughts into the captivity of Christ then and only then can we experience His complete peace.

He becomes the one who holds the enemy prisoner and He alone can keep the enemies' words from destroying us. We need to pray about not challenging God's will for our lives. We want His view of life's difficulties. Have I doubted His love for me? His love for me is perfect. He alone can save me. Disobedience and rebellion are not Godly fruit. It is important that I seek His wisdom and pray fervently not to challenge it!

A beginning place for prayer today:

You know how easily I am lied to by the enemy. Please direct my thoughts and hold them in prayer. Help me to run to You in prayer and not let my thoughts be captive over me. I want the strength of Your Spirit and the growth I'll get if I can just see life through Your eyes. I am so limited in what I can understand. Help me to let go of all my fears, don't let me be in charge of my life. I know the foolishness of that, spare me that foolishness Lord.

Discussion Questions for today:

1. What thoughts do I let the enemy hold me in bondage with?

2. What part does scripture and prayer play in my ability to see when I am being deceived by the enemy?

DAY 51

LET US SEARCH OUT AND EXAMINE OUR WAYS AND TURN BACK TO GOD. LET US LIFT OUR HEARTS AND OUR HANDS TO GOD IN HEAVEN. LAMENTATIONS 3: 40-41

READING FOR TODAY– EXODUS 16: 6-9 AND PHILIPPIANS 4: 4-9

God is the ultimate recipient of our complaints. Have you ever considered that complaining is being ungrateful to God? We must constantly remind ourselves that everything that comes to us must pass before the throne of God first. The translation of this is that everything in my life is something He has allowed. This biblical principle is thoroughly explored in the book of Job. Job's comforters were caught up with trying to explain Job's plagues. Job did not doubt God's love for him and his faith accepted the plagues. He had made up his mind to trust God no matter what the circumstances of his life were.

It is critical to our faith that we turn our complaints into prayer requests. Complaining gives the enemy a toe-hold on our basic sin nature. That toe-hold can turn our focus from the love of Christ to all consuming self-pity and fear. It is not without good reason that Matthew 6: 34 tells us to put our energies into the moments of this day only. While we are in this day we need to look critically at our attitudes and our motives as we move through the day. God has control over us only if we give our attitudes and motives over to Him. Those attitudes and motives are who we are in Christ. We're either hopeless or full of hope about each day simply by Who we are in Christ.

The Israelites had their faith in Moses and Aaron, not in God. Moses and Aaron try to get the Israelites eyes on God for the answer to their concerns: BUT WHAT ARE WE THAT YOU COMPLAIN AGAINST US? They are saying in other words to the Israelites: Speak to God; this is His show! Whatever it is that upsets you; speak to God first. Complaining says to everyone who hears it: "It doesn't matter what God's purposes are for my life, I want life on my own terms!

How limited we are in our perspective of the whys and wherefores of today. How could we possibly ever understand the entire future of our days? We don't understand how God will make something good out of something that is meant to harm us. By past evidence we have seen Him work in that way and we have been prospered despite our discouragement and fears at the time. There is great comfort in letting go and letting God do the work. I am responsible for only those things I can control; everything else is God's responsibility. Thank You Jesus!

God listens to complaints, but they need to be in a format of prayer. LET YOUR REQUESTS BE MADE KNOWN TO GOD. It does not say let your requests be made known to man. Generally speaking, when people ask how you are they don't really want to know. The complainer finds people eventually running away from him. A prayer partner is a great gift. They can be the people who can help us form our complaints into prayers. They can even be someone who can come alongside and pray for and with us.

But, we must remember; only God has all the answers, so I must remind myself that I need to be careful who I put my trust in!

A BEGINNING PLACE FOR PRAYER TODAY:

Lord, help me to stop complaining and start praying more. Help me to listen and look expectantly for Your answers. You alone hold the keys to an abundant life for me and those I love. Nothing I possess can really help when trouble comes my way. Only You can handle everything and make it completely for my benefit. I want You pleased with me. Help me to not let you down Lord. Thank You for this day.

DISCUSSION QUESTIONS FOR TODAY:

1. What have I learned about myself today? Am I thankful or am I a complainer? If I have discovered that I am a complainer, what do I need to do about that?

2. Do I have a prayer partner now or have I ever had a prayer partner? What character traits would I look for in a potential prayer partner?

DAY 52

....AND YOU SHALL KNOW THAT I AM THE LORD YOUR GOD. EXODUS 16:12C

READING FOR TODAY– EXODUS 16: 10-12, ISAIAH 46: 3-4 AND ISAIAH 49: 16

Do I know that God is the Lord MY God? Sometimes life gets so complicated and even hurtful that we forget that God says "Your name is engraved on the palm of my hands."(Isaiah 49: 16) That doesn't mean it's written in something that can be washed away—it is engraved—never to be washed away or made to disappear from His palms!

We are important to Him. He hears us and He loves us and He is always there for us. Life here on earth puts us often in the middle of problems and pain that are sometimes not even of our own making. Our mates, our children, our parents, our family and friends affect our lives every day. Because we experience love and give love we must also expect the downside of loving. The only way that we could eliminate this pain from our lives would be if we were to stop loving and thank God that is not possible!

Love experiences the unavoidable joy and sorrow of life. We don't have any control over our unconditional love or its' emotions. When someone we love hurts we hurt. We cannot turn off the emotions of love without God's intervention. The Holy Spirit is the perfect instrument for intervention when we have become overcome with emotions. He alone can calm our fears, soften our pain and strengthen our lives to enable us to cope with what we must endure. Often the road is paved way ahead by God in preparation for tragedy. He alone knows what we will need to survive a tragedy.

A new friend of mine who became the single parent of her two small granddaughters through the fatal car accident of her son and daughter-in-law confirmed to me once again my belief in God's faithfulness as she shared: "It gives me shivers to think how for the last two years God has molded my life. He led me to and through changes that I thought were my choices, to make me financially secure after my husband divorced me."

She told me that she thought these changes were just for her. Turning her home into a bed and breakfast came to be her dream. It would allow her to work from home. Doors opened freely to her. New avenues got wider and to her amazement when the tragedy happened, she was prepared to meet it because the foundations of her life were in place. Today she praises God for His preparation and peace in a situation she never knew would happen – but God knew. With all her heart she proclaims and knows that God is in charge of her life and her granddaughters, and that He will take care of them.

Tragedy of this magnitude does not befall all of us. Yet I am sure if we review the tragedies of our lives we will see that our survival was accomplished by God. He provided those unexpected people, places and events and ultimate peace through things that only He could orchestrate. We are safer and more securely in His hands because of His provision and our knowledge of it. When we are weak He is strong. It is a wonderful thing to know: I AM THE LORD YOUR GOD!

A BEGINNING PLACE FOR PRAYER TODAY:

Lord, do not let me forget—I am not in charge of anything. You are my strength and my shield and You alone have given me my provision. It is foolish for me to worry over people and things. Help me to quickly commit today's worries to You. I cannot handle these emotions and only You can calm me. Thank You Father that You love me so much that I am always written on the palms of Your hands and You simply look down at those hands and You see me.

DISCUSSION QUESTIONS FOR TODAY:

1. What tragedies have I survived with the help of the Lord?

2. How has God miraculously supplied my needs when I didn't even know that I would need His provision?

DAY 53

I WAS YOUNG AND NOW I AM OLD, YET I HAVE NEVER SEEN THE RIGHTEOUS FORSAKEN OR THEIR CHILDREN BEGGING FOR BREAD. THEY ARE ALWAYS GENEROUS AND LEND FREELY; THEIR CHILDREN WILL BE BLESSED. PSALM 37: 25-26

READING FOR TODAY– EXODUS 16: 13-20, PSALM 37: 21-29 AND LUKE 6: 38.

Man is always fearful of tomorrow if he has no faith in God. Moses trusted God; the Israelites were learning to trust. God is a patient teacher. When He gives commandments or precepts He knows we might take halting steps of faith so it seems with these steps he gently reassures us with gifts of necessity. Our faith in God will lead us to righteousness and righteousness will lead us to God's prosperity or what we Christians call: the abundant life.

Righteousness is defined as meeting the standard of what is morally right. Morally right puts us in the character of doing what is right in Christ like character and behavior. The doing of what is right becomes our responsibility to God and then to the people around us. God prospers the righteous and no matter what we have when we share it or use it as God requires we are blessed.

I personally love the statement "You can't out give God" because He has over the years proven this to me to be abundantly true! If I let go freely of what God has given me, I am always blessed. When I think of generosity I think of a special friend of mine named Isabel. She is not a wealthy woman, but she never hesitates to bless people with her time, talents or possessions.

She has no hidden motives for her generosity; she simply loves the Lord and wants to honor Him. Isabel and her family have known serious times of illness and job loss and yet they have never pulled back from their commitment to loving and caring for the brethren and even new found friends who don't know the Lord. By the same token I have heard her bless God's name for surprise provision when times for her family were quite bleak by worldly standards.

There will always be those who stock pile and in their hoarding way they stack it up (money, possessions, and self-interest, whatever) and they are never satisfied. God calls us to keep a light hand on the things of this world. He gives and He is capable of taking it all away because all that we have is His. Our job is simply to be good stewards of what He has given us. Of course, we are to be faithful and responsible to pay our bills and to save for our families, as well as to put food on the table and clothes on our backs, but once we have done these things we need let the rest go easily for His righteousness sake.

The one thing we cannot be assured of is tomorrow. Today is the time to work and play and share (sharing love most of all) for tomorrow is not a guarantee. Using our possessions as tools to bless others is in itself a great blessing. Christmas seems to be the only time we as a nation focus on this, but Christians need to focus on this every day.

We need to be consciously aware that God has blessed us and it is our responsibility to bless others. After I have been responsible, I need to be generous and this behavior blesses God. If I stack up my possessions they may someday stink! Grumbling, mumbling unhappy people are usually those who do not know how to share, much less trust God. As we see in the scripture passages of today, God is teaching the Israelites about His faithfulness and His generosity. He wants them to be less grumpy and certainly lessen their tendencies to mumble. The real blessing of giving is the joy it gives the giver and God definitely wants them to be happy.

AND IF THOU DRAW OUT THY SOUL TO THE HUNGRY, AND SATISFY THE AFFLICTED SOUL; THEN SHALL THY LIGHT RISE IN OBSCURITY, AND THY DARKNESS BE AS THE NOON DAY: AND THE LORD SHALL GUIDE THEE CONTINUALLY, AND SATISFY THY SOUL IN DROUGHT, AND MAKE FAT THY BONES; AND THOU SHALT BE LIKE A WATERED GARDEN, AND LIKE A SPRING OF WATER, WHOSE WATERS FAIL NOT. Isaiah 58:10-11

A BEGINNING PLACE FOR PRAYER TODAY:

Help me to focus on You Lord. Take my eyes away from financial concerns. Let me be a good steward of all You have blessed me with. I need a light touch on the things of this world. Help me to trust You for all the needs of my family. Let me left up others needs before my own; taking the focus off of myself and putting that focus onto them. My blessings are so many I cannot count them all. Thank You Father, for how much I am loved and provided for because You love me and always seek what is best for me. Now help me to look about and see the needs of others that I can fill today.

DISCUSSION QUESTIONS FOR TODAY:

1. Am I a good steward of what God has given me? What areas do I need work in?

2. Do I bless people with my generosity of time, talents or possessions or am I stingy and mumbling?

DAY 54

BEAR IN MIND THAT THE LORD HAS GIVEN YOU THE SABBATH; THAT IS WHY ON THE SIXTH DAY HE GIVES YOU BREAD FOR TWO DAYS. EVERYONE IS TO STAY WHERE HE IS ON THE SEVENTH DAY; NO ONE IS TO GO OUT. SO PEOPLE RESTED ON THE SEVENTH DAY. EXODUS 16: 29-30

READING FOR TODAY– EXODUS 16: 21-30, JOHN 6: 35 AND ISAIAH 30:15

In verse 23 of Exodus 16 it says: TOMORROW IS TO BE A DAY OF REST, A HOLY SABBATH TO THE LORD. As we look at Sundays in our present day and age it becomes perfectly evident it is not a day of rest. In fact it has become just one more day of "gathering" included in an already hectic week of commercial endeavors. What a shame!

God's plan was perfect, but we have added to it and now it's almost lost. Attending church on Sunday should be a celebration of the week that the Lord has allowed. It should set us apart from non-believers. Turning our eyes to God and honoring Him for even an hour can give us peace and then perspective on our lives. It should be a time of reflection, but sometimes it doesn't happen because we just can't get up, we'd rather sleep in!

Heaven knows we need to slow down at least one day a week. We don't need to be like the legalistic Jew, but we do need rest and God has provided that in His commandments. When our eyes are taken off of our daily tasks they can be refocused on the people in our lives. For life to be a joy to live there has to be time spent realizing the blessings of God, His love and tender care for us and our families and friends.

To see my family healthy and together in the pew beside me gives me a strong sense of God's love for me, but it also makes me think on them as individuals. As a parent, I ask God to help me be a better parent. What have they needed from me this week? What have I given of myself to them this week—not money, possessions or entertainment—what have I given them of me in patience, understanding, sympathy, empathy and direction? Do my family members know I love them? What have been the meditations of my heart and the words of my mouth for them to God?

Groceries can be bought, cars can be washed, and laundry can be done on Saturdays. Sundays need priority. To look about and see the blessings of God raises my spirit in thankfulness. Sharing a Sunday dinner allows for laughter and fellowship. Family outings allow us to interact and understand why we work so hard during the week. All our accomplishments are by His hands to glorify Him and our children are not our accomplishment; they are His! For a brief time these gifts called our children are ours to share with God and then they're gone and have their own lives. Each Sunday that slips away without this intimate fellowship in Christ is a waste of precious time, never to be reclaimed.

We desperately need to worship God at least one day a week. It allows us to prioritize our lives and get our eyes off the world and on Him. My maker desires me to know His magnificence and power in my life. I'll never fully realize it until I rest and give Him time to speak to me. He only desires what is good for me and those I love, but I'll never find it asleep in my bed, in the mall or playing golf on the day He has asked me to rest in Him. God was discouraged by the Israelites who would not rest and be a part of a "holy Sabbath" surely He is even more discouraged today with us!

MY SON, ATTEND TO MY WORDS; INCLINE THINE EAR UNTO MY SAYINGS LET THEM NOT DEPART FROM THINE EYES; KEEP THEM IN THE MIDST OF THINE HEART FOR THEY ARE LIFE UNTO THOSE THAT FIND THEM, AND HEALTH TO ALL THEIR FLESH. Proverbs 4: 20-22.

A BEGINNING PLACE FOR PRAYER TODAY:

Lord, help me to clear the week from my mind with the devoted act of worshipping You each Sunday. Help me to put everything aside so I can hear from You and keep my eyes on You. I get so lost in the weekly cares of my life. You are in charge of everything. Why do I think I am? Cleanse my heart Lord, set me on the right path. Keep my priorities Your priorities. Thank You Father.

DISCUSSION QUESTIONS FOR TODAY:

1. What can I do to make Sunday a Sabbath day that my family and friends can enjoy and see Your blessings in?

2. What prayers do I need to offer up for my mate and my children on Sundays?

DAY 55

"Take a pot and put an omar of manna in it, and lay it up before the Lord, to be kept for generations." Exodus 16: 33

READING FOR TODAY– EXODUS 16: 31-36, DEUTERONOMY 6: 6-9

Traditions are a way of helping your family find God in their own personal lives. Many a teenager becomes rebellious toward church because he is allowed to have his way. God's order requires respect for tradition, not for the tradition, but for the truth of the tradition. God is the truth of the Sabbath tradition.

When we were raising our children, Sunday was a fun day for our family. We always went to the late service so they could sleep in, especially helpful when they were teenagers. On our way to church, we'd stop for donuts, chocolate milk and juice. After church we went out to lunch together. We spent time with one another, we talked, we laughed, and we shared what we had learned that morning and how the week past had gone. When we got home from church, we had no big plans; we were just available to them.

In the putting of the manna in a jar, the Lord requested that future generations understand Him and His provision for us. Sundays are a big part of keeping that respect alive and there will come a time when our teenagers will recall the roots of their God in their lives—but, there have to be roots first!

Words are empty without action. Actions are the fruit of the Spirit in our lives. Taking time to listen to our teenagers gives us an opportunity to see life through their eyes. It's important to listen, even when the conversation isn't so much directed at you the parent. Sometimes the most important information we can get is when we listen to dinner tables dialogues between our children. In our household there was a lot of laughter, but in that laughter was often truths about ourselves and our children. Even laughter needs to be listened to by parents.

One thing is for certain; if we never spend time with our children we will never be a part of their lives or their traditions. Sunday is the tradition which can become a weekly constant in our children lives. Everyone wants to feel important. We are important when someone wants to spend time with us. Making time is another tradition God has built into the Sabbath as a priority.

In Deuteronomy He instructs us to bind His words on our hands and bind them on our foreheads so that we will impress them on our children when we sit and when we walk along the road. Everything of importance God has instruction for in His Word. Our children need to know those principles and that our rules are God's rules. There is a lot of weight in "God says" as opposed to "I (your Mother) think."

The principles of God are found in the Bible. A good Bible teaching church experience every Sunday will equip us for all of our struggles. The traditions of God become firmly planted in us and their sharing will become second nature if we can set aside the Sabbath. We will be better equipped to arm our children against the world if we honor Him and His truths with the family tradition of the Sabbath.

A BEGINNING PLACE FOR PRAYER TODAY:

My family and friends need Your truths in their lives. Help me Father to get deep into Your Word so I know Your character. I want to share Your love with others, but I can only do that if I study Your words to me and look clearly through Your eyes at the people I love and those I meet in my life. Help me always to relate Your words as opposed to my words. My words have no strength or power; only Your words will change lives and mold traditions of You in my life and the lives of those I love.

DISCUSSION QUESTIONS FOR TODAY:

1. Am I building strong traditions for the Lord in my family? What are they?

2. Are the teenagers in my life running the household or am I strong in my stand to build traditions with them even when they are unhappy with me?

DAY 56

THY MERCY, O LORD, IS IN THE HEAVENS; AND THY FAITHFULNESS REACHETH INTO THE CLOUDS. PSALM 36:5

READING FOR TODAY: EXODUS 17: 1-7, PSALM 36: 5-12

Here we go again, the Israelites are grumbling against Moses. They still aren't trusting in God. All their reasoning remains in the worldly realm and all their energy is expended on trying to manipulate Moses into solving their problems. Moses can't believe they don't understand, but God does. Patiently, God puts into operation yet another plan to help their unbelief.

Every day of our lives God seeks to improve our relationship with Him and lessen our unbelief. He desires to have us know Him. We know Him best when we learn to talk to Him directly about our problems. I'm sure He'd like to hear our praise reports, but man just doesn't seem to go there as often as he should. God is always ready to support us and I am sure He is working on us little by little so we can be stronger and wiser in Him. He wants the Israelites to trust Him, but He is willing to give them time to grow and to learn to trust Him.

That's what a wilderness experience is all about—it is a personal encounter with the living God. No matter what our circumstances God can be in the middle of them if we allow it. The question is—do we put God in the middle or do we go else where for help? It's not that God doesn't want us to be resourceful. He wants us to use all our human resources to solve issues, but He'd like to be talked to first! We need to apprise Him of our needs and ask for His wisdom. He wants to communicate with us daily.

The Israelite's are very much like us when we forget who holds the keys to our very existence. We get upset, frightened and disturbed and we needlessly stay in that place. It almost seems at times that we are comfortable in the turmoil and rather than execute change we prefer to stay in our familiar turmoil rather than accepting the reasonable peace of mind we could find in Jesus if we would just talk to Him.

When my oldest son contemplated planning his wedding with his bride to be he said, "But … it's so big!" Yes, I had to agree it was, but I reminded him of the question: "How do you eat an elephant?" And the answer: "One bite at a time!" Problems are like this when God's in charge. He'll give you just enough for today and that's your responsibility. Then He'll work on the rest. Some days your responsibility is just to SIT, you physically cannot do anything at all except hold your position in Christ. Sometimes your job will be just to OBSERVE and THINK to get a better picture of the people or the events of your crisis. A PLAN cannot come together effectively until God has His say in it. The plan will probably take some time to shape itself. Our responses will always be like the Israelite's until we reach maturity in Christ on each subject or crisis He allows in our lives. The alternative to STOP is CONFUSION.

C=Coming unglued. (I Corinthians: 14:33)

O=Open to the enemies words. (James 3: 16-18)

N=Negative thoughts running through your mind. (Philippians 4:6-8)

F=Floundering about in despair. (Isaiah 50: 7)

U=Unbelief in God and His power in my life. (Proverbs 3:5-6)

S=Sinful behavior on my part. (Psalm 119: 11)

I=Indecision—frozen even. (Isaiah 30: 21)

O=Offensive behavior toward others. (Ephesians 6: 10, 11, 16)

N=No progress. (Romans 7:19)

You can make your own analogue out of the letters in confusion, but they'll be just a frightening as mine. One thing is for certain – confusion reigns when God is not a part of the battle plan. God is not the author of confusion (I Corinthians 14:33). If we're running around confused, guess who's in charge? God needed to stay real basic with the Israelites to build their confidence in Him.

He's doing the same for us every minute of every day. He loves us, He wants the best for us and He'll accomplish it if we will just STOP! It is wise to know that we cannot trust the easy or the too obvious solutions of the world. We want complete deliverance from our problems, not just hiding places that will make our problems eventually even more complicated. It is best just to assume there are no easy ways out of life's dilemmas and let the Lord have the last word on everything!

A BEGINNING PLACE FOR PRAYER TODAY:

Oh Lord, forgive my mistrust. Clear my mind of worldly perspectives. Speak to me about me as You see fit. Don't let me get caught up in fear. Let me be caught up in Your provision for my life. I want you to show me Your ways so I can apply them to my life and avoid unnecessary pain. Thank You that You allow upsetting situations to darken my landscape. Help me to see Your growth expectations for me. Help me to keep my eyes on my short comings and overlook those of others. Thank You Father for this day.

DISCUSSION QUESTIONS FOR TODAY:

1. Which scriptures that were listed as combating CONFUSION did I find to be the most helpful to me?

2. Have I ever considered myself to be armed with scripture when the enemy comes to do battle? What scriptures have I used in the past?

DAY 57

I CAN DO ALL THINGS THROUGH CHRIST WHO STRENGTHENS ME. PHILIPPIANS 4:13

READING FOR TODAY– EXODUS 17: 8-13, PHILIPPIANS 4:19 AND I PETER 4: 12-13

As believers in Christ we are not above trouble, pain or sorrow. But we are not like the unbeliever because we have our Savior to come alongside and be a part of our needs. He alone will strengthen me to meet the needs of the battle before me. (Philippians 4: 19).

In my own strength I am weak. My emotions can run away with me. My fears can overwhelm me. I am lost. But…when Christ comes alongside I am renewed and restored. I become focused on the tasks of the day. Strength can come to me through others, but I must be willing to do what God calls me to do first. I cannot run or hide, I must accept and then receive from Him.

The most painful experiences are the most fruitful. God's economy is so different from the worlds. The world says: "Avoid pain and personal suffering at all costs!" and God says: "Embrace this trial or this situation for out of it I will make you more Christ like!" (I Peter 4: 12-13)

Moses took on the battle. He did not retreat. He chose Joshua to be the leader of the army and he put his trust in Joshua's choices. Then he did what the Lord commanded. He held up the staff for all to see. When he was weary he took steps to keep on doing what needed to be done. He sat down and he allowed others to help him hold up the staff.

God gives us people and solutions to our problems on a moment by moment basis. Christian fellowship is never sweeter than when it comes together to assist in the needs of another brother or sister in Christ. To accept help is not to be weak it is to be wise. When someone upholds the same Godly principles that I do it is such a blessing to have them as my personal prayer warrior. Interceding for someone else or being the one interceded for is the personal experience of seeing the power of prayer in our lives. When we pray God gives us the strength to uphold His will for us.

Being righteous requires more than human strength. Illness and disappointment are two things we will never comprehend, but God knows their purpose. The things the enemy means for our demise are the very things God can use for our good. In Romans 8:28 it doesn't say SOME THINGS GOD USES FOR GOOD, it says ALL THINGS.

If I am faithful to hold up God's principles and life commandments as a true believer I can expect the help I need to meet the challenges I face: BEING CONFIDENT OF THIS, THAT HE WHO BEGAN A GOOD WORK IN YOU WILL CARRY IT ON TO COMPLETION UNTIL THE DAY OF CHRIST JESUS. (Philippians 1:6).

A BEGINNING PLACE FOR PRAYER TODAY:

Lord I get so discouraged. I need your help every moment some days just to hold my head up. Help me to not be discouraged about important things in life. Don't let me dwell on the insignificant. When I look at things with your perspective I have a clearer view of what's important to me and to others. I desire to know what those things are and to work harder at them than all the world's priorities which are spread as confusion before me. Help my unbelief Lord, strengthen me this day. Thank You Father.

DISCUSSION QUESTIONS FOR TODAY:

1. What things are happening in my life this day that I do not understand, but I fully expect God to turn into something good?

2. Do I need prayer warriors on something in my life today or do I need to assist someone I know who is also in need of a prayer warrior?

DAY 58

NOT THAT WE ARE SUFFICIENT OF OURSELVES TO THINK ANYTHING OF OURSELVES; BUT OUR SUFFICIENCY IS OF GOD. II CORINTHIANS 3:5

READING FOR TODAY– EXODUS 17: 14-16, EPHESIANS 6: 10-18 AND ISAIAH 51:11

THE LORD IS MY BANNER is the name of the altar Moses erects in honor of God's deliverance of the Israelites from the Amalekites. It is extremely important to note that Moses is instructed to "write these events on a scroll as something to be remembered and to make sure Joshua hears it." Why would Moses need to be sure that Joshua would hear it?

Man can easily get caught up in the victories of life and start claiming them as his work if he doesn't keep a right perspective. Joshua would one day succeed Moses. He needed to keep a clear perspective on WHO was really winning the battles in his life. He needed to hear and store in his heart the true general of the army. Without God, nothing would have been accomplished. God needs to be given the glory in our battles of daily living so we don't fall into the trap of thinking we can take care of our lives and our destinies.

Too much is at stake in our lives to assume we are self-sufficient. As parents, mates and as brothers and sisters in Christ we need to be strong in the gifts of the Lord and marvel everyday at their abundance. But…we must never forget the source of those blessings. When we forget the source we become self-centered and not God-centered. Many battles are lost in the pages of the Bible because God was not the center of them. In some cases He never even asked the participants to take place in a battle.

God needs to be the center of our lives, not just the person we call on when everything else fails. If we fail to check in with Him every day and we fail to search the scripture we are going to be unprepared for battle and we might even be in a battle that God has not called us to! We cannot fight a good fight without the weapons of Ephesians 6:10-18. It is hard to hold the line of peace in our lives if we don't even know the source of peace in our lives.

The enemy is always trying to steal our peace. For if he can do that he can undermine our faith. Peace is a fruit of faith. When my faith is strong, my peace is assured. War is the devil's playground. Personal, small battles that are won or lost make us who we are in Christ and determine who is winning the war. Someone once pointed out to me that the devil is at war only with Christians, he has already won the rest of the world and they are on his side. Therefore it is always wise to remember you are Satan's target!

God is interested in our battles. In God's eyes there is no battle too small or too big where we are concerned. We are His child and He wants us fit for all our battles. *But…those battles have to be turned over to Him or we will be the general. I must ask. .*

myself: "Why do I want to be the general over any of these battles?" Never forget; we never lose when God is our strength. (Isaiah 51:11)

A BEGINNING PLACE FOR PRAYER TODAY:

Lord help me to let go and rest in Your strength. I get so discouraged sometimes and I wade into battle without Your permission and without Your armor. Lord, give me patience. You will win in the end, so I just need to be available, well armed with Your Word and prepared to sit quietly if necessary on the sidelines praying "Thy will be done!" For all my battles, big and small, keep me in Your strength. Thank You Father.

DISCUSSION QUESTIONS FOR TODAY:

1. Am I consistently putting on my armor and, if not, what part of my armor am I forgetting most of the time?

2. Should I be surprised that the enemy is always stocking me like a roaring lion? (I Peter 5: 8)

DAY 59

IF ANYONE SERVES ME, LET HIM FOLLOW ME; AND WHERE I AM, THERE SHALL MY SERVANT ALSO BE; IF ANYONE SERVES ME, THE FATHER WILL HONOR HIM. JOHN 12: 16

READING FOR TODAY– EXODUS 18: 1-7 AND PSALM 37: 3-11

What a picture of love and respect between two men as Moses bows down and then kisses his father-in-law. Jethro is a Midian priest, not a Jew or a believer, but Moses loves and respects his father-in-law. Actually, Jethro was impressed by Moses at a time when Moses did not even respect himself. He was running away from Egypt because he was a murderer. When Jethro heard of his kindness in securing water at the well for his daughters he sent for Moses. Jethro saw compassion in Moses. He invited him into his home and gave Moses a place in his family when Moses needed a family and safety.

The two must have had many long conversations over the years before Moses returned to Egypt. He sent Moses back to Egypt with the blessing "Go in peace". (Exodus 4:18) He trusted Moses' judgments. The two are now reunited after Zipporah has visited her father and told him her eyewitness accounts of God's miracles in Egypt for the Israelites. I can only imagine how Jethro's feelings of confidence in Moses and in the God of Moses must have been confirmed.

Moses wasn't intentionally setting Jethro up to win him to the God of the Israelites. God was setting up Jethro and had been ever since he had extended his hospitality to Moses. Our best source of influence for persuading others to seek the Lord in their lives is often the evidence of God in our lives. Someone sees how we live, how we minister to others and how we value others and they begin to respect us. Once someone respects us they want to seek our advice. When they learn we are who we are because of our belief in Jesus and that our life is biblically based on His righteousness, they often begin to seek Him for themselves.

There are many good men out there in the world. The only difference between them and us is that we're going to heaven and they are going to hell. With all that is within us, we must accept the challenge of being there for the person who needs the Lord. Being there does not mean judging them and preaching to them. Instead, it is more often than not, just patiently waiting to see the fruits of God's character in our lives affect them. God will work in them as they observe us.

Seeing the fruit of Christianity is the best witness for a non-believer, words are always just words. An unbeliever can even desire to accept Christ because he wants what we have. The unbeliever will see security and balance in the righteousness of God at work in us. We are not responsible for the salvation of others, but we are responsible for living the life God has set before us as believers in His righteousness. When we trust and dwell in His righteousness we exercise and then exhibit His hope, peace and salvation. Our job is to value others as much as God values us and treat other people as God has so graciously treated us.

A BEGINNING PLACE FOR PRAYER TODAY:

Father, help me to see that I am a witness before man of Your righteousness working in me. Let me seek Your will in my life today to make me the servant You need. I desire to bring others to a saving knowledge of You, but You are the only one who knows the season of each of us. Let me not be judgmental of others, for everyone belongs to You whether they know it or not, just give me a loving heart and let me dwell in the fullness of your righteousness today. Help me Father. Thank You.

DISCUSSION QUESTIONS FOR TODAY:

1. Which people in my life are the most successful at witnessing for the Lord? What are the principles that they have that makes them admirable?

2. Why was Jethro impressed by Moses?

DAY 60

AND MOSES TOLD HIS FATHER-IN-LAW ALL THAT THE LORD HAD DONE TO PHAROAH AND TO THE EGYPTIANS FOR ISRAEL'S SAKE... EXODUS 18: 8.

READING FOR TODAY– EXODUS 18: 8-12, GALATIANS 6: 1- 10 AND VERSE 14

Sharing the Lord with others every day is Jesus' great commission to all of us. On this Exodus journey of life people will come and go, but it is our job to look for those who God is sending our way—husbands, relatives, friends, co-workers or even a boss. I need to ask myself: "What will they hear me speak of today in their presence?" God's timing is always right so we just have to be open to share—not preach—the blessings of our relationship with Christ.

When we share with others we share who Christ is. Even when we just listen we share the Spirit of Christ. Words are important. They reflect who we are in our hearts and where our focus lies, but more importantly they are our representation of Christ to other people. It is important to have an awareness daily of where we are standing in Christ. It should be a hopeful spirit of faith that we exhibit for the world. If that spirit does not exist in us then it is time to check in with our Lord Jesus and have Him eliminate the spirit of fear or doubt or anger or unforgiveness or whatever other spirit has over taken us. The enemy attacks our minds every day. There is a war going on, but when we lead our battle with the standard of praise for our Lord, the enemies' inroads are on the road to defeat.

Moses is leading and has been leading this Midianite priest, Jethro, to God from the day of their first meeting. The basis of their relationship is mutual respect. Moses did not say: "He is a gentile and I'll have nothing to do with him!" And Jethro did not say:"He is a Jew; I'll have nothing to do with him!" They have simply come together under a banner of mutual respect. But, Moses has something far beyond just good character. He has the Lord. He has strength and wisdom and power and he has been changed into an even stronger man before Jethro. It's not that he wasn't a good man before, but now Jethro sees where all this growth has come from.

Moses doesn't share from "See all that I have and all that I am", he shares from "See all that God has accomplished in my life and all that God is to me in every situation." Jethro says: NOW I KNOW THAT THE LORD IS GREATER THAN ALL THE GODS. (Exodus 18:11) Jethro becomes a believer.

Well, of course, you say: "Why not?" It still remains a miracle though because it is the saving knowledge of the Lord that has been given to Jethro through his associating with Moses. Nothing was crammed down his throat. He accepted the Lord because he saw the fruit of the Spirit in Moses' life and he wanted that fruit in his life. You and I come under the same responsibility as Moses. We are to share in the great commission:

MATTHEW 28: 19-20 – GO THEREFORE AND MAKE DISCIPLES OF ALL NATIONS, BAPTIZING THEM IN THE NAME OF THE FATHER AND OF THE

SON AND OF THE HOLY SPIRIT TEACHING THEM TO OBSERVE ALL THINGS THAT I HAVE COMMANDED YOU; AND LO, I AM WITH YOU ALWAYS, EVEN TO THE END OF THE AGE.

Our words are important, but it's really our praise in those words that gets the attention of people for the Lord. We can never underestimate the power of our words before man because we speak on God's behalf whether we seek to or not. We are His ambassadors the very minute we accept Christ as our Savior and Matthew 28: 19-20 becomes our personal commandment and we are responsible for doing what it says.

A BEGINNING PLACE FOR PRAYER TODAY:

Oh, Lord help me to be openly giving out Your praise. Let people who experience my presence today feel the presence of You in my life. Let them see, You are all they need and life will be filled with hope and blessings if You are apart of them. I do not know who I'll meet today, but let me be an encourager and let them see Who encourages me!

DISCUSSION QUESTIONS FOR TODAY:

1. How is my spirit of praise today? What comes out of your mouth in the presence of believers and non-believers alike? On what does my heart dwell today?

DAY 61

THE STEPS OF A GOOD MAN ARE ORDERED BY THE LORD, AND HE DELIGHTS IN HIS WAY. THOUGH HE FALL, HE SHALL NOT BE UTTERLY CAST DOWN; FOR THE LORD UPHOLDS HIM WITH HIS HAND. PSALM 37: 23-24

READING FOR TODAY– EXODUS 18: 13-16, I THESSALONIANS 5: 16-17

How often have you taken on too much? Jethro sees what Moses is overlooking; Moses is wearing himself out. He has taken on too much. It is safe to say that all of us at one time in our lives have tried the experience of being super woman. Nothing worked as well as it could or as we had expected, we were exhausted and eventually we moved to martyrdom. Moses has just begun the long journey with these people and He will be required to go the distance. He can't do it alone, for surely he will burn out.

What does it require to go the distance? That's a pretty scary question when you don't know the distance. Some of us have a short term trial and others of us have longer ones and even life time trials before us. Wearing out before the end of the race is usually our greatest fear. It is also a lie from the enemy, because trust in God is the answer to what is required. The more we turn over to Him the longer we can go the distance.

Prayer is the sustaining power for being able to complete the race. Giving up the responsibility for something and accepting God's strength and wisdom allows us to be able to see the situation to its end or accept that we might not see its final end. By faith I must accept that God knows the solution and He alone can solve it and my job is to do only what He has set before me—one day at a time. It is much easier said than done, but what I do know is that some days will require short and even hourly prayers to keep us in His strength and totally defended against the enemy. His Holy Spirit can keep fear and fatigue from taking over, but it will surely set in if we do not pray without ceasing and keep His peace flowing in us.

Other people can help us if we let them. Christian friends make such a difference. They know what you need sometimes before you can see it. It takes a humble heart to accept help. Cultivating a humble heart will deliver us from pride and allow God to help us. A humble heart will also allow God to place wise people in our presence when we need them. Thank God for even the new believers like Jethro, because sometimes they are allowed wisdom when we are too far under the trial to see up!

Moses has a humble heart. He respects Jethro's advice and he listens. Listening is another tool for going the distance. God speaks to us through people, but more often than not He speaks to us through His Word. Proverbs is a wonderful place to gain wisdom and strength; it is also a wonderful place to receive humility. Please notice that the word I used here is humility, not condemnation. If we are condemned by the Word it is the work of the devil, but if we are humbled by the Word it is God who is speaking to us. A humble heart receives the conviction of God's wisdom and moves forward to make changes. Moses is accepting the counsel of Jethro and he is going to be able to go the distance!

A BEGINNING PLACE FOR PRAYER TODAY:

Lord, keep my heart soft. Let me not strive in my own strength. I will wear myse[l] out if I do this day alone. Help me to seek your face—even moment by moment if I need to. Keep my ears open to truth and keep my pride out of the way. I desire success. Please be in the middle of this day. I want to go the distance with You. Thank You Father.

DISCUSSION QUESTIONS FOR TODAY:

1. Have I been feeling condemned lately or do I know someone who has fallen unde[r] condemnation? Is there something I can do about condemnation?

2. What decisions have I made today about going the distance?

DAY 62

THE WORK IS TOO HEAVY FOR YOU; YOU CANNOT HANDLE IT ALONE. EXODUS 18: 18B

READING FOR TODAY– EXODUS 18: 17-23, ISAIAH 6: 1-10

How much do I do each day in my own strength? It is way too easy to take on more than the Lord intends for us. When was the last time I asked the Lord to look at my load and evaluate it for me? Do I know or have I forgotten what I really am to do in life for Him?

We need to take the time to lay all of our concerns, relationships, household matters and business before Him. Something is wrong if we are overwhelmed—scripture says HIS BURDEN IS LIGHT and we know confusion and darkness are not of Him. Isaiah heard the voice of God because he took time to listen. We need to take that time—even if we think everything is on the right track. Unfortunately, we can think we're on the right track and be overwhelmed. Moses was doing good things for the people, but Moses was overwhelmed. He had taken on more than God had intended.

Each of us needs to stand ready to hear where God needs us to be for the day or moment or even hour, but ours is a daily responsibility to hear from Him. We are responsible for no more than one day at a time according to scripture (Matthew 6:34). Isaiah and Moses were not the only people God could use. God just needs willing hearts. If we cannot or will not do what God calls us to do He will move on to someone else and pass the blessing on to them. God used Jethro to make changes that were healthy for Moses. If life is too overwhelming it is time to check in. We could be standing in the way of someone else's growth and our own peace of mind because we just won't take the time to check in.

Oswald Chambers says "Get out of your mind the idea of expecting God to come with compulsions and pleadings." God works "quietly" in each of our lives and if there is too much on our plate, there's usually too much noise in our lives to hear His voice and do His will. Not all good service is His will, especially when our families suffer. A good measure of whether we should take on more is how effective we are with what we already have.

Our families should not suffer because of our jobs or our church responsibilities. We need to show our pastors and those over us that we know that jobs and ministry are important, but our family comes first and our jobs and ministry will never be more important than our family and our marriage! God is honored by our faithfulness to His priorities and in return He will give us strong marriages and great family units. Remember Jethro's words: THE WORK IS TOO HEAVY FOR YOU; YOU CANNOT HANDLE IT ALONE and when we feel overwhelmed we need to check in with God.

A BEGINNING PLACE FOR PRAYER TODAY:

My life can get so complicated Father. Forgive me for allowing it to be that way. Help me to prioritize my time with you. Help me to listen after I ask if my agenda is Your agenda for the day. Keep me from big commitments until I ask You first. Let doors close quickly when I am convicted or not that I know Your will. Help me to step aside with the prayer THY WILL BE DONE. Thank You Father for your presence in my life.

DISCUSSION QUESTIONS FOR TODAY:

1. Is a need a call that I should always say yes to? How do I know when I should take on a new job in ministry?

2. Have I evaluated my priorities lately and are they the order God would have them in?

DAY 63

AS FOR GOD, HIS WAY IS PERFECT; THE WORD OF THE LORD IS PROVEN HE IS A SHIELD TO ALL WHO TRUST HIM. PSALM 18: 30

READING FOR TODAY– EXODUS 18: 24-27, PSALM 18: 20-30

IF YOU DO THIS THING, AND GOD SO COMMANDS YOU, THEN YOU WILL BE ABLE TO ENDURE, AND ALL THIS PEOPLE WILL ALSO GO TO THEIR PLACE IN PEACE. (Exodus 18: 23) In some trials "endure" is all we can hope for, but our endurance will not last unless we listen to the words of the Lord concerning our lives. Moses stepped aside from the burdens he was assuming and began to look closer at the leaders around him. He wasn't the only one God could use; bottom line: he needed help!

God allows special people to be in our presence. We need to listen to the words of other Christians who are speaking God's word to us. We don't need the wisdom of men; we need the proven word of God for setting our path. To make wise decisions we often need the confirmation or the correction of other godly men as we set out on "our path." Moses eliminated the weight of his responsibilities by handing some of them over to capable people—but he never relinquished his responsibility completely because he constantly observed those to whom he had given the responsibility.

Communicating our weaknesses to one another is important. When we've chosen those people in our lives that are capable, because we know they seek God, then we have wise counsel. Our burdens become lighter because we counsel and pray with those who can help us make decisions and in some instances share the responsibilities of our lives. We only get into trouble when we will not let go of a problem and we will not communicate our needs with God and with man. We suffer in silence and even upon occasion move to martyrdom.

Moses had to let go. We have to let go. First of all we need to give our concerns to God. Then we need to listen to and observe what God is showing us. It is also important to seek within the treasure of His scripture for the answers we need. When we have prayed and sought scripture then we can step out one day at a time expecting God TO HELP US RUN AGAINST A TROOP or even LEAP OVER A WALL. If our purposes are righteous (they are His commandments and promises found in the Bible), then we can be confident we will endure. Winning for the moment isn't really the answer to the problem; bringing honor to the Lord is the true measure of righteousness in our service for Him and that is the real endurance which we can share with others.

Jesus is the one who needs to be raised up before man. What we think, what we want, what we accomplish needs to be replaced by what God thinks (Bible truths) and those actions will set forth Biblical principles for all to see. Peter tells us in Philippians 4:9: THE THINGS YOU LEARNED AND RECEIVED AND SAW IN ME (Christ like actions and the teaching of Jesus) THESE DO, AND THE GOD OF PEACE WILL BE WITH YOU. The GOD OF PEACE WILL BE WITH YOU—what a promise! We have a way of judging the correctness of our journey if we learn, receive and observe the actions and sayings of Jesus in the scripture. If we learn everything there is to know about Jesus then we will know God. Decisions will become surer in our hearts because we know the side Jesus would choose. Please note, surer is the word I used not easier as the description of how we will experience our decision making because right decisions are sometimes the hardest to make, but their reward is great for they are THE PEACE THAT SURPASSES ALL UNDERSTANDING. (Philippians 4:7) We must never be afraid to seek help from our heavenly Father and admit our needs to our Christian friends.

A BEGINNING PLACE FOR PRAYER TODAY:

Lord, help me to let go and let this day just happen. Where ever I am, whatever You have allowed in my life is my ministry. I don't need to seek my ministry, I need to be open to the day and just experience it in your powerful righteousness. Thank You Father for allowing me to run against a troop of the enemy and even helping me to escape over the walls of the enemy. Guide my thoughts to reasonable people of God who can help me accomplish Your purpose for my life in a way that is an honor and a blessing to You. Thank You Father, for this day. Thy will be done!

DISCUSSION QUESTIONS FOR TODAY:

1. Do I have strong Christian counsel in my life when I make decisions?

2. How should I choose the people I want to be my advisors? What character traits are important in an advisor?

DAY 64

I HAVE LEARNED THE SECRET OF BEING CONTENT IN ANY AND EVERY SITUATION, WHETHER WELL FED OR HUNGRY, WHETHER LIVING IN PLENTY OR IN WANT. I CAN DO ALL THINGS THROUGH HIM WHO GIVES ME STRENGTH. PHILIPPIANS 4: 12B-13

READING FOR TODAY– EXODUS 19: 1-6, PHILIPPIANS 4: 4-7 AND PSALM 18: 30-40

I CARRIED YOU ON EAGLES' WINGS AND BROUGHT YOU TO MYSELF. That's how God gets us through life on His "eagles' wings". But note they are camped in a desert. Deserts are dry places. Periodically, our living has to take place in a dry land, but God carries us through those dry places. And He further says: NOW IF YOU OBEY ME FULLY AND KEEP MY COVENANT, THEN OUT OF ALL NATIONS YOU WILL BE MY TREASURED POSSESSION. (Exodus: 19: 5) We are carried by Him and we are treasured by Him if we keep His commandments.

It doesn't mean we'll lose our salvation if we fail to keep His commands, but is it healthy for us to keep striving in the direction of keeping them. The scariest part of living is not knowing something, so we try hard to know as much as we can. When we focus on Him as the carrier and us as the passenger on our way to heaven then we are in a sense in control of our lives. We have chosen to give Him complete control and we have chosen to be Christ like in our words and deeds and to let God chose our landing spots.

If we are in a great landing spot we're happy campers today, but if we're not; are we still a happy camper? It appears God is using Moses to remind us all that we need to remember all He has delivered us from so we can keep a right perspective on the present and not worry about the future. Why does God keep reminding the Israelites of what He's brought them through? Can't they remember? Of course they can, but they are human; they get worried. They get fearful. The longer we walk with God the easier it is to turn those fears about living over to Him, but it doesn't mean that fear goes away completely.

Paul says he HAS LEARNED; this means even Paul knew fear could get to him, but he has seen God at work and he knows God is faithful. He knows God gives him the strength he needs. The fact that he refers to being strengthened lets us know we will need that too. The best time to prepare for battle is before the battle begins. So…there is no coasting time in life! We need to be prayed up and studied up so that when the Carrier stops in the desert we can survive until He lifts us up and puts us into another place.

Discouragement is a powerful tool of the enemy. We have to pray daily for ourselves and other believers that they stay strong in their faith and that they experience God as their Carrier. We don't choose sickness, unemployment or failure. God allows these landings. But, we'll take off again because the Carrier will lift us up and over the places of battle and we'll be able to rejoice in that. (Psalm 18: 30-40) Discouragement can't have a hold on us if we praise Him for our blessings. Sometimes it takes deep digging to resurrect those blessings when we've landed in a desert, but when we dig into those blessings we dig a bunker of God's love to get us through this place and this moment. There will be less digging if we keep the bunker dug everyday instead of digging in only when the landing lasts longer than we had planned. BE PREPARED! The Boy Scouts' motto should also be the Christian's motto.

A BEGINNING PLACE FOR PRAYER TODAY:

Lord, keep me in Your Word. Arm me for the future if today is sweet and keep me praising You even if this day is not sweet. Help me to encourage others to be prepared by praising You before them and lifting up their needs to you. Lord we need each other everyday. We're all on this journey together with different side trips and yet one final destination. Help us Father to please You. Help me to dig that bunker of love, deep and wide so I can be like Paul and be content because I know You.

DISCUSSION QUESTIONS FOR TODAY:

1. What deserts have I landed in and learned from and then been carried on into sweeter places with so much more knowledge than before I had landed in that desert?

2. What are the things I value most when I am in the desert?

DAY 65

NOW IF YOU OBEY ME FULLY AND KEEP MY COVENANT, THEN OUT OF ALL THE NATIONS YOU WILL BE MY TREASURED POSSESSION. EXODUS 19:5

READING FOR TODAY– EXODUS 19: 7-9, JEREMIAH 2: 1-12 AND PHILIPPIANS 1:6

IF YOU OBEY ME FULLY is quite a lead-in phrase to the promise that follows in the above scripture. If we obey, we respect, we honor and we love the Lord our God, but how easy it is to get caught up in the respect and honor of the things of this world. The very things that will rob us of our fellowship with God are the things we prefer over fellowship with God.

God sees our hearts and He is quick to notice (Jeremiah 2:11b) BUT MY PEOPLE HAVE EXCHANGED THEIR GLORY FOR WORTHLESS IDOLS. It's easy to say: "Oh Lord, not me!" But... truth would have me see I put Him often behind my job,the household chores, the needs of my husband or children and He gets the back burner as I take on tasks of my making and my choosing.

Sometimes the biggest idol in our lives can be ourselves. We worry more what the world thinks than if we are pleasing to God. Jesus has been sacrificed upon a cross to make us holy in the sight of God. Through Christ we have complete forgiveness so one day we can enter into heaven, yet absurdity of all absurdity, we are striving to earn that free gift! We unfortunately volunteer our time sometimes to let others see that we are working for Jesus and we know this is true because we don't have any real joy in what we're doing; we're just burdened by one more responsibility. We let others know we are studying—we carry our Bible to church and that may be the only time of the week we take it off the shelf. We might even have a bumper sticker on our car. Our children, our homes, our relationships all get a super amount of attention and they have become our idols. We may even have a profession in which we seek respectability. These are idols to us, about us and for us if we are not careful to dedicate them to God and His glory.

The ultimate question is: Who is getting the glory and are these things in my life idols or are they expressions of how much I really love the Lord? If I really love Him I will sit at His feet, pray and study before I do anything. I cannot obey Him if I don't know what He wants of me. My priorities are to be set by Him and I can expect them to change from day to day. It's okay if a ministry changes in my life. Growth produces change. If everything in my life stayed static then I would not be growing. What God deemed good for me yesterday may now be complete. I cannot hold back time or constantly prove myself with deeds of the past. It may be time to move on to the new things of God. What are they? I don't know, so it may be time for me to check in on the subject. I might be in a rut.

Everyone hates change. It's uncomfortable to change, to see ourselves in a new light. We get pretty comfortable hiding behind our comfortable images of ourselves. Routine is good; it produces fruit. But, the routine can become the idol if we're not careful. To ask God each day what He thinks I need to be about will keep me from the

"I" problem. "God says", "God wants", "God is pleased with"---these are the phrases I should hear myself say every day before I say:"I think", "I want", and "this pleases me."

We want to be His "treasured possession". So, it's time to put the treasured possessions of self and pride on the altar and burn them. We need to be appalled at the charges of God in Jeremiah. Turning and repenting of those idols is really the only way we can stay honest with ourselves before God. It would be great to be a part of that "kingdom of priests and be a holy nation", but none of that will happen unless we first take ourselves out of the position of being an idol.

A BEGINNING PLACE FOR PRAYER TODAY:

Lord, thank You for this fresh look at me today. It isn't pretty and I repent. Put me on Your path today and keep me always looking to You for the changes I need to make that will honor You. Thank You that You love me so much, that You keep my image clear and bright even when what I see devastates me and causes You pain. Keep Your light on me Father. Search my heart and make me clean and pure in Your sight. The world's opinion is second to Your opinion of me. Thank You that You love me so much that You will always be working on me.

DISCUSSION QUESTIONS FOR TODAY:

1. What have been my idols in the past and are there idols in my life right now? What can I do about these idols?

2. Do I have an "I" problem? What is my need in this area?

DAY 66

I AM THE LORD AND THERE IS NO OTHER. I HAVE NOT SPOKEN IN SECRET, IN A DARK PLACE OF THE EARTH: I SAID NOT UNTO THE SEED OF JACOB, SEEK ME IN VAIN: I THE LORD SPEAK RIGHTEOUSNESS, I DECLARE THINGS THAT ARE RIGHT. ISAIAH 45: 18B-19

READING FOR TODAY– EXODUS 19: 10-15, ISAIAH 45: 18-25 AND ISAIAH 55: 8-9

Modern man is constantly running about seeking truth from various belief systems. God clearly says back in Isaiah: I AM THE LORD AND THERE IS NO OTHER. What foolishness to seek for ages what has been as plain as the nose on your face! The Old Testament is easy, because God is accepted, but the New Testament, Jesus, now that is a problem? Man seems to accept the Old Testament because it appears to be more of a historical record, but he questions the New Testament.

It is said that even the devil knows God exists. His existence isn't the question of real importance. The question is will I surrender MY will to Him. God wanted the Israelites to know He was real. Moses needed the people to know who God was, that He was real. In Isaiah 45 God says who He is and gives all His accomplishments. Mount Sinai is the perfect place to impress the Israelites of His presence in their lives, however, a burning bush would not even be convincing enough at this time! He knows them so well, just like he knows us today.

In His divine plan He wants their full attention so He tells Moses to have them clean themselves up for three days so they'll be ready to be in His presence. If we had three days to clean-up for the Lord, what would we clean-up? We might start with our outward appearance, but eventually wouldn't we begin to look at our hearts, our minds and even our souls. We'd be examining everything wouldn't we? God knew this. He wanted the hearts of these people prepared. It was to settle once and for all that He existed.

Jesus existed. He is a historical figure and as academic and scientific searches progress, much has been discovered to prove this fact. But, man is still skeptical about His link to God. It seems all so simple to us as believers, but not every man will choose to believe. We owe it to others to give an accounting of what we believe. The Bible is a strong position to stand on. I don't have to say merely: "I believe"; I can say: "the Bible says." If man can be convinced to read the Word of God his life will change.

We don't have the great shows of the Old Testament, but we do have the records of them. When we read them we discover how hard God has worked through the ages to get our attention and keep us focused on Him. He loves us above all the things He has created and He wants us as His own. Ultimately we must choose Him and accept His Son, Jesus. Then we must seek Him daily and stay in His presence by serving Him. He puts boundaries of protection on us, just as He did the Israelites, but one day we'll come into His presence and see Him and the boundaries will no longer be necessary.

I need to be like the Israelites. I need to understand that He is omnipresent and I can listen for His voice and seek Him whenever I need Him. He still loves as He loved in the Old Testament, but in the New Testament He has even broadened His love because He has made a perfect, once and for all sacrifice in His Son for our sins and He has given us the indwelling spirit of the Holy Spirit. Because we have accepted His Son's sacrifice for us on the cross we are forgiven and now acceptable in His sight; we have been made holy. Nothing has changed since the beginning of time; He is the Lord of all and He is Lord even of the unbeliever. The difference between the unbeliever and us is how each of us will spend eternity!

A BEGINNING PLACE FOR PRAYER TODAY:

You are an awesome God. I need to remember Your power, Your strength and Your magnificence in my life and the world about me. All of this You have set in motion and at any time You can return. Lord, I want to be ready. Help me to look up, to look past the cares of my small world and to share You with anyone who'll listen—be they a child or an adult. Everyone needs You, Father; everyone will be lost without You. Help me Father. Keep me in awe of You everyday and let me be a blessing to You Father. Thank You Lord for who You are in my life.

DISCUSSION QUESTIONS FOR TODAY:

1. Can man really understand everything there is to know about God? Is He only an intellectual pursuit or is He real? Why does man's understanding run into problems when it seeks to know and understand everything about the ways of God?

2. How can I really know God?

DAY 67

ALL THE WAYS OF THE LORD ARE LOVING AND FAITHFUL FOR THOSE WHO KEEP THE DEMANDS OF HIS COVENANT. PSALM 25: 10

READING FOR TODAY– EXODUS 19:16-25, PSALM 25: 1-10 AND JOHN 16: 7, 8, 13, 14

God for the most part does not do things in secret. He is who He is for all the world to see. But, blindness and deafness are the mark of a non-believer. They cannot see nor hear, because they choose not to know God. Paul argued before Festus and King Agrippa in Acts 26 that God always had the plan of Christ Jesus as Messiah and that the plan of salvation for Jew and Gentile was NOT DONE IN A CORNER. It was perpetuated and displayed in scripture and then acted out as historical fact right before the eyes of the Jews and the Gentiles alike.

God wants the Israelites to see His presence in their lives. The sound of the trumpet, the smoke and the fire upon Mount Sinai could not be mistaken. Moses was the mouthpiece of God, but they needed a complete reverence of God, not a reverence for Moses. God wanted the Israelites to trust Moses because they believed he was the ambassador of God.

Moses is completely dedicated to God. He naively thinks the Israelites also are as devoted as he is, but God knows the heart of man. He warns Moses that he must tell them to stay back from the foot of the mountain in verse 12 of Exodus 19, then He repeats it in verses 23 and 24. Man can easily take on too much, be caught up in the show and spectacle of the spiritual and be destroyed by his own enthusiasm.

Obedience produces integrity and uprightness. Left to our own devices we can bring shame to ourselves. God is an awesome God who requires complete obedience. He does nothing in half-measures. He always keeps us in boundaries that are for our own safety, but His words need complete obedience. When He starts a work in us it is never left half-accomplished—we can bear witness to its' progress, but God will complete the work in His timing and in His design. That's hard for us sometimes. Patience is not our favorite thing and the possibility of emotional or physical pain is even less appealing. But…God knows what each of us requires and He sets the safety limits for our growth.

An obedient heart is a prepared heart for whatever God will put before it. God is never taken by surprise, He knows us. We cannot fail Him. He expects it, but He then requires repentance. Repentance can become a watered down word if we are not careful.

It is not just the words, "I'm sorry Lord." It is the action that responds to that repentance that the Lord surveys. It is turning completely away from our sin and being washed up and set on a new path which God approves of and it is not necessarily a path which always pleases the believer. God does not want us caught up in the religious spectacle of the moment, He wants us steadily growing within His limitations

A beginning place for prayer today:

Lord, help me to be obedient. Your Holy Spirit constantly reminds me of what I should do. Let me be obedient to Your Spirit within me. Help me to do Your will. Keep me from the religious spectacle of the moment. Focus me; center me, on You so my heart does not become foolish or anxious. Never let me take Your safety for granted. Hold me within Your perfect limitations. Thank You, Father.

Discussion Questions for today:

1. Why are there safety limits set for our growth and can I think of some that God has put on me while He has worked situations out in my life?

2. How do I know for sure that I am sorry about something in my life and that I am going to make a change in my life?

DAY 68

*For the Lord is King and rules the nations. Both proud and humble
together, all who are mortal—born to die—shall worship him. Psalm 22: 28-29*

Reading for today– Exodus 20: 1-3, Psalm 15 and Psalm 16

I AM THE LORD YOUR GOD WHO BROUGHT YOU OUT OF EGYPT, OUT OF THE LAND OF SLAVERY. YOU SHALL HAVE NO OTHER GODS BEFORE ME. (Exodus 20:2-3) If for no other reason God is worthy of being worshipped because He brought us all out of our own Egypt when He saved us! He has taken us out of the world and separated us unto Himself to save us and to keep us for Himself. (Colossians 1:13, 21-23) How do we repay Him? Do we worship other gods?

Sometimes we choose to worship our own intellect. God's laws are okay if they don't get in our way. We determine what's best for us. We make choices and we stand firm on our choices because we really like being the masters of our fate—until of course, things start going wrong! Then, we turn back and we question God: "Where are You?" He is always present, but we have chosen to overlook His importance in being involved in our decisions. FOR A MAN'S WAYS ARE IN FULL VIEW OF THE LORD, HE EXAMINES ALL HIS PATHS. THE EVIL DEEDS OF A WICKED MAN ENSNARE HIM; THE CORDS OF SIN HOLD HIM FAST. HE WILL DIE FOR LACK OF DISCIPLINE, LED ASTRAY BY HIS OWN GREAT FOLLY. (Proverbs 5: 21-23) It is wise to remember that the Bible says that the heart of man is deceitfully wicked and that a disobedient heart can keep us from giving God His rightful place in our hearts.

Being a Christian is dying to self. It would be wonderful if once we accepted Christ as our Savior this problem of self went away. Actually, it becomes the biggest battle ground for believers when we are truly sold out to the Lord. When we were unbelievers we never noticed our selfish natures much, but now we notice that it crops up daily. We are often appalled at our sinful nature and the frequency with which it can appear. It is a constant battle to have the mind of Christ and let the mind of the world be put aside to have no power over us.

If we are successful at keeping the idol of self under control, then we have to allow God to help us deal with the idols of the world. We can get caught up with the pursuit of money, the pride of our accomplishments; we can even be ungrateful to God and seek our own pleasures. The world can become powerful and controlling in our priorities. The world values that our own needs take priority over everything, so we value these things and they rob us of our fellowship with God. Sometimes people can even attend church more for appearance and position in the community than for the love of God. We can easily be trapped into letting the opinion of the world be our focus.

Loving God is the full-time pursuit of being a successful Christian. He is to be the beginning and the ending of all things. He is to have dominion over us, not us over Him. In Him is strength and power for our daily struggles, but even beyond what He can give to us is the fact that He created us, we are His. Whether we acknowledge it or not

He owns us and can do with us as He pleases and this is true of non-believers too! He can even mock the unbeliever and laugh at him, calling him a fool. (Psalm 14:1)

Do I want to be a fool in God's eyes? If I have set other idols before God I had better question the value of them. What good is it if a man gains the whole world and loses His soul? (Matthew 16:26) Life is so temporary and so short that it passes before we know it. God is a jealous God. He wants both feet firmly planted on His side of the fence. It would be terrible to hear Him say: "Go away, I never knew you!" because you spent your life in church on Sundays, but you served other gods your entire life.

A BEGINNING PLACE FOR PRAYER TODAY:

Dear Father, be gracious to me and forgive my foolishness. It is far too easy to put other people, things and situations on Your throne. You alone sustain and keep me if I am faithful to heed Your Word and to do Your will in my life. Help me to pass everything before Your throne before I prioritize it. I desire to dwell within Your boundaries and in your pleasant places. Keep me strong in You Lord. Thank You Father.

DISCUSSION QUESTIONS FOR TODAY:

1. What am I allowing in my life that might become a god if I am not careful?

2. What is the priority of my life today?

DAY 69

OH, THAT THEIR HEARTS WOULD BE INCLINED TO FEAR ME AND KEEP ALL MY COMMANDMENTS ALWAYS, SO THAT IT MIGHT GO WELL WITH THEM AND THEIR CHILDREN FOREVER. DEUTERONOMY 5: 29

READING FOR TODAY– EXODUS 20: 4-6, LUKE 6: 47-49 AND DEUTERONOMY 8: 11-14

YOU SHALL NOT MAKE FOR YOURSELF AN IDOL IN THE FORM OF ANYTHING IN HEAVEN ABOVE OR ON THE EARTH BENEATH OR IN THE WATERS BELOW. Idols can be anything and sometimes they start out as good intentions for service in the kingdom of God. But, when the service begins to take on a life of its' own it becomes an idol.

Husbands can become idols. Everything can be done for the love of a husband, but do I love him more than God? What happens when the idol no longer loves the worshipper or the idol passes away? Sometimes everything is done for the children. Is God pleased with the way we're bringing them up?

Who do those children really belong to and how much of our ego is tied up in the job of "making a child perfect" by "being the perfect parent?" What do I do when the child fails me or leaves me? How about my job? Once it was a means to provide for my family, now it is "who I am", it can become my complete ego! Sacrifices are made for the boss which just happen to put everyone and everything else in my life on hold while I worship my job.

Possessions can become idols: our home, our car, our boat, our jewelry, our bank accounts or our stocks and bonds. More attention is paid to them than the Word of God. We no longer read our Bible, we clean our house, wash our car or boat, polish our jewelry or spend hours figuring ways to buy, sell and save our wealth. (Deuteronomy 8:11-14) The earthly becomes our focus; the heavenly is a place we go to only when the earthly things are falling apart.

Is it no wonder that God sometimes has to take things away from us, just to get our attention? It isn't that He doesn't want us to succeed; He wants us to have a right perspective. "Love Me", He says, "and all these things will be taken care of when you have given Me control over them." Matthew 6: 34 says not to take care for tomorrow and Matthew 6: 19 tells us not to store up things because our heart will be so full of them that we run the risk of not having a place for God in our hearts.

Worshipping idols does not produce peace or joy. If this day finds us lacking in peace and joy, then something is wrong. Close examination will probably show there are idols in our lives. The lack of peace and joy can simply be caused by the problem that our priorities in life have slipped over to the priorities of the world. Is God trying to pull something from us that we are stubbornly holding onto with a death grip? Should I let go of my husband, my children, my job, my possessions, my accomplishments and be free to hear God speak to me again? The answer is too obvious to give, isn't it?

A BEGINNING PLACE FOR PRAYER TODAY:

If any idols have come into my life, I give you permission Father to take them away. Create in me a heart which longs to worship only You. Keep me mindful that You provide and You can take away whenever You choose for my own benefit. Let me easily let go of all the things that are offensive to You Father. Let this day honor You in my word and deed. Thank You Father.

DISCUSSION QUESTIONS FOR TODAY:

1. Has something become an idol in my life? What are my excuses for letting it have priority over serving God?

2. Is it easy for an idol to establish itself in our lives and even take over before we even know it is an idol?

DAY 70

You shall not take the name of the Lord your God in vain, for the Lord will not hold him guiltless who takes His name in vain. Exodus 20: 7

Reading for today– Exodus 20: 7, I John 2:4 and I John 3:7, 10, 16-18

Do I attach the Lord's name to things I shouldn't? Is swearing the only way to take the Lord's name in vain? Can harmful personal interpretations of scripture be my way of taking God's name in vain? We can take God's scripture out of context and use it to beat up other Christians. This is one of the worst offenses of taking His name in vain and an offense that many of us prefer to overlook.

God is first love, then truth and at all times the ultimate authority in our lives. All He does for us or allows us to go through is a form of His love for us. God does not and cannot lie to us; whatever He says is true. His truth always proves out. We have no way around it, the consequences of disobedience makes this very clear. But we have no right in the name of God to be cruel to anyone with our words. Quite the opposite is true –we are required to love in truth and expect God to produce the truth of who He is in the consequences of our obedience or even in our disobedience.

Truth should be heartfelt, but not harmful. No one likes the truth at all times, but for a season it is painful and then it rewards us. If we attach God's name to anything it should be for a righteous purpose. When God confronts us with our sin He is gentle and patient with us as we repent and turn from the sin. How do we extend gentleness and patience to our family and friends when they experience sin in their lives?

Our work as fellow Christians is not to save souls, that is God's job. Our mission begins where God has united us in the fellowship of Christianity as we minister to one another in that fellowship. That means I do not take His name and beat up other Christians; instead we are to use His name to help others and ourselves become totally devoted to Him. We should pray always that we set a good example of God's love for our brothers and sisters in Christ so that God's family can prosper righteously, just as He works in us personally to make us more righteous in His sight.

Life on earth is full of personal tribulation and I personally think that we as Christians should not add to it. God disciplines, He restores and He blesses, these are not our powers nor can we use His name as a hammer to get others made righteous by constant pounding. People run away from churches when the leaders and the members take on the powers of God rather than the mantel of discipleship and private prayer for one another's needs.

Instead of building up the body of Christ we can actually tear it down as we attach levels of sin to sin and claim one sin greater or lesser than another and do it with His precious name attached to it. All have sinned and come short of the glory of God and no sin according to scripture is greater or less than another. Have we used His name in vain to pursue our own understanding of righteousness on someone else? God forbid!

A BEGINNING PLACE FOR PRAYER TODAY:

Lord let me use Your name wisely. Help me to be a disciple who seeks to come alongside others when they need You. Give me wisdom and help me to judge wisely before I speak and act on Your behalf. When I do not have answers for people let me learn to pray with them and for them so that You can provide the answers they need. Help me to not run from my responsibilities of being a disciple of Yours, but also help me to be just a disciple and not a Pharisee. Let me be caught up in Your love and not claim for myself Your power to discipline, forgive or restore others.

DISCUSSION QUESTIONS FOR TODAY:

1. Have I ever seen a church torn down by its own self-righteousness?

2. Do I need to seek forgiveness in this area? (It might be a husband, child, relative or friend of mine that I have harmed.)

DAY 71

REMEMBER THE SABBATH DAY BY KEEPING IT HOLY. EXODUS 20:8

READING FOR TODAY– EXODUS 20: 8-11, JAMES 4:13-15 AND PSALM 32

If I do not have a day of rest from my labors, the focus being on "my labors", I run the risk of losing God's plan for my life. To set aside one day a week for the restoration of the soul and the mind produces great fruit. To use every day to accomplish something diminishes my energy and stops the flow of fellowship with Him.

It is vitally important to take one day and just focus on the blessings of the week. We need to thank Him for what He has accomplished and to listen a little harder for His voice so we can get some perspective on what we should or should not do in the coming week. Our peace of mind depends completely on our relationship with the Lord. How can we enjoy the fruits of our labor if we don't stop and quiet our hearts before Him so we can focus on the events of the weeks' labor?

I, like you, know from experience the value of doing things God's way. We have all experienced the ease and also the power of His strength in the good and hard times of our lives. It is wisdom to know that there are no bad times in life there are only hard times. The hard times produce more character in us and therefore we should not despise the hard times but examine them closely for their hidden blessings. I can take comfort and confidence in Him as He comes alongside of me to guide me through the inevitability of those hard times. I lose the blessing of His focus on my life when I choose to be in charge of the hard times.

I can plan my life, but the question remains: Is He in the plan with me? Only a day of rest, a slower pace and some reflection can cause me to turn my eyes from myself and put the focus on Him and His desires for my life. His plans are always perfect—my plans are just plans! If being successful as His disciple is my goal I'd better rest up and reflect on the past week before I rush into the next. My peace of mind depends on it!

If He doesn't get the Sabbath for His glory, then I can expect the week that follows to be in my vain glory! Within a short time I will discover that His plans are on the back burner and I am on my way to burn out. No matter how righteous my motive, if my motives are not His and I have not checked in for the day, then all my labor becomes a burden. My labors will surely burn like wood, hay and stubble and I will more than likely dissipate with them, because I do not have His blessings.

I want what I do to count for something! How about you? I want my labors to be valuable in His economy. What riches am I storing up in heaven? Will all the things I value matter to God when I stand before Him on judgment day? I don't know unless I cease from "my labors" and seek His face for HIS labors. Will it all be vanity as Solomon says in Ecclesiastes? Will I one day be blessed with a store house of heavenly treasure? God's wisdom says "Remember the Sabbath day and keep it holy." That which is Holy belongs to God. When I set aside the Sabbath to be Holy I am separating myself from the things of this world and releasing the chains that hold my mind to have that mind be finally exercised by Him and set apart for His service. I am thanking Him for last week and giving Him the control of the next week. I need to heed His words: SIX DAYS YOU SHALL LABOR, BUT THE SEVENTH DAY IS A SABBATH TO THE LORD YOUR GOD.

A BEGINNING PLACE FOR PRAYER TODAY:

Today may not be the Sabbath, but until I get there I'd better check in with You for this day Father. Do not let my plans get ahead of Your plans. I need your vision for this day. Help me to set aside Your Sabbath. Let me plan to rejoice in your blessings this coming Sunday. Help me to be absolute in my resolve to plan to thank You for the week, hear Your voice, receive Your new vision and be refreshed by You. Thank You Father that You love me so much that You want my life to be a personal relationship of intimate fellowship with You and Your Word. Oversee this day until my Sabbath day comes. Thank You Father.

DISCUSSION QUESTIONS FOR TODAY:

1. What have I learned about the Sabbath today and what do I need to re-evaluate?

2. What have I learned about planning my weeks?

DAY 72

Honor your father and mother, so that you may live long in the land the Lord your God is giving you. Exodus 20: 12

Reading for today– Exodus 20: 12, Psalm 5 and Proverbs 3: 1-7

It is easy to honor those who are honorable, but not all parents are honorable. Perhaps the real essence of honoring is giving honor in the power of the Spirit of God. Because God says I must; I will honor even those I know I don't feel that obligation to and in time, God will make me honorable in His sight. The best way I can honor the Lord is to be the parent that would honor God. If I come from less than perfect parenting I need to study His word diligently to learn what it is to be a parent of honor. Also as I practice kindness and concern for my parents, my children will see it. Perhaps my life will mark the beginning of honor in my family tree.

It is easy to honor parents who have truly loved you. You can think back on the things they did for you and suffered for you. Life is truly a circle, where you started is where you will end up. My parents began taking care of me and now at the end of their lives I find myself trying to help them take care of themselves. As I raised my children it became clearer to me what my parents had sacrificed for me because now I was doing it for my children. And, now that my parents are older I see more clearly the responsibility of being a parent never leaves us. No matter what age I may become, my parents will still be my parents. Their concern is still for my best and because of it I love and honor them.

The only parent who is perfect is God, the Father. The rest of us are just trying to not to be too human! It is a constant war of His Spirit over our spirit of pride to keep us on the right track of becoming the parents we need to be. Our children are simply a gift from God which He shares with us for a season. Most of the time our children have long lives with us, but others are given to us for only a short time. It is important to remember that our children will return to Him, as will we, in His timing. No matter how long our lives have been they will always seem short when it comes to the end of our days.

If I am building a legacy of honor for my children, then I must honor my children. They are unique and gifted by God for specific purposes and it is my job to direct their path in God's way. I cannot determine their success or failure in endeavors of my choosing. They were not put on this earth for my prideful and selfish pleasure; they were put on the earth for God's pleasure and purposes. I need to know God's perspective of them. My job is to love unconditionally, but I must look at them carefully to see their needs for growth and then set boundaries that will give them safety in the Lord's care. Discipline has become almost a dirty word in our society—but discipline by definition is not corporal punishment, it is training. If we train up a child in the ways of the Lord we instill honor and respect for God's ways and for ourselves as parents.

The ultimate parent is God and when we disobey His commands we are not honoring Him and we can expect punishment. No school, institution or book can train up a child. Creating honor for God and us as parents lies in our constant and devoted prayers to God about our children. Prayer is the cornerstone for wisdom in all relationships.

Secondly, we must become worthy of our children's honor—because we honor them our discipline must be understood by them to be our way of keeping them safe from spiritual, physical and emotional harm. Our disciplinary actions should have nothing to do with personal pride or ego. Discipline for any age child requires consistency. Children are apt to be less anxious or fearful when they know that we will be like our heavenly Father in that we will never leave them or forsake them and forgiveness is always available to them no matter what the offense. Great families don't just happen, they are the product of a parent or parents who pray without ceasing and provide unconditional love and boundaries of discipline.

Children are free will beings, but if we continuously speak in our homes of our awesome, powerful and loving God, our child will have the opportunity to see and experience how He works in our lives. Our goal is that they will come to know that God loves, honors and values everyone. We want them to understand that they are loved by God as much as we are loved by God. It is our prayer that our children will come to honor Him and respect His commandments not only out of fear, but because they have developed a true sense of just how wise and loving God's intentions are for their lives. The family unit is the perfect training ground to practice honoring and loving our God.

A BEGINNING PLACE FOR PRAYER TODAY:

Father, thank You for my parents. Help me to honor them as I go about my life today. Teach me to be unconditional in my ability to love all the people in my life so I can be an honor to You. Our seasons of life are all too short so let me love my family in word and deed for as long as You allow me to have them. Thank You for all the blessings within my family and give me wisdom to honor all the members of Your family Lord.

DISCUSSION QUESTIONS FOR TODAY:

1. Were my parents the kind I could honor? Why or Why not? What is my responsibility to them now?

2. Are my children learning to honor their parents? How and if not, why not?

DAY 73

And the words of the Lord are flawless, like a silver refined in a furnace of clay, purified seven times. Psalm 12:6

Reading for today– Exodus 20: 13, Psalm 119: 129-135

YOU SHALL NOT MURDER. (Exodus 20:13) I can easily accomplish this commandment we say to ourselves. I have never murdered anyone nor can I ever see myself planning the murder of someone. Well, by God's standards, I have murdered and I have even planned upon occasion the murder of someone. Jealousy and anger are murderous tools. And too often our words become the tool of the murderer when we lash out at someone else. Our purpose is to set them straight, but our result can be the murder of their spirit or their reputation.

Murder means to mortally wound to death. Words can give life but sometimes they kill. The spirit of a man can be nurtured by us. We get the opportunity to nurture everyday in our family units, at work, at play and in the general market place. But the words we speak more often can be destructive if we lack the responsibility God requires of us. We need to pray and think before we speak. Psalm 119:130 says: THE UNFOLDING OF YOUR WORDS GIVES LIGHT. When I operate in anger, frustration or selfish motive it unfolds to death, it dumps on the recipient murderous weight. Words can blind and eventually meme and kill if they are not given in love with the purpose to prosper.

Our mates can often receive murderous words and they are only the first for usually in that same vain we blast our children, our co-workers and anyone else who gets in our way if we do not choose to be silent and weigh our words before God before we speak. Proverbs 10: 19 says: WHEN WORDS ARE MANY, SIN IS NOT ABSENT, BUT HE WHO HOLDS HIS TONGUE IS WISE. AN ANXIOUS HEART WEIGHS A MAN DOWN, BUT A KIND WORD CHEERS HIM UP. (Proverbs 12: 25) How do we use our words—do they give life or death to the hearer?

Children especially need God's wisdom in order to inherit life. Pride can be a murderous tool when words are levied for pride's sake rather than for instruction in God's ways. The tone has everything to do with the words. Words delivered in a kind tone are much more easily received than those delivered in anger. Words in anger kill the spirit but wise words build up the spirit. A WORD APTLY SPOKEN IS LIKE APPLES OF GOLD IN SETTINGS OF SILVER. LIKE EARRINGS OF GOLD OR AN ORNAMENT OF FINE GOLD IS A WISE MAN'S REBUKE TO A LISTENINING EAR. (Proverbs 25: 11-12)

Gossip is another form of murder. It is the murder of someone's reputation or the distortion of his motives. We have to be careful what we say and to whom we say it. When I speak about someone am I building up or tearing down their reputation: What is my purpose in sharing information about someone? Do I look more righteous when I stand on the unrighteousness of someone else? We must look wisely at our words, remembering always that they can do permanent damage and even murder the spirit of a loved one or a fellow human being. I need my words purified before I speak; only prayer before I speak accomplishes purification and clarification.

A BEGINNING PLACE FOR PRAYER:

Oh, Father, guard my tongue. Let me pray before I speak. Give me wisdom to spend hours with You before I approach anyone or any situation with my words. I desire Your wisdom so I will not commit murder. Help me Father to see my anger or pride as You see it. Help me to prosper my brother and to love him as I love myself. Thank You that I can come to You and seek Your face when I need peace and a clear mind on a subject. Thank You Father that You alone can make my words of value or completely dismiss them from my mind.

DISCUSSION QUESTIONS FOR TODAY:

1. Who do I need to seek forgiveness from for words I have spoken in haste?

2. What situations cannot change with words, but require prayer and then maybe actions? Are there things only God can handle?

DAY 74

THIS DAY I CALL HEAVEN AND EARTH AS WITNESSES AGAINST YOU THAT I HAVE SET BEFORE YOU LIFE AND DEATH, BLESSINGS AND CURSES. NOW CHOOSE LIFE, SO THAT YOU AND YOUR CHILDREN MAY LIVE…DEUTERONOMY 30: 19

READING FOR TODAY– EXODUS 20:14, DEUTERONOMY 30: 15-19 AND ROMANS 3:9, 19-20 AND 23-24

THOU SHALT NOT COMMIT ADULTRY. (Exodus 20:14) The Ten Commandments are more than just laws they are the boundaries set for us by God so that we might have an abundant life in fellowship with Him. When we choose to live within His boundaries we choose life. When we choose to live outside His boundaries we choose death.

The death of disobedience is to our spirit not to our body – for the body will go on and for the most part, little change may even be noticed in the physical body of man, it may even progress to old age and then die. But, when we choose to live without His boundaries we choose to terminate the abundant life and accept the mundane and the ordinary. Without the boundaries there is limited exposure to the fruits of the spirit: love, joy, peace, patience, kindness, goodness, faithfulness, gentleness and self-control--and without these elements life is truly bleak. (Galatians 6:22)

Raining on my parade is not what God has in mind with these commandments. Instead God wants us to have a parade, but there are choices to be made. Obedience gives blessings; disobedience gives curses upon our lives. SEE, I SET BEFORE YOU TODAY LIFE AND PROSPERITY, DEATH AND DESTRUCTION. FOR I COMMAND YOU TODAY TO LOVE THE LORD YOUR GOD—loving God is obedience to God. IF YOU ARE DRAWN AWAY TO BOW DOWN TO OTHER GODS…YOU WILL SURELY BE DESTROYED. (Deuteronomy 30-15-18). Sin is always the worship of the other gods.

Adultery is a very clear picture of the effect of sin when disobedience is chosen. We see graphically the fruits of the spirit being wiped out by this one sinful act and as its' destruction is played out we see what ALL SIN in general does to us:

1. We destroy a love relationship with a mate and our God

2. Eventually sadness overwhelms everyone involved

3. We lack peace and live in fear of being found out

4. We have exercised our will over God's will for our lives, regrettably we've tried to find the exciting in the forbidden

5. Our hearts are no longer kind, they are hard, greedy and self-centered, fulfilling our lusts

6. Goodness has slipped away and what was once a pure experience is now ugly and cheap

7. We are no longer trustworthy to our mates and even our children and friends lack confidence in us

8. We have harshly pushed our way into an experience which has no other purpose than self-gratification and our gentleness of spirit is lost

9. Our freedom is lost and we are now in the enemies' hands—he rules us, he has his way with us and we serve the master of sin

10. And without the love of Christ and His forgiveness demonstrated on the cross we would stay in this condition for all eternity

No sin is more or less in the sight of God. Sin is sin. Adultery is a good example because the result of it or any sin is always the same, it destroys the fruit of the Spirit in our lives and terminates the abundant life of freedom we have in Christ Jesus. All sin is an infection of our lives and never affects only us—it is like the proverbial rock in the pond.

The ripples of sin move out and eventually touch everyone in our lives. God warns us not to move out of His boundaries because He loves us too much to see us sin. He does not want us to reap the sadness of sin and we have the choice to sin or not sin. Will we choose life or death? Only a fool chooses death and yet all about us today we see man choosing death!

BEGINNING PLACE FOR PRAYER TODAY:

God, let me look squarely at the sin in my life as I pray for Your will in my life today. Cleanse my heart, oh God, and create in me a spirit of obedience. Make me not an adulterer to You. Keep my heart pure. I desire You to be my first love. I desire to choose life and blessings. Let me not disappoint You Father. Guard my thoughts, my words and my deeds—direct and light my path moment by moment today. Thank You Father.

DISCUSSION QUESTIONS FOR TODAY:

1. What have I learned or been reminded of about the consequences of sin today?

2. Can we take any sin in our lives and justify it when we know the consequences of sin?

DAY 75

*HUMILITY AND THE FEAR OF THE LORD BRING WEALTH AND HONOR AND LIFE.
PROVERBS 22:4*

READING FOR TODAY– EXODUS 20: 15, PSALM 24: 4-5 AND PSALM 25

THOU SHALT NOT STEAL. (Exodus 20: 15) Stealing something is taking something or accepting credit for something that is not yours. We all would like to have wealth and honor and life, but we are all given different talents to accomplish such things. Abundant life comes with wealth that is not measured in money or in possessions. Honor comes to the powerful and the poor alike when God is the determiner of what is honorable.

When we lack the fear of God we can steal without conscience. On the first inspection of my heart stealing seems to be a character trait I don't personally exhibit, but on the second inspection I just might be giving it a limited look. Supposing I do not give my boss a day's fair labor for his wages, I steal from him. If my nature were to keep heaping up credit card debt—I would be stealing, because I have no way of ever paying my debts; I just want to fill my life with adventures and things. If I don't pay my fair share of taxes I steal from my government and therefore from my fellow citizens. If I don't tithe to the church I steal from God and set up store houses for myself. If I am a Christian I should seek to have a good name before God and man. A thief of anything does not possess an honorable name. God should be able to trust me with all my responsibilities and any kind of stealing should be out of the question for me.

When I cut corners I am stealing from God the full measure and rightful approach to becoming the honorable person He desires me to be. Cutting corners and getting away with things does not honor or please God. I Timothy 6:9 says," PEOPLE WHO WANT TO GET RICH FALL INTO TEMPTATION AND A TRAP AND INTO MANY FOOLISH AND HARMFUL DESIRES THAT PLUNGE MAN INTO RUIN AND DESTRUCTION." Stealing can be just one of the traps which wanting to be rich can produce. It can take us into the trap of measuring whether it's "really harmful" or "just a little harmful" to someone else. The Bible also says in Proverbs 18:9: THE LORD DETESTS DIFFERING WEIGHTS, AND DISHONEST SCALES DO NOT PLEASE HIM. To me it means that every man, rich or poor, is worthy of my honesty in God's economy

HE WHO WORKS HIS LAND WILL HAVE ABUNDANT FOOD, BUT HE WHO CHOSES FANTASIES LACKS JUDGMENT (Proverbs 12:11). A fool spends his time dreaming of ways to beat the system, only honest work produces something that will honor God and allow Him to honor us. When we day dream or waste time we're lost in a trap that is destroying our productive hours. For example, we only have so many hours to set good examples and train up our children. When we wish we weren't stuck in the boring things of this life we grow deeper into them; instead of just doing the work and getting through the boring we are stuck in it! I am thoroughly convinced that getting through the mundane and unexciting produces a reward. WHATEVER YOU DO, DO IT WITH ALL YOUR HEART, AS WORKING FOR THE LORD, SINCE YOU KNOW YOU WILL RECEIVE AN INHERITANCE FROM THE LORD AS A REWARD (Colossians 4:23 and 24).

The definition of stealing has two parts. Did you notice? Of all the stealing I do the most sorrowful one for me personally is not always giving God credit for what He has given me or done for me. Do I give God credit when I speak about "my" accomplishments? Sometimes we just get caught up in life and we take everything for granted and worse yet, as a result we don't daily share what God is doing or has done. It appears to the world that "we" have accomplished much! Do my children think I have accomplished my life single handedly because I never give God credit? Subtle, well yes, but stealing is stealing. How hurtful and nonproductive this is to the discipling of others. How sad God must be because I don't take the time to share His blessings with others. Do I steal? Well, yes, if I don't give to God the credit He is due, I steal from Him!

A BEGINNING PLACE FOR PRAYER TODAY:

Lord, help me to use my time wisely. I do not wish to lose my reward from You because I steal valuable time for foolish things. Help me not to store up treasures here on earth. Let me use what you have given me wisely and let me share my blessings with others. Help me to hold open my palm and let go of the things you have so generously and freely given to me. Do not let me rob others by not letting me share Your blessings. Forgive me when I try to weigh my sin and try to make excuses for stealing from You. Help me Father to fear You more than man.

DISCUSSION QUESTIONS FOR TODAY:

1. Have I been guilty of stealing? What is my definition of stealing? Has my limited understanding of stealing been a stumbling block for me?

2. What is an abundant life in God's perspective?

DAY 76

A MAN OF KNOWLEDGE USES WORDS WITH RESTRAINT, AND A MAN OF UNDERSTANDING IS EVEN TEMPERED. PROVERBS 17:27

READING FOR TODAY– EXODUS 20:16, JAMES 3:13-18, PSALM 26:2-3

"You shall not give false testimony against your neighbor."(Exodus 20:16) This is another straight forward command of God and yet each day it is ignored or not even considered before we begin conversations. Frequently we speak before we think about what we're saying. We couch gossip in phrases like "We need to pray for So and So because did you know…?" Sometimes we are acting on raw emotion instead of sound judgment when we speak before an audience of one or two or even more. If we don't have all the facts we may not be impartial and we are certainly not speaking complete truth without those facts.

Scripture is very clear: "A man of knowledge uses words with restraint, and a man of understanding is even tempered." This scripture must then be underlined with the scripture from James 3:17 that says: "The wisdom that comes from heaven is first of all pure; then peace-loving, considerate, submissive, full of mercy and good fruit, impartial and sincere." James 3: 17 is an important scripture because it outlines the guidelines for purposes of speaking wisdom. Before we speak, we must be sure that our motives are pure. The qualities of wisdom are our measuring stick, if it lacks any of these traits then we need to question our motives, cease our conversation or not begin the conversation at all.

"But if you harbor bitter envy and selfish ambition in your hearts do not boast about it or deny the truth."(James 3:14) Sincere concern is never the motive when we are jealous or are trying to build ourselves up. Honest and sincere concern can be best served if we pray for someone in our own prayer closet alone. We don't need to look for validation of our point of view with anyone other than God.

If our testimony causes strife and disorder and leads to others performing "evil practices" such as slander, condemnation and down right destruction of someone else's words, deeds or motives then we know for certain that it is not Godly wisdom. "Speak and act as those who are going to be judged by the law that gives freedom, because judgment without mercy will be shown to anyone who has not been merciful."(James 2:12-13) According to this scripture it would seem wise to be silent rather than to be unmerciful to someone and run the risk of having that act of behaving unmercifully be put to our account.

Before we worry about someone else's reputation we would be wise to worry about our own reputation before God and most earnestly desire to be wise in His sight. "Who is wise and understanding among you? Let him show it by his good life, by deeds done in humility that come from wisdom" (James 3:13) and that wisdom comes from above. (James 3:17) "The words of a gossip are like choice morsels; they go down to a man's inmost parts." (Proverbs 18:18) God forbid that we would slander or share the faults of others and leave the person who hears these words with a permanent picture of someone else's sin. We are the press agent of every individual that we know. What we say about other people will be remembered about them every time they are seen by others. It is important to be careful that we are considerate of others hearts, that they are not polluted by our thoughtless words.

A BEGINNING PLACE FOR PRAYER TODAY:

Lord, forgive me if I have spoken without thinking in the past. Keep me mindful of my own heart's motives. Let the words of my mouth be helpful, constructive, loving and merciful or keep me still in the presence of others. Help me to be the one you can count on to not listen to nor pass on gossip. Father be with me always and guard my mouth so that I will be a blessing in Your sight.

DISCUSSION QUESTIONS FOR TODAY:

1. Has the Lord brought anyone to mind that I may need to seek forgiveness from? How can I go about this?

2. When we speak what must our words of wisdom accomplish according to scripture? What should we do if we find our thoughts fall short of being wisdom from above?

DAY 77

Sell your possessions and give to the poor. Provide purses for yourselves that will not wear out, a treasure in heaven that will not be exhausted, where no thief comes near and no moth destroys. For where your treasure is, there your heart will be also. Luke 12: 33-34

Reading for today– Exodus 20:17, Luke 12:22-34 and Luke 16:14-15

YOU SHALL NOT COVET. (Exodus 20:17) Webster's dictionary says this means to desire enviously the possessions of someone else or to wish for excessively and longingly" or "crave something that belongs to another." You don't crave something unless you feel like your missing something and to know God is to be content. Paul says, "in whatever circumstances I have learned to be content" because "I can do everything through Him who gives me strength." (Philippians 4: 11-13)

Coveting then must be the opposite of resting confidently in God. The question then that we must ask ourselves daily is: "What are my wants and what are my needs? God always provides my needs, so I wisely should be concerned about my desires. Are they the desires God wants in my heart? Are they selfish or generous in nature? Are they acquisitions to my character or my possessions that will further the gifts of the Holy Spirit in my life or in the lives of those around me?

Whatever I desire I want it to be what God desires for me. My personal prayer has always been: "Lord, please close the door quickly on opportunities or ideas when they are not Yours!" Our sinful nature always manages to rear its ugly head when we least expect it. But if I am thankful for all the Lord's blessings my heart stays closer to my needs and then the realization that all my needs are met by God becomes a predominant theme in my life. My job is to diligently do the work of each day and God will take care of the rest.

It would be nice if every day were fun or easy. But, God has work to do in us. He is transforming us into His image and that transformation requires work. The fruits of the Spirit are not measured in the possessions of outward wealth; they are inward rewards which allow us to serve our Savior and His people. If we are blessed with wealth we have a responsibility to make it grow and then share it so that is available to anyone who needs it.

Keeping a light touch on things and realizing it will all burn as wood, hay and stubble if it is not for Christ's sake keeps my mind a little more focused when it comes to needs and wants. (I Corinthians 3:10-15) Life has taught me, thus far, that the more I have the more I am responsible for and although I want to be a good steward of what God has given me, I don't want it to rule over me. We need to keep the store houses in heaven more stocked up than the ones here on earth!

A BEGINNING PLACE FOR PRAYER TODAY:

Father, the words of Your scripture instruct me not to covet, help me to be content, to know Your peace and set aside foolish longings for things of no value to Your kingdom. Bless me with your presence Lord. Keep me mindful of Your path for my life. Help me to put aside my desires and my plans—give me Your desires and Your plans for my life. I need You in the middle of my life; I don't want You to be the spectator for my foolish choices. Thank You Father that You love me and desire the best for me.

DISCUSSION QUESTIONS FOR TODAY:

1. What is the strongest desire of my heart today? What is the value of that desire in God's economy today for me and ultimately for the people I serve for Christ?

2. Do I have a right perspective on my needs and my wants? Do I know the difference?

DAY 78

THEY STAYED AT A DISTANCE AND SAID TO MOSES, "SPEAK TO US YOURSELF AND WE WILL LISTEN. BUT DO NOT HAVE GOD SPEAK TO US OR WE WILL DIE." EXODUS 20: 19

READING FOR TODAY– EXODUS 20: 18-19, PSALM 139 AND PSALM 39

Why do we choose to stay "at a distance" where God is concerned? All scripture tells us to draw close to Him and yet we often keep Him at a distance. We sometimes think we will die if we hear too much truth. Sunday sermons are as close as some of us choose to get to the truth. We can listen and get second hand revelations through a pastor's study of the Word. Is that what we are to do: get second hand information only?

God needs our ears every day. He cannot speak to us unless we go to Him. Yes, we can be spoken to and convicted in large crowds, but it is even better to speak to Him one on one! That's why Christ died for our sins. We are no longer separated by ours sins from God, we are new creatures in Christ who can go before the throne of God boldly and seek His face.

We can read His Word, expect Him to speak directly to us and expect Him to produce good fruit in our lives. Standing far off is not what God intends for us. He has given His only Son for our sins so that we are made righteous and can enter into His presence whenever we choose.

Fear of the truth is often an excuse for not drawing close to the Lord. We want answers for our lives—sometimes! The answers we shy away from are the hard ones. Part of us will have to die to self occasionally to get what needs done in our lives accomplished and only God holds the answers to the when, where and how of that. Scripture says "Whoever finds his life will lose it, and whoever loses his life for my sake will find it." (Matthew 10:39) We actually need to die to ourselves daily so that we can see what God has for us.

When I read Psalm 139 I realize how completely He knows me. That He holds the keys to a successful life for me. How foolish we are if we will not go and speak directly to Him. I can know what I am to do or what I am to say. I can know how to live my life, but I must take the steps toward Him to be enlightened and to be made peaceful in my decisions. My days are very short in the world, Psalm 39 says so, and I want to know what I should be about to make those days count.

We cannot pray "Search me, O God, and know my heart" from a distance. There can be no way of getting rid of my "offensive ways" if I don't let God show me what they are! And...there will certainly never be a time in my life when I can be led "in the way everlasting" if my God does not speak to me personally, daily. It is imperative that I get up close and personal with God. He would have it no other way because He loves me!

A BEGINNING PLACE FOR PRAYER TODAY:

Help me to stop playing church and keeping You at a distance. Help me to draw close to You. You love me and want to hear my prayers. Everything about me is important in Your sight. Help me to see myself as You see me. Let me be your witness before men that You are alive and speak to us if we will just draw near. Bless me with Your fellowship Lord, I desire Your wisdom and Your perspective on my life. Have Your way with me, make me a useful vessel in Your sight. Thank You Father.

DISCUSSION QUESTIONS FOR TODAY:

1. Am I afraid to seek the truth about any areas in my life? Why would that be?

2. What does "drawing close" mean to me where God is concerned?

DAY 79

GOD HAS COME TO TEST YOU SO THAT THE FEAR OF GOD WILL BE WITH YOU TO KEEP YOU FROM SINNING. EXODUS 20: 20B

READING FOR TODAY– EXODUS 20: 20-21 AND PSALM 27

The fear of God keeps us from sinning. It is a healthy virtue to fear God. Without the fear of God there would be no safety on this earth or in our lives. Fear is a healthy respect for God because we are acquainted with his commandments. We know He has the last word on everything. He holds me in the palm of His hand and in Him is life and death. I am appointed a time in my life to die just as I am appointed a time to experience life. I can choose life or death for my experience here on earth. I can choose to be a friend of God or His enemy.

If I fear God I can keep short accounts with God and know when I have sinned in His sight. It is foolish for me to look for validation from this world. Every day this world changes its value system. Responsibility for self has all but disappeared in our world today. Man today, if he does not fear God, does what he pleases and looks only to himself and his needs. "Me first!" has become the cry of modern man.

To be free from sin I have to face it straight on. I need to step into the light where God is and seek His face so He can shine His light on my needs and direct path.(Psalm 27) He is to be my shelter and my fortress in times of need. No man can take His place. He has things to teach me that will save me from the harm of today and the future things that could harm me if I don't come into His presence today.

I desire "to be set high upon a rock"; to be put in a place of safety. My mind can put me in danger, but God can transform all those fears and put me "high upon a rock: so that danger will come close, but pass by me. When the tests of life come I can hide in His tabernacle and sing His praises because my focus is on Him and not on me or this world. I am to the world inconsequential, but to God I am of great importance. He wants to teach me His ways. He wants me to be confident in Him as a source of strength. If I run to Him, I am not weak; I am wise. In Him there is long life and goodness, my fear of Him is my respect for Him and a wise man seeks the Lord and knows His commandments. "The fear of the Lord is the beginning of knowledge, but fools despise wisdom and discipline." (Proverbs 1:7)

A BEGINNING PLACE FOR PRAYER TODAY:

Dear Father gives me a healthy fear of sin in my life. No matter how dark things look let me step through that darkness into your light. Be with me this day in all the testing you set before me. Let me see clearly those tests and commit them to Your care. I need you present in this day and in this moment. Be with me and let me be a blessing to You Father. Thank You for the fears of this day for through them I will grow close to You as I lay them at Your feet. Thank You, Father.

DISCUSSION QUESTIONS FOR TODAY:

1. Are there areas in my life that I do not fear God in and have become too comfortable in my sin? How does this happen?

2. Can fear overwhelm me? Should fear overwhelm me?

DAY 80

I KNOW THAT THE LORD IS GREAT, THAT OUR LORD IS GREATER THAN ALL GODS. PSALM 135:5

READING FOR TODAY– EXODUS 20:22-26, PSALM 115 AND COLOSSIANS 3: 16-17

I need to know my place in God's economy. When I first understand His place and who He is then I have a better picture of myself. God wants me to know that I am loved and treasured by Him, but...He desires that I love Him first above myself and then that I love others more than I love myself. I come in third!

JOY—Jesus, Others, Yourself—don't ask me who said it, but it's a sure prescription for true joy. The Israelites didn't quite know God yet. They were learning in fearful, orchestrated baby steps. All relationships take time to grow, but God has an order for us finding a right relationship with Him and being caught up in ourselves puts a giant road block to that relationship being what it should or could be.

So God says: "You have seen for yourselves that I have spoken to you from heaven."(Exodus 20:22b) God is in charge of everything. The sooner we get this through our heads the more relief and fellowship we will have with God. He plans, He orchestrates and He purposes all things in our lives when we allow Him into our lives. Conversely, when we orchestrate and we purpose all things, that's when we don't know Him. He allows that, but it's not very productive—it's a walk we take alone becoming totally responsible for the consequences of our choices.

"Do not make any Gods to be alongside of me." (Exodus 20:23) Unfortunately, I am usually the god I put alongside of God. A right relationship with God says that NOTHING, no one or no thing stands beside God. We are the clay, He is the potter. We have not fashioned ourselves nor have we given ourselves our talents or our gifts. God has allowed our growth and given us our talents. We are recipients of good gifts, not the maker of them.

There is a natural reverence and awe that builds in us when we finally get it through our heads: "We are blessed by God" and He gets the glory and honor for EVERYTHING in our lives.

"Make an altar of earth for me and sacrifice on it your burnt offerings and fellowship offerings, your sheep and your goats and your cattle. Wherever I cause my name to be honored, I will come to you and bless you." (Exodus 20: 24) Then He says about the altar "do not build it with dressed stones" and "do not go up to my altar on steps, lest your nakedness be exposed."

Our altar is our lives. How we live is the altar seen by others and we need that life to be the exhibition of everything God has allowed in our lives so He receives the honor. We are not to present His work as refined by us nor are we to take credit for our blessings, the honor and praise is to be His. And if we try to add to His blessings by giving ourselves credit we will be seen with all our prideful faults exposed. He cannot bless us, nor come to us if we're busy taking prideful credit in the eyes of the world. Perhaps a healthy positioning of ourselves in Christ can be best achieved if we use verse one of Psalm 115 as our life motto:

NOT TO US, O LORD, NOT TO US, BUT TO YOUR NAME BE THE GLORY, BECAUSE OF YOUR LOVE AND FAITHFULNESS.

A BEGINNING PLACE FOR PRAYER TODAY:

Lord, help me to feel Your blessings everyday. I want my altar to be built high by You and for You. Let me be quick to give You glory, honor and praise for all that You are in my life. Keep my heart always mindful that You are the source of all good gifts and they must be given back to You freely for Your use. When I assign value and position to myself—keep me in the third place—I want to know your Joy in my life. Thank You Father for Your faithfulness to me. I cannot praise You enough!

DISCUSSION QUESTIONS FOR TODAY:

1. Have I taken credit for something that God should have received full credit for having accomplished?

2. What are some of the ways I can implement praise in my life so that God gets the glory for all His blessings in my life?

DAY 81

SINCE THEN, YOU HAVE BEEN RAISED WITH CHRIST, SET YOUR HEARTS ON THINGS ABOVE, WHERE CHRIST IS SEATED AT THE RIGHT HAND OF GOD. SET YOUR MINDS ON THINGS ABOVE, NOT ON EARTHLY THINGS. COLOSSIANS 3:1-2

READING FOR TODAY– EXODUS 21: 1-11 AND COLOSSIANS 3: 1-14

God speaks to Moses: "These are the laws you are to set before them." This is a new nation that God has begun and He now needs them to know His laws for them. At first when you read these verses you begin to think: "Well, what does a Hebrew slave have anything to do with my life and how is this relevant to me?" If I read between the lines I begin to see God establishing the virtue of integrity in His pattern of living for His people. Integrity is His nature and it is to be ours if we are to be an honor to Him.

When Christ becomes a part of our lives, integrity and fairness move in so that our consciences are put into a completely new attitude. What was once a "me first attitude" now becomes: "What would Jesus do?" God starts with the basics of everyday life in their society and builds in accountability. We have the written word as our guide, they did not. You become aware quickly that these people, God's people, will stand for integrity and attitude training begins the minute we accept Him into our lives.

We are reminded in Colossians that we must set our minds on Him. What does He want of me? It is no longer: What are the world's standards? His Word never changes and His approach to life for us is to be righteous and He intends to make sure that we wrap our hearts in His truth. Old ways are to be put aside and new attitudes are to be practical and yet full of integrity.

When we read Colossians we see that we are to put aside the old self and rid ourselves of the old nature which always relates back to the earthly nature of man. As we study His Word daily it is a day by day journey into seeing ourselves as clearly as Christ would see us through His eyes—we need this view of ourselves if we are to have integrity. His laws for the Israelites are very specific and detailed.

God is always specific, He never clouds truth and that is one of the reasons the Bible is always new and fresh for each season of our lives. Words like "evil desire" and "greed" are just words, but when God turns them inward to our hearts they become specific for us and for our seasons. The work He has begun in us is specific to us and He alone holds the timing for the work in each of us.

"Whoever obeys His command will come to no harm, and the wise heart will know the proper time and procedure. For there is a proper time and procedure for every matter, though a man's misery weighs heavily upon him." (Ecclesiastes 8: 5-6)

And as a reminder I keep well before my eyes Ecclesiastes 7:20: "There is no righteous man on earth who does what is right and never sins."

God begins in integrity with the small matters and builds a strong and righteous heart in each of us if we allow Him time in our lives. I personally love the promise in Philippians 1:6 that He who has begun a good work in me and will continue on in that work until I see Christ face to face when this life here on earth is over. This promise is definitely a promise of faithfulness on the part of God toward man.

A BEGINNING PLACE FOR PRAYER TODAY:

Dear Father here is my heart. Let me be a person of integrity. I love the constancy of Your righteousness. When I am confused I can come to You for answers. Thank You Lord. Help me to stay in Your word and deal with honesty and truth in all that You are showing me. Thank you for being specific. I am accountable for me in Your sight. Keep my heart pure and cleanse it every day. Forgive me this day my trespasses. I love You, Lord.

DISCUSSION QUESTIONS FOR TODAY:

1. What areas in my life are of a concern to God where integrity is a necessity? What changes have I made or been forced to make because God has challenged me?

2. Is the concept of integrity and its' importance in the life of a Christian something that perhaps I have not given great thought to? Are integrity and righteousness one in the same?

DAY 82

FOR IF YOU FORGIVE MEN WHEN THEY SIN AGAINST YOU, YOUR HEAVENLY FATHER WILL FORGIVE YOU. BUT IF YOU DO NOT FORGIVE MEN THEIR SINS, YOUR FATHER WILL NOT FORGIVE YOUR SINS. MATTHEW 6:14-15

READING FOR TODAY— EXODUS 21: 12-14, PSALM 16 AND PSALM 139

God allows for accidents and mistakes. Often it is not the intent of our heart to harm or even kill another (emotionally, spiritually or physically) but death is the end result. God knows the intent of our hearts and He sees motive clearly, He is always ready to forgive us.

To have a clean heart, we must be ready to face the failures of our hearts and to seek His heart. I need His perspective on what it is that I am about. Realistically looking at ourselves keeps us humble and keeps our own judgmental spirits under control. God is the judge of each of us. He has the final say. Thank goodness He provided Jesus for us or we would all be lost in our sins.

I need to depend on God's power to overcome the sins of my life. I cannot always make right the wrongs I have done or that have been done to me. Only God can produce permanent change in my life. He knows a repentant heart because it turns away from the sin and seeks it no more.

My actions will speak for themselves. I can be misunderstood or even purposely assaulted by others, but God remains the ultimate judge of my innocence. By the same token I can expect repercussions from my sin. But…God will give me the strength to bear up under them. He is my hiding place. When man fails me God still holds on and lifts me up by His grace, His power and His faithfulness because I am a child of God.

When I choose to serve God, He chooses to bless me with His presence and in Him is the fullness of life. I can expect sorrow, disappointment and even tragedy in my life, but I can also expect Him to be there. Oswald Chambers says, "It is not true to say that God wants to teach us something in our trials; through every cloud He brings, He wants us to unlearn something."

The turn of the phrase "He wants us to unlearn something" says to me that my natural tendency to sinful behavior has to be completely and totally changed by my encounters with my sinful self. I need to unlearn "me" and learn the new nature of the new creature in Christ that God intends me to become. Nothing hurts more than failing God, but nothing is sweeter than His forgiveness as we rush into His waiting arms to take away the pain of it all.

A BEGINNING PLACE FOR PRAYER TODAY:

Lord, You are my hiding place. You are the mirror for me and you show me as the sinner that I truly am. It is hard to see myself that way, but it is a true and honest image. Father, I desire to better myself in Your sight. Work with me, move me close and closer to Your image and forgive me this day of all my sins. Create in me a clean heart so I can serve You wisely and represent You well this day as Your servant. Thank You for this day and even for my failures—in these failures I will grow. Thank You Father.

DISCUSSION QUESTIONS FOR TODAY:

1. Is there any sin in my life that God cannot forgive me of if I am a believer in Christ?

2. Why is it important to be forgiven and to allow forgiveness for others to be a part of my life?

DAY 83

AND TO HIM WHO ORDERS HIS CONDUCT ARIGHT I WILL SHOW THE SALVATION OF GOD.
PSALM 50:23

READING FOR TODAY– EXODUS 21: 15-25, PSALM 50: 15-23 AND PSALM 51

After reading these excerpts of man's sinful nature you become aware that God sees everything and for everything there is an answer, a judgment and a consequence. God is the final judge and the final word of truth for all things. He sees all and knows all. He does not judge by our outward sacrifices and nothing redeems us before Him, but the meek and quiet spirit of a repentant heart.

The best I can offer God is a sincere desire to follow His laws and be ready to accept that I will fail and I will be forgiven. My suffering depends only on how long I try to deceive myself or seek my own ways. There is only destruction in the life I choose to live for myself. When God cleans me up I am truly clean. My spirit is restored and I am encouraged to go on.

There will be broken bones as God deals with my sin. Like the lamb that the Lord carries on His shoulders, my legs must be broken so I do not keep running away from Him. Harsh treatment, you say, well, yes, but what are His alternatives when we seek to destroy ourselves by our sinful acts?

It is important to remember—no sin is greater than another. SIN is SIN. The reward for sin is death. If I kill with words or with physical harm—the sin is the same and the penalty is the same if we do not seek forgiveness. Our God is a holy God, nothing less can He tolerate in His presence and so we were bought with a price so dear to God that we can personally never repay it or stand in His presence without the Saving Grace of Jesus His Son.

How long does it take me to accept responsibility for my actions? Am I the master of excuses: God says there are no excuses; there is only sin, the acceptance of my responsibility and the turning of my heart to repentance? The strongest thing we deal with is the old man. He will continually raise up his ugly head when we least expect it.

I was born with a sin nature; no one had to teach me to be sinful. I knew what I wanted when I wanted it and I made life miserable for everyone with my cries until they picked me up! My sinful nature always tries to make me first—but God is first and I am not even a close second. The order of importance is JOY—Jesus, others and You. This is not the natural order of the world—every day is a battle to keep the order right!

A BEGINNING PLACE FOR PRAYER TODAY:

Father please put my focus in the right order. Put me at the bottom of the list. Father, I desire You to be on the top of the list. I want to do Your will and serve You. You love me and will take care of me, but first I need to have a responsible heart. Help me to seek a clean heart and right motives today. Forgive me, I keep usurping Your throne. Wash me with hyssop and make my sins whiter than snow. Allow me to not conveniently overlook the seriousness of my "little sins", forgive me Father. Thank You.

DISCUSSION QUESTIONS FOR TODAY:

1. How does God know when I am truly repentant?

2. What part of forgiveness is the hardest for me?

DAY 84

THE LORD WILL FULFILL HIS PURPOSE FOR ME; YOUR LOVE O LORD, ENDURES FOREVER—DO NOT ABANDON THE WORKS OF YOUR HANDS. PSALM 138: 8

READING FOR TODAY– EXODUS 21: 26-36, PROVERBS 6: 16-19 AND PSALM 139: 23-24

At first glance these verses look like an insurance policy written for the victims of accidents. There are stated specifics of how the victims will be paid. Closer inspection shows us that God separates accident from responsibility. With every accident there is responsibility for lazy and thoughtless acts which cause permanent harm. The payment is higher for those victims.

When we deliberately sin—the consequences are greater for us. At the time of the sin we are thoughtless as to the full consequences of it. We do what we do without thought to anyone else. It's always easy to create a mess: "dig the pit and leave it uncovered for someone to fall into" or "let the bull gore, rather than destroy it". Why is that?

Our sin nature is our self nature. It is lazy and irresponsible. A wise person prays every day for wisdom. Wisdom should really be the choice to just look around us. Am I creating pits for others to fall into, am I goring someone on a daily random basis? What havoc am I responsible for? We need to be always in control of our sphere of influence. Actually, that's the only thing we can control or change. God stands by waiting to help us if we ask for those changes.

We cannot avoid the consequences of sin; the bigger the rock in the pond, the bigger the ripples. One sinful act reaches far out and affects more things and people than we ever dreamed possible. But…If we are faithful to pray each day about our sinful selfish behavior God lets the Holy Spirit come between us and our sinful nature. He alone can help us recognize our sin, curb our nature, grant forgiveness for it and help us to accept the responsibility and then make permanent changes in our character.

When we study the word of God we learn the character of God. God wants us to have His perspective on sin. He wants us to know that He is just and there is justice in all things because He makes it that way. There will be "no digging of pits" or "goring of others" without a payment being made. God's character does not compromise or bend. He is unchangeable and exact in everything He does. God keeps good books and if we are faithful to pray about our sins He will forgive us and keep us on a short leash for our own safety.

A BEGINNING PLACE FOR PRAYER TODAY:

Oh Lord, forgive me for my unconscious sins. Let me be squarely responsible for the things I see in myself. Help me to not overlook what I want to overlook. Work on my heart. Clean it up and give me good motives. Thank You that I am work in progress. I have so much to learn about myself and the way I treat others. Everyday Father keep me mindful of how and what I do. Thank You Father that You do not abandon me and You work with me through Your Holy Spirit every day. Thank You Father for Your care and Your faithful love.

DISCUSSION QUESTIONS FOR TODAY:

1. Can we escape the consequences of sin?

2. What is the best way to deal with the sin in our lives?

DAY 85

I SAID, "I WILL CONFESS MY TRANSGRESSIONS TO THE LORD"—AND YOU FORGAVE THE GUILT OF MY SIN. PSALM 32: 5B

READING FOR TODAY– EXODUS 22: 1-4 AND PSALM 32

"When I kept silent, my bones wasted away through my groaning all day long." (Psalm 32: 3) Being the sinner that we are we are like the thief of Exodus 22. Sin must be paid for as quickly as it is done or we will live our lives groaning. Silence between us and God does not clear the heart of the guilt of sin. So…we must ask for forgiveness every day or we will groan every day.

God does not persecute the thief; He persecutes the act of the thief. Paying up quickly allows me to be cleaned up. I am not condemned, I am forgiven. In Psalm 32 it says: "For day and night your hand was heavy upon me; my strength was sapped as in the heat of summer." God demands payment for sin; i.e. confession and repentance. They are old fashion words to us, but they are the only way to regain our strength for living. I do not want the weight of my sin heavy upon me, I want it lifted and gone for good, as soon as possible.

Sin is usually either blatant or subtle, but none the less it is sin. I can start with a small sin and then deliberately increase the scope of it by trying to hide it or excuse it in the sight of myself or others. Even if I do the sin in relative darkness (or private) and I am clever and no one even sees it or recognizes it, it will still grow and become a heavier burden as the days pass.

We can end up as the thief who must be sold for his debt in verse 2 if we remain stubborn in accepting Christ. No one sets out to back slide. It happens little by little, it is subtle but it is all consuming. "The lord's unfailing love surrounds the man who trusts Him," but "many are the woes of the wicked." When I confess my sin I am forgiven of the guilt of it. The sin will be paid for, the consequences will exist, but I can then move on to restore the victim of the sin, even when it's me, as God teaches me the way I should go.

To have a spirit that has no deceit before God is a marvelous gift to oneself. To go before God every day and confess what we know are the acts of our sinful nature allows us to be taught anew every day. When we have no deceit in our lives we have the gift of having God watch over us and counsel us. We may sin, but…we do not deceive ourselves and we become the one who can "rejoice in the Lord and be glad." We will be able to sing about life instead of groan about life.

God's touch is either heavy or light upon our life because of what we do about our sin. What sins beset us today? It is important to cast them before God or we will never know the light touch of God. We are either teachable or we are like the mule that God must put a bridle in his mouth and yank along. Do I want to be taught or yanked along through life?

A BEGINNING PLACE FOR PRAYER TODAY:

Lord, I am so sorry for my foolishness. I carry burdens I have no right to have. You alone can lighten my load. I need to confess my sin and let You teach me your ways. Thank You that You love me so much that You save me Your Son and set my sins far away from me. You have delivered me from needless guilt. Help me to see clearly what I need to do to have a clean heart before You, Father. Thank You for saving me.

DISCUSSION QUESTIONS FOR TODAY:

1. Why do I need to confess my sins to the Lord on a daily basis?

2. Does God want us to carry around a sack of guilt daily?

DAY 86

FOR THIS GOD IS OUR GOD FOREVER AND EVER; HE WILL BE OUR GUIDE EVEN TO THE END. PSALM 48:14

READING FOR TODAY: EXODUS 22:5-9, PSALM 27 AND PSALM 48

Restitution is the key word in our verses today. The word literally means to pay something back and restore it to its' original state. Sometimes things in our lives are destroyed by our lack of care or concern and God is saying here that it is sinful to destroy anything. We are responsible for getting it back into its original state. Have you noticed that it is not enough to recognize our sins and confess them; we must do something about them. Unfortunately, repenting is a verb, it is an action word. Personally, repenting before God is always the easy part for me, but our sin is made much more real when we have to go out in the world, before friends, family and even enemies and restore through our words and eventually our deeds the sin we have created. It is clear that restoration requires an inward change in my attitude and then an outward change in my actions.

The outward steps that produce change are not always the easiest steps to take. They require faith that sometimes seems so out of reach, but reaching down inside of us for the strength of God is what faith can produce in us. When we have hurt someone, even unintentionally, it is difficult to find the right words or actions, but the steps must be initiated if the restitution or restoration is to be complete. I find the biggest obstacle to restoration is the "I" part of the equation.

How "I" will look in the public eye is not really important, God requires us to "seek His face" and restore or make restitution. It has been proven over and over in my life that no one goes forward unburdened unless they will turn from their sins and seek a new path by laying the burden down at the feet of God and then taking the strength of God and doing something publicly about it. In order to get the strength necessary I have found that it is important to pray it through, before I act, and then start praising God for what He is going to do with my situation.

A new path takes conscious work on our part and that new work is often foreign territory—we just are not comfortable in foreign territory. Foreign territory might be being friendly in unfriendly circumstances or it might be looking at an old situation with new eyes which puts us in an unknown and uncomfortable place. Loving the unlovable or even being hopeful when in reality we feel fearful or downcast is foreign territory. In all of these circumstances it is placing our faith in the hands of the God we trust. We can rest in God because He promises: I WILL BE YOUR GUIDE EVEN TO THE END.

To see a problem clearly, to see it as God sees it, is to examine it upside down and backwards through God's eyes and we must allow the Holy Spirit to change our heart's focus to what God says restoration requires. Restoration requires true maturity in Christ. The immature Christian looks for someone else to blame and someone else to solve the problem, but the mature Christian looks carefully at himself in God's perspective according to scripture. As we study the word we see what God's standards are and we begin to understand what a pure heart before God looks like. God's standards require a right heart and a right attitude and God's standards cannot be attained without the active participation of the Holy Spirit. To me that is the best part of being a Christian—I am never working alone because I have given the Holy Spirit permission to work within me to pursue God's standards. The best motive I can have for living is to pursue God's motives for me and then step aside and let the Holy Spirit work.

Sometimes I forget that my rewards are not here on earth, they are in heaven, but by following the leading of scripture and making restitution as God requires, I can experience the blessings of God's love each day while I'm here on earth. Scripture says that faith produces a feeling of being strong and safe. God is my fortress in time of trouble and a rod of stiffness to be strong when all within me fears the worst. Not of my works, but because of the Holy Spirit's active work of restoration in my life I can expect in God's timing to be transformed into Christ's image. Thank You Jesus!

A BEGINNING PLACE FOR PRAYER TODAY:

Lord, please help me to get my eyes off of myself and on to the well being of others. Restore in me a will to make restitution to You and others for all my failures. Help me to focus even on the little things. Restore my countenance for I have much to be thankful for and I owe you much praise for your faithfulness to me. Let there be an openness about me that draws people to me so I can share You with them. Help me to step aside and get out of the way as You have Your perfect will with me. Restore me afresh and anew with hopefulness for all that You are capable of doing. Thank You Father that You care so much about me and let me not be afraid to make restoration where restoration is needed.

DISCUSSION QUESTIONS FOR TODAY:

1. Is there anyone I need to make restitution to in my life? Is that restitution just to the Lord because I have been offending Him or is it a person near to me in my own family?

2. What are the actions that God requires of me to restore my heart to His standards?

DAY 87

Therefore if any man be in Christ, he is a new creature: old things are passed away; behold all things are become new. II Corinthians 5:17

Reading for today— Exodus 22: 10-15, Colossians 3: 13 and Isaiah 55: 6-13

Can we always affix blame for things that happens in our lives? I don't think so. Only God knows why something has been allowed to touch us. To search for why or who to blame is an impossible search. I believe that accepting the reality of our lives and then moving forward with hope is the Lord's true blessing to us as believers.

Things can be given away, stolen or torn to pieces, but we are not to seek someone to blame. Our job is to accept the truth of the loss and deal with any responsibility we have in the matter. I cannot know someone else's pain at the loss of a loved one, but I can hold up their heart and ask God to give them peace and love during their pain. I can forgive those who tear things apart in my life so I can be free of anger. I can turn over my fear to God and let Him deal with it, but I cannot overcome fear on my own.

My responsibility is to seek God's perspective on all things. I am to search the scripture to see how He resolves things and then to stand firm on the knowledge that only God is in charge of my life. He has the total picture of my existence. His purpose and His plan for my life will move forward. I can make it either a hard or easy transition through this life by choosing either to seek blame or accept the reality of my circumstances. Nothing will ever turn back the clock—no words or actions can be retracted. What is done is done and I must focus on the present. Even the present is in my hands for a short time and even that "present" has limitations.

I must use the gifts of today as wisely as I can. Who has the Lord put in my path today? What task must I carry out to be of service for Him? Today, without blame, is my hope for tomorrow. To not regret today, to not waste today; that is my part and that is my service before the Lord. Wisely, carefully, hopefully, prayerfully I do not seek blame, but my responsibility for this day is to be in Christ and know that He is creating in me a new creature. Creating me into a new creature can be painful at times, but it will also always be hopeful. Ultimately the work will prosper me to the end of my days when God's work will finally be completed. Praise God for His faithfulness to me!

A beginning place for prayer today:

Today is a new day Lord. Let me lay aside the sins of yesterday, even the triumphant of yesterday and begin a new day. Put in my path Your duties and Your perspectives for this day. Take away all my preconceived ideas of who I am and make me new today. I desire to see life through Your eyes and have Your heart of service, Jesus. Help me Father for I am weak and I wish to be strong for You. Don't let me give up and settle with a heavy hand on the things of this earth. Help me to let go of it all. Thank You, Father.

DISCUSSION QUESTIONS FOR TODAY:

1. Is there anything in my life today that happened in the past that keeps me from being the new creature God has intended me to be? Does holding on to the past produce good fruit?

2. What are the fruits of seeking blame?

DAY 88

YE SHALL WALK IN ALL THE WAYS WHICH THE LORD YOUR GOD HATH COMMANDED YOU, THAT YE MAY LIVE, AND IT MAY BE WELL WITH YOU, AND THAT YE MAY PROLONG YOUR DAYS IN THE LAND WHICH YE SHALL POSSESS. DEUTERONOMY 5:33.

READING FOR TODAY– EXODUS 22: 16-17, COLOSSIANS 3:23-24 AND ROMANS 8: 35-39

God loves me, even when I sin terribly against Him. He loves me and nothing I can do will separate me from His love. Why does God lower Himself in these verses in Exodus to write about such immorality? He writes about it because it happens and it must have an answer. Nothing is new when it comes to sin. There has been and there will always be reckless disrespect for what we know is wrong. In our own lives the sin may not be as obvious as this one, but we will sin and we do sin because we are human.

The redeeming quality of following what God says is right and doing it allows us complete repentance. And even if we repent things may still not be good for us. We may suffer for a long time because of the consequences of that sin, but after a while we will live again. To be out from under the guilt of our sin I believe is the only way God can use us again.

Guilt is the enemy's greatest weapon against us. We are truly foolish to try and stand on our own righteousness. How many minutes or seconds can we go without sinning before God? I think it is important to accept the fact that we are weak and that God is quick to forgive us and clean us up. If God sees us as righteous the devil will have a harder time condemning us.

We cannot possess the land God has given us if we stand condemned by the devil and believe his condemnation. I can always be convicted of my sin and seek God for forgiveness, but condemnation is always of the enemy and I must actively try to discern condemnation and conviction. Condemnation always puts us in a place where we cannot accept the love of God. That is the ultimate goal of the devil—to separate us from Him!

Possessing the land is what life is all about. My life is the land God has given me—these are the circumstances I find myself in and the people that surround me. These circumstances are what God has either given me or has allowed in my life because of my choices or the choices of others. There are not always easy answers to my life, but when God is in charge I need not fear the future or experience condemnation. I need to be right in God's sight. Man can look at me anyway he wants, but God must see me as obedient to Him or I will surely live in the devil's condemnation. Under condemnation I can never be free to live fully and accept the joy of life.

I think we have to accept the fact that we cannot live a sinless life, it is impossible, but we can know victory over sin when we are faithful to confess our sins, repent and accept God's forgiveness. Repenting is a 180 degree turn toward responsibility for my actions. I am to look squarely at the reality of my sin and desire to make what I have done wrong right, even when it won't be pleasant or even satisfactory to me because of the feeling of shame I may have to bear for my actions. With repentance I am righteous before God and I am free to possess the land even if for a season of time it is a valley.

A BEGINNING PLACE FOR PRAYER TODAY:

You know the sins of my life Lord, all are equal in weight. All sin is destructive and I need your cleansing power. Help me to be obedient, to confess my sins to You Jesus. I know that You are my advocate before the Father. I desire to honor You and be a good witness. Help me Father to possess my land so I am a blessing to You. Wash me white as snow. Thank You Father for Your Son Jesus, because of Him I can be righteous in Your sight.

DISCUSSION QUESTIONS FOR TODAY:

1. Is there any sin I can commit that will separate me from the love of God?

2. What is the difference between being convicted of sin and being condemned by a sin?

DAY 89

BLESSED ARE THEY WHICH DO HUNGER AND THIRST AFTER RIGHTEOUSNESS FOR THEY SHALL BE FILLED. MATTHEW 5:6

READING FOR TODAY– EXODUS 22: 18-20, JAMES 4: 13-17 AND JAMES 1: 12.

"Do not allow a sorceress to live." (Exodus 22:18) A sorceress is one who practices the supernatural; one who manipulates the natural. Each one of us can have at any given time the mentality of a sorceress over take our hearts. We are all capable at times of trying to manipulate God, the provider of the natural flow of our Christian's life. We can pursue all manner of things to avoid the natural flow of God's will in our lives. Here the scripture says to kill the sorceress, do not do evil things like try to get your own way and do not worship anything except God.

Nothing that we manipulate is righteous. If God has a new course for us, the mark of righteousness in our lives is to submit and obey God's choices for us. Cover up and short cuts mark the course of the manipulator. Our full potential as believers cannot be realized until we accept willingly the ways of the Lord. We can question Him directly, but once the answer does not change then it is time for us to adapt to the new circumstance. I need to explore with a sense of adventure the unexpected in my life. Even the bad things in life give me the opportunity to make lemonade out of what appear to be the lemons in my life.

A wise man consults God on everything and that is not manipulation. Scripture says, "Now listen, you who say, 'Today or tomorrow we will go to this or that city, spend a year there, carry on business and make money!' Why, you do not even know what will happen tomorrow. What is your life? You are a mist that appears for a little while and then vanishes. Instead, you should say, 'If it is the Lord's will, we will live and do this or that. As it is, you boast and brag. All such boasting is evil. Anyone who knows the good he ought to do and doesn't do it, sins.'" (James 3: 17)

To kill the sorceress is to kill the evil intent of not doing what is hard to do and choosing to avoid doing what is right by scripture. One of the fruits of not being submissive to God is stagnation. I believe we retard our growth in Christ with each adventure into manipulation as we choose to short cut or alter God's choices for us. According to scripture self ambition causes disorder and evil practices. "But wisdom that comes from heaven is first pure; then peace loving, considerate, submissive, full of mercy and good fruit, impartial and sincere."(James 3: 13-17)

How often do we hate a circumstance? The very circumstances we loathe can often be the circumstances which will produce the most spiritual growth. I think the whys of life are deadly. When we seek an answer to why we can often find ourselves trying to manipulate a situation. When a door closes it has been my experience that kicking and pounding on it is futile. Submission to God's will has always led me to blessings. I've discovered over the years that the most fruitful question I can seek God with is: "How can I live victoriously in this circumstance?" When submission and obedience are in our lives, there is little place for the sorceress to become the author of our lives. Our personal growth in Christ is in God's hands and the rewards are great!

BLESSED IS THE MAN WHO PERSEVERES UNDER TRIAL, BECAUSE WHEN HE HAS STOOD THE TEST, HE WILL RECEIVE THE CROWN OF LIFE THAT GOD HAS PROMISED TO THOSE WHO LOVE HIM (James 1: 12).

A BEGINNING PLACE FOR PRAYER TODAY:

Help me, Father, to kill the sorceress who seeks to kill me with fear and temptation. Help me to keep my eyes focused on You. I need You, Father, to stand guard over my heart so I don't manipulate my way out of Your will. Help me to be patient and not seek shortcuts. Let me have strength and wisdom in all my adversity so I will daily kill the sorceress and rejoice in my trials, because You are my fortress and my God. Thank You, Father.

DISCUSSION QUESTIONS FOR TODAY:

1. What are the circumstances in my life today that I am having trouble letting God take over or have I had difficulty in a past circumstance?

2. How has God worked in the past or is He working right now and because of it I have peace, but I don't know how it will all work out?

DAY 90

YOU ARE TO BE MY HOLY PEOPLE. EXODUS 12: 31A

READING FOR TODAY– EXODUS 22: 21-31 AND PHILIPPIANS 1:6, 9 AND 10

A holy person is a man or a woman of God who stands out in a crowd as someone who has the qualities of God. Our example for living is Jesus. His behaviors are clearly the behaviors of God because He was God incarnate and therefore these are to be our characteristics. These verses of Exodus today tell us we are not to mistreat people or oppress them regardless of who they are because a holy person does not take advantage of anyone—rich or poor. We are to be compassionate in all our dealings and by this we are known as God's people. Being compassionate is always easy when it doesn't really cost us anything, but oh how we fear being taken advantage of by people!

Benevolence is not Christ like when we always have to be sure that we won't be taken advantage of by another person. One of my good friends once came across a couple who stood with a "we are hungry, can you help us sign". She had no money with her so she found out where they were staying and bought groceries for the couple and their children.

Unfortunately, when she arrived at their motel she found them high on drugs and the children nowhere in sight. She gave them the food. Her instincts of compassion were not wrong, they were Christ- like. She was also glad she did not have money in her possession at the time of her compassion for it was obvious the money would have gone to buy drugs. She didn't feel taken advantage of, but to this day she always carries McDonald's gift certificates in her purse.

As a Christian I have social responsibilities and God uses these responsibilities to keep me humble and pure. Nothing that I have is mine—that must always be firmly planted in my heart. Everything I have is a gift from Him. My time, my talents, all of it is His to give or to take away. To open up my hand and give away what God has given me allows God to have an empty hand to refill. I have discovered and I am sure you have too that you cannot out give God.

Each of us, at one time or another, has been in a place of needing forgiveness or a second chance and God freely gives that. To be compassionate to one another is not always easy, but it can have the added benefit of purging our hearts of unforgiveness, anger, frustration and even anxiety. To keep a right perspective, to remain committed to Him requires that we submit everything to Him.

Our burdens become light when He carries them. Sometimes the opportunity arises here on this earth that we can be the hands, the ears, the eyes or even the barn full of goods that needs to be shared. When the opportunity arises, it is our job to be Christ-like and give. Our giving is the tangible expression of mercy and grace that attracts nonbelievers to Christ, especially when the giving is done in His name.

Only the Holy Spirit can mold us into holy people. Without an active prayer life and the reading of scripture daily we become dry and empty of faith. When we lack faith, we can also lack compassion and a desire to serve others. Our faith needs constant watering. Fellowship with God keeps us from living a dry and barren life. We have judgments to make concerning our compassion toward others, but those judgments must be examined by a heart of love rather than heart that measures the cost first. When our heart becomes a calculator it loses its compassion.

BEGINNING PLACE FOR PRAYER TODAY:

I need Your compassion in my life, Lord. Teach me to use Your compassion wisely and liberally. Take away my selfish nature and let me give away everything You have given me. Let me keep a light hand on everything. All that I have is Yours to give away; especially love and compassion. Change my heart toward those who disappoint me simply because they are not who You have intended them to be yet. I am also a work in progress; let me turn my eyes to that before I condemn others. Lord, I know that I am needy, please refresh me today. Teach me to pray and hold my tongue for another time or another day. Thank You, Father, that You are so patient with me.

DISCUSSION QUESTIONS FOR TODAY:

1. Are there areas in my life that I am too afraid of being taken advantage of that and therefore I cannot allow compassion to flow freely to others?

2. Where do I find I am most critical and in what circumstances would I not be compassionate? Are these places reasonable places where God would want me to use wisdom before I stepped forward to help another person? Is it true that in some instances a person must work something through by himself so that God's work is complete in him and to help him would not allow him to grow?

DAY 91

WHOEVER OBEYS HIS COMMAND WILL COME TO NO HARM, AND THE WISE HEART WILL KNOW THE PROPER TIME AND PROCEDURE. ECCLESIASTES 8:5

READING FOR TODAY– EXODUS 23: 1-9 AND PROVERBS 29: 20

Am I impartial when I make judgments about people? Do I try to speak impartially of people looking for the good first or do I dwell on the negative first? If I were to step back and look at my dealings with others, what would I see?

I have learned that prayer should supersede all verbalized criticism. Having God hear my complaints and allowing Him to sort out my judgments before I speak is a wise course of action. It has been my experience that God puts those complaints in a lot better perspective when I present those complaints to Him first.

Surprisingly, sometimes after the complaint has been spoken to God I find that my heart is the one that needs the work, but by praying about it first God is able to give me peace where otherwise I would have sown seeds of destruction. God and I have had many morning shower talks. It is funny how when I share my complaints with Him first, the less of those complaints I actually verbalized to my prospective targets.

Some thoughts are correct and need addressing, but most of them are my own personal judgments and they match my real or imagined comfort levels. Our motives for confrontation can be selfish or petty and our own sin natures are capable of blowing things way out of proportion if we are not careful. I have found that successful personal relationships are a delicate balance of knowing which is a major offense and which is a minor offense. Experience has proven to me that it is always wise to major on the majors and minor on the minors—especially where children and mates are concerned!

Life can be lived and enjoyed in many different ways, but not all avenues are what we as individuals would choose. That's why they are called choices. Priorities and choices are a matter of personal preference and they are acceptable and reasonable to God as long as they are moral choices. God will be the ultimate judge of motives and it has also been my experience that we have enough on our own plates without verbalizing our dissent over things that really don't concern us.

Choices are made every day; some good, some bad, but they are the choices God has allowed us to make. My prayer is that my choices in the things I say and do where other people concerned will be an honor to God and produce something of value for God's kingdom. If God is not in the business of condemning me then how can I be in the business of condemning others? For scripture says:

NOT RENDERING EVIL FOR EVIL, OR RAILING FOR RAILING: BUT CONTRARIWISE BLESSING; KNOWING THAT YE ARE THERE UNTO CALLED, THAT YE SHOULD INHERIT A BLESSING. FOR HE THAT WILL LOVE LIFE AND SEE GOOD DAYS, LET HIM REFRAIN HIS TONGUE FROM EVIL, AND HIS LIPS THAT SPEAK GUILE. I PETER 3: 9 AND 10.

Life can be full and enriching for everyone if we are blessings to one another whenever possible. To choose to guard my tongue and speak only truth when asked for my opinion is a blessing to others. The unnecessary strife that is eliminated by my adherence to prayerful conversations with God will be a blessing for me and that is promised in scripture.

A BEGINNING PLACE FOR PRAYER TODAY:

Lord, You know when I am destructive with words. Please help me to hold my tongue and let me speak to You first before I speak. Help me to keep my judgments to myself and let me only speak when it will be a blessing to a situation. Keep me especially loving and understanding toward my immediate family. They need my support and comfort and only wise words will accomplish that end. Thank You Father that You love me so much that You desire me to keep my heart at peace because I first check in with You and then I speak.

DISCUSSION QUESTIONS FOR TODAY:

1. Can I think of a situation where I wish I would have prayed before I spoke?

2. How should we judge our criticisms before we speak? Are motives to be a consideration?

DAY 92

FOR THUS SAITH THE LORD GOD, THE HOLY ONE OF ISRAEL; IN RETURNING AND REST SHALL YE BE SAVED; IN QUIETNESS AND IN CONFIDENCE SHALL BE YOUR STRENGTH. ISAIAH 30: 15

READING FOR TODAY– EXODUS 23: 10-13

It seems evident through scripture that God knows we get too caught up in "our" plans and we lose sight of His plans. He commands us to rest from our labors and come away with Him. The Sabbath is the perfect day for that; it is a day of total reflection, or it can be if we allow it. When we take time from our business we can reflect on all our blessings. If we foolishly keep moving and never stop to reflect or listen to God's voice we lose sight of the Lord's accomplishments.

Ideally, to sit at His feet is the better part of life. All I hear when I move about is my own noise. If the noise is happy, it feels great, but if I'm in a place of heavy noise I become weary. And, it seems, heavy noise is more the rule of thumb these days. So I need to set aside the day, rejoice in the week past and renew my spirit with His Spirit. I need to see my accomplishments and failures, my joys and my sorrows and all my blessings in His perspective. I must force myself to be still. Sitting quietly and reflecting is very much against our human nature. For the most part, we don't reap the benefit of God's renewal because we just are not quiet before Him.

Each morning, I am an even wiser person if I rise early to study His Word and then listen for His voice. He has a plan for me, but I can't hear it if I don't listen. The Sabbath is a good time for reflection and communion with God over the past six days of labor, but it is even more beneficial for me to be renewed afresh each morning. It seems needlessly foolish to struggle with my plans when I can easily commit them to Him each morning. He can order them or throw them out before I've wasted too much precious time on the wrong plans. When doors close on my efforts I look forward to seeing what door God will open next.

Arrogantly, we can sometimes view our prayer time as simply "plan approval time"; we aren't talking with Him about our plans we are telling Him our plans. If we allow ourselves the privilege of asking His advice, we are sometimes surprised when He puts before us a new dream and His scheme for accomplishing it. When my desires are set aside and I submit willingly to Him, He has the opportunity to do a much better job with my life and certainly a more perfect work than I had ever thought possible.

When our boys were looking at college football scholarship opportunities they always had their choices in mind. We respected those dreams, but we always prayed for God's choice first. We encouraged them that God would make the final and best choice for them, even if they didn't think so at the time. Our oldest son was disappointed not to go out of state on his football scholarship. After two years of college football he wanted to drop out of football and concentrate on his academic pursuits more. He had been playing football since he was eight years old and he discovered he was burned out. We were close at hand to help him deal with his new dream. Our youngest son was disappointed that at the last minute he wasn't picked up by a large prestigious football college out of state. God's choice gave him a great football experience out of state in a smaller college atmosphere. In that small environment he met his future wife, as well as getting his college degree. Both boys agree that God really knew what He was doing. As adults, with wives and jobs, they are still comfortable with letting God open and close doors for them. They have tasted the success of letting God be in charge of their lives. When they call for advice from us on their latest decisions, it's most often to ask us to pray for God's best for them.

I can sow and I can harvest, I can even feed people or give blessings because of my harvest, but only God can refresh me. Daily I can be refreshed and daily I can bless others if I'll just "be still". In quietness I am renewed by the confident assurance that God has ALWAYS met my needs and been there for me. I know He will be there for me today if can just be still and wait.

A BEGINNING PLACE FOR PRAYER TODAY:

Dear Father, I look forward to Sunday, to keep your Sabbath, but I desire to be refreshed daily. Take me into your presence with Your scripture. Restore my soul with a look back at yesterday's blessings. Give me your guidance for today. Please set aside my plans and help me do Your will and set my will aside. I want to dwell in confidence in Your strength.

DISCUSSION QUESTIONS FOR TODAY:

1. Why is it important to read the Word and pray when I'm looking for direction in my life?

2. Where there ever times in my life when I wouldn't let go of things or I was disappointed? Did I discover I'd wasted too much time banging on doors and God really did know best?

DAY 93

HONOR THE LORD FROM YOUR WEALTH, AND FROM THE FIRST OF ALL YOUR PRODUCE. PROVERBS 3:9

READING FOR TODAY– EXODUS 23: 14-19 AND DEUTERONOMY 8: 7-14, 18

Everything I have is the Lord's. How easy it is to receive the blessings of this life and forget the giver of those blessings. God tries to give man a right perspective on his holdings. If we consider everything to be God's, we don't hold on so tightly to our possessions and they are easily shared or even given away.

God prospers me because He loves me. He also allows misfortune because He loves me. When I am too well off I have a tendency to be self-reliant, when I am in need I talk to God. In talking with Him, I am reminded of His previous blessings and His consistency in my life. His intent is not to make me rich for the sake of making me rich in other men's eyes. *Sometimes my wealth cannot be not measured by man, because my wealth is found in the intangible fruits of the Spirit. (Galatians 5 22-23)*

God desires me to share my riches with others so that the gospel can be shared. Ultimately, He chooses to make me rich in Him, and that allows me to be able to have a heart for giving and serving. As His servant I bring honor to Him in these acts.

Everything I put my confidence in should be a reflection of how much I honor Him. The easy flow of blessings to others is evidence of God's work in my life. If I hold on too tight to the riches of my life they will never prosper the kingdom of God. We need always to remember that it is "the Lord thy God that giveth the power to get wealth that He may establish His covenant which He swore unto thy fathers."(Deuteronomy 8:18). Giving is not always the giving of material goods and the benefits of giving are best received when our motives are not to get more for ourselves. The most valuable store houses are the ones filled with the gifts of the Holy Spirit.

I have discovered that nothing is more valuable than the joy I feel when I give of my time and my talents in places where there is no material gain. To come alongside a friend who needs her garden tended because she is overwhelmed by having her husband in a nursing home, to fix a meal for a family who has a new baby in the house or a funeral at hand, to take time to visit a shut-in, to help out at vacation Bible school with crafts and see the delight of a child as you help his little fingers work a wonder; these are gifts to others that often bless us more than the ones we try to bless.

Anonymous giving is really a fun thing to experience. I remember one time that a single mom in our Bible study needed glasses immediately, but she just couldn't afford them. Writing a check for the amount at the time was really an easy thing for me to do from my business account. But, I didn't want her to feel like a charity case, especially, if it meant she felt beholding to me. God had provided my funds and I wanted to give it as a gift from Him. The check was written out to the church and the head of our women's group let her know after the study that the glasses would be paid for as a love gift from

God. It was fun watching her over the weeks share how God had blessed her. She couldn't believe the caring nature of God, over even the smallest of her needs.

Three times a year the Lord requests of the Israelites to bring their offerings to God—not because God needs them, but because man needs to be reminded of His blessings to him. If man will set aside his own strivings he can reflect on the blessings of God as he gives those blessings as an offering. Anything that is given to another in the name of God is a blessing to God. I think each of us needs to look closely at our wealth and decide whether we store it up or give it away and get an even bigger blessing. Yes, I believe some blessings are stored in heaven as treasure for us, but life can be ever so sweet this very day if we just give without personal gain and then experience those blessings in other people's lives.

A BEGINNING PLACE FOR PRAYER TODAY:

Father, please forgive me that I often look at the material things in my life to verify Your love for me. Help me to see what gifts of the Holy Spirit you are storing up in me. Let me value everything in my life as a gift from You. Perhaps, even one day, I might have an opportunity to share some of those gifts with others. Please help me to see those around me who are in need of Your touch in their lives and let me share wisely from my storehouse Your blessings with them. Thank You, Father for this day and all the possibilities of sharing that will exist in it.

DISCUSSION QUESTIONS FOR TODAY:

1. Which one of God's blessings should I be sharing today?

2. Have I become so fearful of not having enough that I have forgotten who the gifts I am hoarding have come from? Do I have a guarantee of a long life here on earth? So what am I saving things for?

DAY 94

YET THIS I CALL TO MIND AND THEREFORE I HAVE HOPE: BECAUSE OF THE LORD'S GREAT LOVE WE ARE NOT CONSUMED, FOR HIS COMPASSIONS NEVER FAIL. THEY ARE NEW EVERY MORNING; GREAT IS YOUR FAITHFULNESS. LAMENTATIONS 3: 22-23

READING FOR TODAY – EXODUS 23:20-23, ROMANS 5:5 AND JOHN 16: 7, 13.

As we travel through our personal wildernesses we need a guide. The Angel of the Lord was the guide of the Israelites. Our guide is the Holy Spirit. He leads and speaks to us each individually. The Holy Spirit is in us and therefore we are the temple of the Holy Spirit. (I Corinthians 6: 19)

Because the Angel of the Lord spoke to Moses, the people had hope in the future. Today, now more than ever, we need hope. Through Christ Jesus we have eternal hope, which is heaven through salvation, but even more glorious, we have that same hope for each day we live here on earth. Living is the hard part of salvation, but we don't have to wait for death to experience hope, our loving God provides that each day with the fellowship of the Holy Spirit living in us.

God does not want us walking around wondering what awful thing will happen next. He wants us to focus on His love for us. His best love gift is the Holy Spirit. (Luke 11:3) Knowing the beginning from the end, the good and the bad we will experience, He guides us with His love for us. Jesus knows our personal enemies— such as sorrow, disappointment, lack of patience, unforgiveness and fear. Just as the Angel of the Lord helped the Israelites defeat their enemies so through the power of the Holy Spirit can He defeat our personal enemies.

Hope keeps us going like nothing else can. It allows us to overlook the evil and painful things in life and gives us a quest to find the good that will come of it, because "greater is He that is in you than he that is in the world."(I John 4:4) As we mature in Christ we learn to set aside the WHY question and rush to seek the answer to: HOW will God use this in my life? The constant presence of hope in our lives assures us that we are never alone and all things can be used by God for our good, even the things the enemy wants to destroy us with. Our despair at the presence of evil and pain in this world will only be for a season, if we can remember the promise that "joy comes in the morning". (Psalm 30:5)

Sometimes "the morning" of our sorrow takes a while to come. It has taken my dear friend Barb three years to experience "the morning" of her sorrow after the sudden passing of her husband. Little by little the sorrow of her aloneness has been replaced with the loving memories of their life together. She has learned to rejoice in the joys of her children and her grandchildren and to marvel at the family unit God has given her. It has been a slow and sometimes painful journey, but God has held her in His arms and the blessings have finally washed away the magnitude of the sorrow. Our expectation of what the Lord is doing in our lives is our steadfast knowledge that our hope, the Holy

Spirit, conquers pain and evil. The more scriptural truths we can commit to memory, the stronger our hope will be in the Lord.

A BEGINNING PLACE FOR PRAYER TODAY:

Lord, thank You for the hope I have in You. With Your hope I can put fear in its place. Help me to see You have a plan for me and for those I love and become so fearful over. You will keep me going and move me through this life. I need not be afraid of my enemies for my enemies are Your enemies. Thank You that You have already made a way of escape for me. Help me to see each new day as You see it. Please let my hope and expectation be a joy to You and let me freely share it with those who do not know You. Thank You, Father.

DISCUSSION QUESTIONS FOR TODAY:

1. Have I known great sorrow and how did the Lord give me hope for tomorrow?

2. What does joy look and feel like when sorrow and fear have been overcome with the hope we have in Jesus?

DAY 95

MY SOUL MELTETH FOR HEAVINESS; STRENGTHEN THOU ME ACCORDING UNTO THY WORD. PSALM 119: 28

READING FOR TODAY – EXODUS 23: 24-30, PHILIPPIANS 4: 6-7 AND PSALM 130:5

It is easy to say, "The Lord's timing is perfect" when the answers to our prayers are quickly met. But …what about the lingering time, the God's waiting room time of prayers which seem unanswered and endless? God's timing is perfect, but it's not our timing so it is often fretful for us. Even though we are personally okay it just doesn't help much when children or dear friends suffer—we can easily feel helpless. It is times like these that we need to pray through a subject and then leave it at His throne and expectantly wait for His perfect answer. Hope lies in verse 30 of Exodus 23:

I WILL DRIVE THEM OUT BEFORE YOU LITTLE BY LITTLE, UNTIL YOU BECOME FRUITFUL

AND TAKE POSSESSION OF THE LAND

A complete work takes time. "Little by little" until you become fruitful is the key phrase. God knows what each of us needs and He gives us the tools to get that need met little by little. Even when we pray for someone else He is working through a land that needs possession of in our lives. While He is orchestrating a solution to our prayer request for someone else He is even at that time defeating an enemy we might have and replacing it with His growth for us.

We see only the surface of a problem; God sees it from all sides. He does not deliver bandages. He delivers healing, purification, peace, insight for us and the restoration of confidence in Him with each trouble or sorrow that touches our lives. Sometimes we even hinder Him by rescuing ourselves or others with quick remedies, when what we really need to do is take our hands off a situation. We can actually lengthen the time to answered prayer by attempting to take care of it ourselves instead of becoming fruitful in hope, patience and faith in the One, the only One, Who can give us "possession of the land."

When days are particularly black we need to hold tight to Jeremiah 29:11-13:

FOR I KNOW THE PLANS I HAVE FOR YOU, DECLARES THE LORD, PLANS FOR WELFARE AND NOT FOR CALAMITY TO GIVE YOU A FUTURE AND A HOPE. THEN WILL YOU CALL ON ME AND COME AND PRAY TO ME, AND I WILL LISTEN TO YOU. AND YOU WILL SEEK ME AND FIND ME WHEN YOU SEARCH FOR ME WITH ALL YOUR HEART.

When we search for Him with all our heart we gain the greatest wisdom and the greatest peace. The question of Why? is not ours to search for, but the acceptance of the fact that He has a plan, a multi-level perfect plan, which He will work out in our lives for "a future and a hope" in all things and that understanding or piece of information must become our ultimate goal for living. Our constant prayer needs to be: "Thy will, not my will be done!"

A BEGINNING PLACE FOR PRAYER TODAY:

Father, forgive my anxieties and let me look to Your perfect plan for my life. I only see limitedly what this day has and I need a hope for the good things in life that You have planned for me and those who love You. You know my needs and You are gracious now as you have been in the past to give me Your strength and courage.

I need not worry about the future for You are in charge of that. Bless me with Your peace and strength for this day: One day at a time, until Your plan for me is accomplished. Thank You Father, I want to love and trust You with all my heart and I know Your Holy Spirit can accomplish that in me if I will just let go and let You be God. Thank You, Father.

DISCUSSION QUESTIONS FOR TODAY:

1. What prayer request has been the hardest and the longest for me?

2. Has an unanswered prayer become an obsession with me and is it destroying my joy? What changes can I make in my attitude toward this prayer?

DAY 96

FEAR THOU NOT, FOR I AM WITH THEE: BE NOT DISMAYED; FOR I AM THY GOD: I WILL STRENGTHEN THEE WITH THE RIGHT HAND OF MY RIGHTEOUSNESS. ISAIAH 41: 10

READING FOR TODAY– EXODUS 23: 31-33, PSALM 16, COLOSSIANS 1: 10- 12

God sets our boundaries. In Psalm 16 He puts us in pleasant places because He "is the portion of my inheritance and my cup". His standards are to be my perspectives on life and because I hold His perspectives I see Him as holding me in a particular place for a season. I am not to be shaken because He is continually before me and He will instruct me throughout my season. I cannot have His perspective if I allow fear to overwhelm me. He has chosen to drive the enemy, fear, from my life. Day after day He works to prove that He is in charge of my life if I allow Him to have that control. My fears can be many on any given day. If I will allow Him, He can beat down those enemies and I can survive the storm of those fears because He has put me in His protective boundaries.

So often in my life I have let fear make me fear the worst in an unexpected situation only to realize at the end of the trial that He has produced great fruit for me and others from the event. Maturity in Christ has given me the perspective that His boundaries are safe harbors for me and that I need not fear, but I must put my trust in Him.

It is not my desire to make you think that I have conquered fear, but I have been able to let go of fear a lot quicker when I remind myself daily that I have not set the boundaries for the protection of my life—He has set those boundaries. Keeping my eyes on Him is my job and I cannot allow the gods of this world to take His place in my life. Power and strength belong to God and each day He gives them to me liberally so I can accept the troubles of the day.

I must totally rely on Him as I do my best to serve His standards for living. The power of this world is short lived, it is temporary and it has been proven to me time and again that I waste my energy when I put my trust in it. I have a duty to Him to not have too heavy a hand on the things of this world.

This morning in the scriptures He reminded me again that He is in charge, but if I give allegiance or show priority to anything other than Him first it will become a snare to me. If I do not trust Him, even that mistrust becomes my snare.

My mother passed away from Alzheimer's, after having been bed ridden for seven years, with the last five years being in a fetal position. My father was her devoted caregiver and there were days that I definitely questioned the Lord's decision to keep her with us and not take her home. Psalm 16 became my prayer for my mother and my father. My strength lay only in my ability to accept His boundaries for her and for him.

Blessings come even within the boundaries of sad circumstances. Because of my Mom's illness I got to experience my father at a very personal level. You see, emotionally, my father had always been a very private man. It wasn't until my Mom's illness that I got to see the truly tender side of my father. My father loved every day that he got to be a part of her life. It probably wasn't until about the last year of her life that he was ready to let her go home. God allowed him time to love her and then to give her back to Him, but it took seven years for God to accomplish that gift to my Dad.

My own fear of the future can be my biggest snare. I look about and I wonder some days how all the problems about me will be overcome? How can life be good for me when all about is the potential for sadness and evil. The answer is: IT IS THE WORLD and because I am His I AM NOT OF THIS WORLD.

I am passing through and God makes the boundaries fixed for me. His scripture says: "fixed"—not flexible or with holes, but fixed. Matthew 6:37, when paraphrased says that today holds enough, tomorrow has not come yet and I can do nothing about the past. All my prayers need to be directed toward the events of today, God will take care of tomorrow.

A BEGINNING PLACE FOR PRAYER TODAY:

How easily Father I seek worldly answers to heavenly problems, please forgive me Father and help me to focus on the important gifts You offer and not question the boundaries of this season in my life. You have chosen where I am to be used by You for my good.

This season in my life is not a snare, but an opportunity for me to grow spiritually in Your economy. Help me Father to be more committed to Your perspective of my life than to the world's perspective. Let me see You clearly today and help me Lord to readily accept that I am always safe within Your boundaries. Thank You Father, I love You.

DISCUSSION QUESTIONS FOR TODAY:

1. What are my biggest fears about the place God has allowed me or my loved ones to be in today? Are these fears something I can do anything about? Who is in charge of my life and do I have comfort in that knowledge?

2. Do I spend too much time thinking about the future? Is today slipping away because of my thoughts about the past?

DAY 97

Thomas, because you have seen Me, you have believed. Blessed are those who have not seen and yet have believed. John 20: 29

Reading for today – Exodus 24: 1-8 and Proverbs 19: 23

What do I believe? The Israelites had witnessed first hand the miracles of the Lord over and over again—so they believed in the power of the Lord. If I am a believer I have begun and will continue to collect evidence of God's faithfulness in my life. I have learned that not all of the events of my life make sense at the time I experience them, but when I look at the collective sum of those events I have seen God's hand in all of them.

Believing there is a God takes evidence gathering, but trusting Him and obeying Him is the result of seeing just how perfectly He has worked in the past and knowing that He will continue to sustain me if I will trust and obey Him daily. The disciples were like us, they collected evidence and little by little they began to see Jesus and the power and strength He possessed. Most of all, they began to see that what He represented was peace and love for them individually, which was manifested in the simplicity of His directives. The Israelites also began to see Him in simplistic terms—Rule #1: Do what He tells you and you will be blessed.

In today's world we still have the opportunity to believe in God. We do not see a Moses in operation, but we still can see the fruit of acting upon what we perceive to be the truths we personally need to address in the commandments of the Bible. Our belief is based on the witness of Christ on the cross for our sins and the truths of the Bible. Our faith must take action to grow, so we must act on the conduct that the Bible sets before us. Our mountain, the mountain we go to is the Bible. It is within the pages of His Word that God speaks to us and we listen to His voice and then seek to do what He commands. The doing says we believe and the blessings that follow are the result of doing what we believe.

Doing is the hardest part of believing. Doing usually requires patience and persistence and quite frankly it does not always produce immediate fruit. But, because we believe God is able to work in us for our own good—He does not work on others for us—He works on us—then the things God says He will provide for us and our relationship with Him becomes a personal relationship. Each individual has to be accountable for himself to be blessed by God. Children for instance will not arrive at heaven's gate because their parents were Christians.

Parents are simply the directors of their children's paths until they, the children, turn their paths over personally to God and become believers themselves in Jesus. The Lord used Moses to direct the path of the Israelites, but each of them were responsible for their beliefs by their own deeds before God. Every day as I face challenges it is up to me to answer to the question: "Do I believe in God and His power and do I trust Him and obey Him today?" When I answer this question with a confident "Yes!" then I can expect God to act on my belief.

A BEGINNING PLACE FOR PRAYER TODAY:

Yes, Father, I do believe in You. I thank You for all that You have allowed in my life which has strengthened my belief in You. Let my belief grow so that it will spill out and become a path to affect someone else to want to know You. Thank You for this day and the people I experience in it. Give me wisdom to see that what You have for me is perfect for this season in my life. I put this day at Your feet and thank You for it. In Jesus name I thank You for this day. Thank You.

DISCUSSION QUESTIONS FOR TODAY:

1. Am I in the middle of a situation today that I question the value of or even wish I could eliminate from my life? If I were to look at it from Jesus' perspective, what could be the fruit of it in the long run?

2. When we trust and believe in God are we guaranteed that things will always go our way and be smooth? Why are trials of value any way? Do they have something to do with the commitment or belief that I have in God?

DAY 98

A MAN'S STEPS ARE OF THE LORD; HOW THEN CAN A MAN UNDERSTAND HIS OWN WAY?
PROVERBS 20: 24

READING FOR TODAY – EXODUS 24: 9-13 AND PSALM 25

God appears to Moses, Aaron, Nadab, Abihu, and the seventy elders of Israel as they gather at the base of the mountain. It further says that He did not lay His hands upon them as they ate and drank. This gathering of men was satisfied to sit with Moses in the presence of God and let Moses be the responsible one. Perhaps the general meaning of "He did not lay His hand on them" is that He allowed them to be safe in His presence as they were obedient to be with Moses, but it reminds me of something else. It strikes me as how we generally view our pastors and teachers today.

It seems to me that we are all too often content to let our pastors and teachers go to the mountain, present us with the fruit of their search through the scriptures and then let that satisfy our lives for the coming week. After all, we went to church, aren't we Christians of the highest order? "He did not lay His hand on them", why? Could it be He saw their hearts were committed to Moses: their trust was in the leadership of Moses, and not God, not yet anyway?

Unless we personally search those same scriptures that our pastors and favorite Bible teachers search we are not getting the real banquet—we are just routinely eating at Sunday's dinner table. The worst part of this is that we give ourselves only one meal for the whole week. Bible study groups are a wonderful source of personal accountability, but it isn't really what the Lord wants from us. Fellowship with other believers is most important, but I think God wants us to desire to establish for ourselves a personal relationship with Him. How often do I go to the mountain (prayer) and then just listen for His voice as I search His scriptures for myself?

Even as we read this daily study, if we don't read the scriptures for ourselves and seek their meaning for ourselves personally—we will get nothing of real value. The value of this study doesn't lie in my words, but in your reading of the scripture and then just listening for His voice as you do that reading. When we do the reading God can lay His hand upon us as we find out what He has for us. Because I have seen Him work in the past I can assure you with all confidence He will speak to you in a very personal way.

Sometimes a scripture is presented to us and we are not quite sure what that means, but later on in the day it becomes of value or it is stored for the perfect circumstance in the very near future. We will feel His presence and His guidance as He lays His hand upon us for this day. He only promises us one day at a time. So we need today's inside information and we need it each and every day of our lives as we seek to find our way with Him. Sunday sermons and Bible study groups are wonderful, but nothing can compare to God's hand on us personally everyday day of the week.

A BEGINNING PLACE FOR PRAYER TODAY:

Forgive me Father if my day is so busy that I forget to give You and Your scripture time in my life. Please create in me a desire to see You each day before I start off on "my" busy schedule. What vision do You have for me this day? How do You want me to spend this day? What is Your plan for this day? Awaken my heart to You, Father and give me Your strength and wisdom to rise to the needs of this day. Please bless me with Your presence all day. Thank You Father, I love You.

DISCUSSION QUESTIONS FOR TODAY:

1. Why is it important for me to have a daily devotional time reading a portion of scripture?

2. Has God ever given me a scripture for a particular day? What was the scripture and how did He use it in my life?

DAY 99

WAIT ON THE LORD, AND KEEP HIS WAY, AND HE SHALL EXHALT YOU TO INHERIT THE LAND. PSALM 37: 34

READING FOR TODAY– EXODUS 24: 14-18, PSALM 37: 1-6 AND PSALM 138: 7-8

When was the last time I waited on the Lord for six days and then sat at His feet for forty days and nights getting His direction for my life? For the most part, short quick prayers are the routine of the day and an expectation of short quick answers is what we desire.

Even Moses used for his people "the phone instead of the throne experience" when he told his followers: "Indeed, Aaron and Hur are with you. If any man has a difficulty, let him go to them". Yes, they were babies in their faith, but even today we run to counselors when we should go to God first.

Solid answers to problems take time and perseverance. Time and perseverance are the two hardest words we have to deal with in the human experience known as life. Sometimes there are no immediate answers to things—we have to just wait and watch. When our daughter- in-law was waiting for her rotation assignments in the lottery at medical school, she was one of 37 students out of a class of 250 who didn't get any of her choices and then had to enter the lottery again. It was probably her first tearful conversation with me as my daughter- in- law.

Our son was a brand new police officer in the state she was attending school in and it looked like she would be going out of state by herself for the next year because of her school and his new position. They would be separated for an entire year. I swallowed hard and said what I believed, but simultaneously I prayed that the Lord was doing what I believed He always did. My words were: *"The Lord has a plan and I don't know what it is, but I'm sure He'll work it out for your good. Dry your tears and pray and we'll do the same!"* And that is just what we did and God worked on the problem.

Sara re-entered the lottery by choosing as her first choice a prestigious hospital assignment that had not been filled in another state and got it. Meanwhile she let others know she was looking for a swap so she could stay in the area with her husband. The Lord provided another student who wanted her assignment and asked to trade with her offering just what she needed to stay near her husband.

It took time (weeks) and perseverance, but Sara got her needs met by God and the truth of God's faithfulness was brought home to Sara in a powerful way. Sometimes we don't understand what the Lord has allowed in our lives, but faith says, "I will wait on the Lord because I have committed my way to Him." Sara's first rotation assignment turned out to be excellent and in the city where her husband worked. God helped to confound the system by giving Sara wisdom and most importantly, the peace to let God work. Blessings upon blessings, Sara got just what she needed and more!

Inheriting the land may not mean that something good will come of today's problems today. It more than likely will mean you will have the peace and wisdom of God to wait while evil or destructive forces in your life move to their end. Having peace and a lack of anxiety or frustration over the things we cannot change is "inheriting the land." The problem, though appearing out of our control, is under control because we can live with it, for however long it takes, because God can will His strength into our lives through His Holy Spirit.

> *"BECAUSE HE HAS SET HIS LOVE UPON ME, THEREFORE I WILL DELIVER HIM; I WILL SET HIM ON HIGH, BECAUSE HE HAS KNOWN MY NAME." PSALM 91: 14*

Waiting is possible only because "we know His name". No power or strength on earth is greater than His. He alone creates in us daily the miracle of peace in our lives. Peace is His greatest miracle and gift to us. When I cast my care at His feet He delivers me into a place of peace that defies all human logic. If I wait on Him, He will give me what I need and I will be richer than richest man in all the earth!

A BEGINNING PLACE FOR PRAYER TODAY:

Dear Father, forgive me for not waiting on You as I ought to. Please keep me from running from place to place to find answers and solutions for my problems. Help me to settle my heart by going to You first with my problems. Let me quickly cast all my care on You and then wait for You to work on my behalf. I desire your wisdom and perspective on all the aspects of my life. Please guard my heart and give me liberally of Your miracle of peace; thank You Father for Your love and support.

DISCUSSION QUESTIONS FOR TODAY:

1. What is the greatest benefit of turning over the "out of control things" in my life to the Lord?

2. Has the Lord ever surprised me by taking the scary things of my life and making them a blessing? Describe that experience.

DAY 100

AS IN WATER FACE REFLECTS FACE, SO A MAN'S HEART REVEALS THE MAN. PROVERBS
27:19

READING FOR TODAY– EXODUS 25: 1-8, PSALM 71:3 AND JOSHUA 1:9

"You will take my offering from anyone who gives it with a willing heart. And
let them make me a sanctuary that I may dwell among them." What is the ultimate
offering we give? And, what is the spirit we should give it in and what kind of sanctuary
will it build?

Consider the concept of setting something material aside, and then giving it to the
Lord. Set aside the concept of a building as a sanctuary. Now, I must ask myself what
gifts am I willingly giving to God? And because I set aside those gifts for Him have I not
discovered that He has become my sanctuary? He becomes a safe place, a place of peace
and harmony, a place where I am accepted just as I am; that is my personal sanctuary and
quite simply that is my personal relationship with God.

We do not have to go to a building to have a sanctuary to dwell in with God. His
presence in our lives is our sanctuary. One of my favorite pastors, Chuck Smith, once
said, "If you came to church this morning to be in the presence of God I need to tell you
that you were in His presence the moment you opened your eyes this morning. He is
always where you are!" If we have a willing heart then we have a place to dwell with
Him and that heart is the sanctuary of God.

Separation from God is never because God moved away from us; it is because we
have moved away from Him. My willing heart is my simple act of prayer. The line of
communication is always open, but I must open it daily. My ears hear if I am silent in
His presence. Asking is easy, hearing an answer sometimes takes searching the
scriptures and waiting to see the evidence of each days happenings. Sometimes it takes
days and even weeks of happenings to put an answer together, but one thing is for certain
God wants to dwell with me and give me peace.

The Israelites were being drawn day by day into a more mature faith—so was
Moses for that matter. God knew they would feel safe with a structure to dwell in so He
would tell them to build a sanctuary and get them used to the idea that they could come
there and be in His presence. We too need the concept of a sanctuary for a gathering
place to dwell with Him, but hopefully by now, we have realized that wherever we are He
is. Throughout the day as we live our lives He is there. If all the sanctuaries in the world
were to be destroyed He would still be with us. We would only need to bring our gift of
prayer and our willing heart and His sanctuary would be open to us.

God knows us because He knows our hearts. Our hearts are either set toward God
or they are set toward the world. The secure sanctuary rests always with the pure in heart
for as Matthew 5:8 says, "Blessed are the pure in heart for they shall see God."

Moses went up on the mountain to see God and God invites all of the Israelites to feel His presence if they will give of themselves freely and help Him build a sanctuary for their mutual dwelling place. God doesn't desire to dwell with just the especially "gifted" believer, He desires to dwell with all of us and He desires to be our sanctuary. Now the question remains: Do I have a willing heart toward God?

A BEGINNING PLACE FOR PRAYER TODAY:

Lord, thank You for this day. Open my heart and make it Your sanctuary. I desire to speak with You today and to see You work in my life and the lives of others. Please take my eyes off of myself and let me see everything of importance around me. You have given so much to me, help me to give back the things other people around me need. Help me to use all that I have to create a sanctuary for You in my life so I can dwell with You all the days of my life. Thank You Father for all Your loving care.

QUESTIONS FOR TODAY:

1. Have I ever thought of my heart as the sanctuary of God? What does this mean to me?

2. When have I experienced separation from God? Is that even possible?

DAY 101

O LORD, YOU ARE MY GOD. I WILL EXALT YOU, I WILL PRAISE YOUR NAME, FOR YOU HAVE DONE WONDERFUL THINGS; YOUR COUNSELS OF OLD ARE FAITHFULNESS AND TRUTH. ISAIAH 25: 1

READING FOR TODAY– EXODUS 25: 9 – 22, JEREMIAH 32: 19 AND PROVERBS 16: 20

AND THERE I WILL MEET WITH YOU, AND I WILL SPEAK WITH YOU FROM ABOVE THE MERCY SEAT, FROM BETWEEN THE TWO CHERUBIM WHICH ARE ON THE ARK OF THE TESTIMONY, ABOUT EVERYTHING WHICH I WILL GIVE YOU IN COMMANDMENT TO THE CHILDREN OF ISRAEL. (EXODUS 25:22)

Look carefully at the heart of God through this verse; I will meet with you, I will speak with you. Where does He place us? He places us between two angels for our protection. How does He judge us? He judges us on the seat of mercy. And why does He put us in this position? He does this so He can give us the commandments we need.

Has He left any need unmet? By His very nature God has no plans but to protect and care for us. It is so easy to get caught up in the worries of the day, but God has them all covered. Nothing can happen to us that He does not allow. We have His protection, His guidance and His care; we are so well taken care of. Non-Christians are on their own; they think they're in charge and they are, but praise God we don't have to be!

As believers, we have a God who plans our days and knows what He desires for us so that He will cause us to thrive in all the areas of need in our lives. We simply have to sit on the mercy seat and listen. His mercy allows us to be free of all fear about the things we have done or said. His forgiveness covers everything.

Simplicity is the most attractive part of Christianity for me. Christianity is being responsible to God, listening to Him and obeying Him and then being blessed by Him for no other reason than He loves me. How much simpler can life be? We complicate life with the WHAT IFS and God simplifies it with I AM WITH YOU ALWAYS, EVERYWHERE YOU GO. The Ark of Testimony is my life based on the commandments of God; I sit with His protection and His mercy. What more do I need to add to this? The answer is that I can add nothing more—HE IS COMPLETE FOR ALL MY NEEDS!

The Ark of Testimony was portable. It went everywhere and covered all emergencies. My God is portable; He is everywhere I need Him to be. That is absolutely marvelous to me. Nothing I do will change His availability to me. Nothing I say will ever be a shock to Him, for He alone understands me. A friend, a mate, nothing can be better than a conversation with the Lord, for He alone understands me and knows my heart and I can never fail to find His love for me, but I can fail a friend or a mate or be failed by them for they are human, God is not. Faithfulness and truth are always waiting for me if I go to the Lord for my daily bread.

A BEGINNING PLACE FOR PRAYER TODAY:

Thank You Father that You are always with me. I need only to turn to You to feel Your presence. I need only ask and You will give me forgiveness and newness of life even when I don't deserve it. You love me and You seek to show me Your ways every day. Please keep my heart before You this day. Make me worthy of Your love and help me to be the servant You need me to be this day. Thank You Father for Your love. I love You Lord; You are too marvelous for me to even comprehend.

DISCUSSION QUESTIONS FOR TODAY

1. Why is a conversation with the Lord much more valuable than a conversation with a therapist, a friend or a mate?

2. What does the Mercy Seat represent to us?

DAY 102

AND GOD IS ABLE TO MAKE ALL GRACE ABOUND TOWARD YOU; THAT YE, ALWAYS HAVING ALL SUFFICIENCY IN ALL THINGS, MAY ABOUND TO EVERY GOOD WORK. II CORINTHIANS 9: 8

READING FOR TODAY– EXODUS 25: 23-30, ISAIAH 58: 10-11 AND COLOSSIANS 3:23, 24

The table to be constructed for the Israelites temple was beautiful in design, but also portable and functional. All the vessels on the table were made for pouring—all the dishes, pans, pitchers and bowls. The vessels were to be made of pure gold—an element that is tried and purified by fire.

Our faith, if it is to be valuable to the Lord, must be portable and functional. If it sits quietly at home and does nothing it is not portable, it serves no purpose, no matter how well made the foundation. Our faith must move out of our homes and our hearts and out into the real world and real life situations to be tested and proven and most importantly to inspire others to seek after their own faith in Christ. A portable faith means it is active and functional—it serves real life situations and has visible purpose for us and for those we encounter.

The vessels on the table were to be made of pure gold. We are the vessels of the Lord's Table. He will purify us through daily life experiences and over time He will make us as pure gold. Fiery trials produce pure gold and we are admonished to think it not strange when we experience tribulation. We can expect it, because through suffering we learn that "suffering produces perseverance; perseverance, character; and character, hope." (Romans 5: 3-4) Each of us needs these qualities to be of service to God, others and ourselves. We are trusted by others if we have character stronger than what the world has to offer. Our perseverance not only produces admirable character, but hope for all to see and be inspired by. We are different from the world because we have a hope in something other than ourselves or manmade institutions. Through service we become the peculiar people God sets upon a hill as a light for the world.

Every vessel that Christ fills with His Holy Spirit is meant only for pouring, not for storing. There are different types of vessels on the table, but they are all made for pouring. Pouring is service—no matter what the vessels are or what they hold they must be able to pour out their contents. Every Christian is blessed with different gifts, i.e. the essence of their lives, and those gifts can either glorify the individual or be a love gift that glorifies the Lord who gave it to us as we share it. How am I pouring out the spirit of God on other people today? Am I storing up my talents or am I sharing them? Is my hand so full of blessings that I choose not to release them? Can God refill this vessel if I refuse to pour freely so He can replace it with new wine?

A BEGINNING PLACE FOR PRAYER TODAY:

Lord, please help me to think of myself as a blessing for others today. Help me to pour out everything You have given me so that I might be able to comfort, aid or come alongside those who are in need. Also Lord, help me not to be covetous of other people's gifts. Let me rejoice in the gifts of others and give me a desire to be inspired and inspire others to service so that the gospel may be spread abroad. Thank You that You have chosen me to be Your vessel. Help me to give You joy as You observe my service for You. Thank You Father for all your blessings.

DISCUSSION QUESTIONS FOR TODAY:

1. What are the ministries I serve in and why is it important to serve with a joyful attitude? If I am lacking joy in the ministry that I have chosen is it now time to start out fresh on a new ministry? How do I begin to make a change?

2. Why is it important to take an honest inventory of our talents and the ways they should be used? It is false humility to say I have no gifts and perhaps even selfish because we do not use our gifts for Christ?

DAY 103

BELOVED, LET US LOVE ONE ANOTHER; FOR LOVE IS OF GOD; AND EVERYONE THAT LOVETH IS BORN OF GOD, AND KNOWETH GOD. HE THAT LOVETH NOT KNOWTH NOT GOD; FOR GOD IS LOVE. JOHN 4: 7, 8

READING FOR TODAY– EXODUS 25: 31-40 AND I CORINTHIANS 13: 1-8A, 13

Am I a lamp stand for Jesus? Do people even know I am His? A lamp stand sheds light and therefore represents the love of God. It is there to help people find their way in a dark place and we know there is much darkness all around us today. Man can be surrounded by so much darkness that he cannot find light unless a lamp stand is provided for him. We need lamp stands all around us every day in every corner of our world and only Christians can be those lamp stands because our source of power is God and He never runs out of energy.

The energy source of the lamp stand is God's unfailing love for us. All we are required to do is to plug into Him and let Him work in us to make us more loving. Love never fails it says in I Corinthians 13. And, it also says in I John 4:10-12: BELOVED, IF GOD SO LOVED US, WE OUGHT ALSO TO LOVE ONE ANOTHER.

It seems to me that the most important starting place for a lamp stand to shed its' light should be in our homes. According to scripture, we are to love God first, then our mates and then our children. Light needs to be shed abroad, but getting it spread out too soon, before our homes are adequately lit can cause problems. Make sure the lamp stand shines brightly at home first. If it shines at home first, we have met the most basic requirement and then we can branch out letting all the bowls of the lamp stand be shed abroad. Look first at your mate and then look to your children. Do they know they are loved? When the light is on at home it is time to extend that light to family, then friends, co-workers and bosses and then to strangers.

How we shed light is unique to each of us. Thankfully, all our life experiences, our interests and our trials are not the same. So…..God covers a lot ground with just the variety of His followers because we are so varied in lifestyles and experiences. We need not worry about whether we are to be uniform and match the other lamp stands, each one of us is unique; just be His light, that's the primary thing!

Sometimes the most obvious place that light is needed is the one that is the hardest to reach, but if I pray for perseverance in one of these troubled places God will honor that. When home is not perfect, it is not an excuse to not go out in the world and serve. We can only do the best we can with our home situations, and as long as they are our first priority, we can be assured that God will honor our desires and He will work it out to His satisfaction and He will do it in His own timing.

It also seems to me that when we focus on others we're much healthier spiritually and emotionally. If I am not so consumed with self, I will be much happier. To remember that I am a work in progress as Philippians 1:6 says, gives me confidence just to go about the business of loving others and letting God love me.

HE THAT HATH MY COMMANDMENTS, AND KEEPTH THEM, HE IT IS THAT LOVETH ME; AND HE THAT LOVETH ME SHALL BE LOVED OF MY FATHER, AND I WILL LOVE HIM AND WILL MANIFEST MYSELF TO HIM. JOHN 14: 21

A BEGINNING PLACE FOR PRAYER TODAY:

Thank You for how much you love me Father. Lord help me to love those closest to me. Help me to seek a better understanding of the irregular people in my life by praying for those who aggravate and hurt me the most. Show me the needs of those I can barely tolerate.

Let me shine light in the hard places instead of moving out where it is easy and personally rewarding. Please help me though to always love You first and to keep my heart pure in Your sight. Thank You Father for all the opportunities You provide throughout the day—keep me alert and keep a smile on my face so that I can be approachable. Thank You Father, for this day filled with all its new opportunities and hope.

DISCUSSION QUESTIONS FOR TODAY:

1. Are there people in my life I need to pour out the love of God on and yet they hurt me or infuriate me so much that I just keep my distance? What is my responsibility in this situation and how can I be used? What do I need to ask God to provide for me so that I can successfully serve Him?

2. How can I get my attitude in line with God, so that I can be a lamp stand? What attitude is closing me off from serving Him? Do I need to ask for His forgiveness right now?

DAY 104

IF YOU HAVE ANY ENCOURAGEMENT FROM BEING UNITED WITH CHRIST, IF ANY COMFORT FROM HIS LOVE, IF ANY FELLOWSHIP WITH THE SPIRIT, IF ANY TENDERNESS AND COMPASSION, THEN MAKE MY JOY COMPLETE BY BEING LIKE-MINDED, HAVING THE SAME LOVE, BEING ONE IN SPIRIT AND PURPOSE. PHILIPPIANS 2: 1 AND 2

READING FOR TODAY– EXODUS 26: 1-30, JOHN 14: 21, I JOHN 1:5-7.

Can you believe how detailed God has made the instructions for setting up the tabernacle? Every corner of the tabernacle has specific instructions for set up. The framework is strong, well designed and the end product will be a tabernacle that man can set up wherever he roams. God has afforded it protection from the elements with a covering of goat hair, rams skin and badger skin. He desires no elements to obscure the holiness of the inner sanctum of His holiness. This tabernacle is to be the dwelling place of God—secure, comfortable and safe. Our churches today should be that kind of place. Every man, woman or child who enters should be able to be secure, comfortable and safe within its' structure. How often we have created environments that are beautiful, but not comfortable or safe?

Our new and even our old believers run from some churches, not to them, because they do not offer them peace and safety. The people who make up the church are actually its' framework. Each individual or group of individuals should provide the comfort of a church for its visitors and members. Our large group gatherings magnify the praise of the Lord, but our small groups should, as in a prayer groups or a home fellowships, inspire security, confidentiality and safety for the hurting.

The freedom to be who we are takes place in small groups that have secure walls of confidentiality and love. Our small groups should be covered over with truth for all who enter. No matter what is shared by the believer, he should be assured that he will always find light in the group. Truth without love, however, has become man's unfortunate adaptation of the church. In Christ there is no condemnation, but that is not always true of the church body. Unfortunately we must be careful that man does not twist or interpret scripture until it looks like the pharisaical times of Jesus' day.

A church should be as safe as the tabernacle of old. The principle of "let he who is without sin cast the first stone" should prevail. Compassion has become a lost art in some places. Pastors and lay people alike do not always listen, nor do they always give sound advice because they deal in their own limited experience and are not diligent to pray and seek scripture for God's leading. We should not be afraid to say: "I don't have an answer right now. I will search the scriptures and let's search the scriptures together."

Dealing with sin can sometimes be the place where the church hides its' head in the sand or worse, has blanket answers and no compassion. For instance, Christians who are facing divorce can be given harsh and even destructive counsel because those counseling have only one aim: "Save Christian marriages no matter what!" On the surface this looks like a righteous pursuit, but it can be a very limited narrow view of the scripture: "God hates divorce!". No matter what the circumstances, no matter how harmful or even potentially dangerous, poor advice can be given when the counselor has already made up his mind to the subject and the outcome. I have actually heard lay counselors and pastors say: "Suffering is part of life; this is your cross to bear." These same people do not want to hear about the long term, life altering affects of an alcoholic, a drug abuser, a wife beater or a child abuser, because they have already made up their minds and they will only counsel to "stay in the home, we cannot counsel you to leave!" Sometimes the stakes are too high for everyone involved, the Christian has no alternative. God knows the sadness and the destruction of divorce, that's why He hates it, but He does allow divorce because He loves us. He wants us spiritually and emotionally healthy. He certainly does not want us living ungodly lives surrounded by sin as the victim of a mate or a relative.

We have to be so careful how we quote scripture. Standing on a scripture out of context or one that has not been thoroughly researched with other scriptures to support our interpretation is dangerous. However, we are also not to soften scripture. I believe that homosexuality is the most blatant tool of the devil in our churches today. We can show compassion for the homosexual, we can love, encourage and pray for him or her as they struggle with change, and even fail and repent and try again, but we cannot accept it as an acceptable form of behavior. Sin is sin, wife beating, child abuse and homosexuality, along with countless other sins, are not acceptable forms of behavior for Christians. Hard as it is for us to face—toxic Christians develop in our churches when the pursuit of loving unconditionally is thrown out the window in favor of legalism. God loves us and He has set His scriptures as the framework for His church, but they are not to be used as tools to beat up the sheep.

Safety, love and truth are God's desire for His church. Once sin is identified, it must be dealt with in a way that allows the sinner to confess, find help in changing his ways and given prayer and encouragement so that the sin can be eradicated by God. If sin is causing harm and cannot be eliminated then the victim should be given aid to protect him from the sinner. Ultimately, the scripture framework of the tabernacle is two pronged—it is first loving and then accountable and responsible in its declarations and actions. There is a great need among all of us within the church to be loving. I think it is incredibly important to be merciful and compassionate toward one another—remember there may come a day when we ourselves will need that mercy and compassion!

A BEGINNING PLACE FOR PRAYER TODAY:

Father because I am yours; hold me to accountability where Your scripture is concerned. Let me speak truth when I am asked or when I encounter sin. But...most of all please give me your love and your compassion for all those you set in my path this day. Lord, please help me be productive and not toxic. Help me to help others remain strong in their faith and take away any judgmental spirit that is not of You. I want my judgments to be wisdom from You, not personal preferences or twisted scripture so I have pat answers for everything. Please watch over my heart and the words of my mouth this day. Thank You Father for Your scriptures.

DISCUSSION QUESTIONS FOR TODAY:

1. When I counsel other people, what should I use as the basis for instruction or guidance? Why is the Bible the only place for wisdom?

2. Do I need to check my motives before I give advice? Do other people always need my advice? When should I be silent in my opinions? When I am silent, what should I be doing in place of sharing my wisdom? Why?

DAY 105

NOT BY WORKS OF RIGHTEOUSNESS WHICH WE HAVE DONE, BUT ACCORDING TO HIS MERCY HE SAVED US, BY THE WASHING OF REGENERATION, AND RENEWING OF THE HOLY GHOST; WHICH HE SHED ON US ABUNDANTLY THROUGH JESUS CHRIST OUR SAVIOR. TITUS 3:5, 6

READING FOR TODAY– EXODUS 26: 31-37, II CORINTHIANS 5: 17 AND ROMANS 6:14-16

The veil of blue, purple and scarlet which God directed the Israelites to make as a separation between them and God's holiest dwelling of His presence is for us today Jesus. Not one of us can stand in the presence of God without Christ as our veil or covering. We are forgiven because we have accepted Christ as the propitiation for our sins. We stand without spot or wrinkle before God because of our acceptance of Christ as our Savior. He is the veil that protects us from God's wrath.

Sin is an ugly thing and the veil covers it if we come to the altar and place our broken hearts upon it daily. The veil can separate us from our sin and therefore we can communicate with God freely. We are not immune to sin because we are believers. Our very nature is sinful because we are human, not gods. The walk of faith is a constant communion with Jesus to keep our hearts pure. Rising with Jesus above fear, anxiety and failure to do and say what will give us the peace of Christ is to be our daily walk. Our walk with Christ is not a walk without trial, life is a series of trials, but without the fellowship of Jesus we would struggle mightily to keep the laws of God.

The laws of God are the guidelines of the moral man, but a Christian is much more than just a moral man. We are helpless without Christ; because He lives in our hearts we wear Him, like the veil, as a suit of protection. We stand behind Christ, He covers us completely. It is only when I try to step out and remove myself from His covering that I am vulnerable to sin and attack from the enemy. Hidden in Christ I live and have my being—apart from Him I am nothing and I am defenseless.

Truth is the lamp stand that sits near the table and illuminates the things I place on that table. All the things I put on the table before God, Jesus will be the veil over, and He will allow the light to shine and make me pure again. The best thing I can put on the table is a broken and contrite heart and Jesus can work with that offering. How freeing it is to know that He will be my advocate, not my works or my words. If I stand before that veil He gives me the truth I need for my daily life and I do not need to fear that I must perform perfectly or be cut off from His presence. He is always with me and nothing can separate me from the love of God in Christ Jesus (Romans 8: 38, 39).

A BEGINNING PLACE FOR PRAYER TODAY:

Thank You Father that You put Your Son, Jesus, upon a cross to die for me. My sin is not before you because Jesus covers me. Thank You that You love me and mark my path for this day. Please help me to not be tricked by the enemy into fear or anxiety. Only You can give me a pure heart and pure wisdom to meet the trials of this day and I desire to praise all of Your blessing toward me. Please let my praises tumble freely from my heart and mouth. Thank You Father for Jesus. Thank You for this new day.

DISCUSSION QUESTIONS FOR TODAY:

1. Are there things I need to put on the altar today, but I am afraid to let go of them? Why would I be afraid to put anything on the table?

2. What would life be like without the covering of Jesus over me? What would my relationship be like without Jesus? Can you recall what life was like before you met Him?

DAY 106

FOR THE LORD GOD IS A SUN AND SHIELD: THE LORD WILL GIVE GRACE AND GLORY; NO GOOD THING WILL HE WITHHOLD FROM THEM THAT WALK UPRIGHTLY. PSALM 84: 11

READING FOR TODAY– EXODUS 27: 1-8, HEBREWS 4: 16 AND EPHESIANS 2:20-22/

Through these verses in Exodus this morning we see God's design for the altar that is to be built for the tabernacle. Sacrifices can be burned here before God for offerings of praise, thankfulness or even forgiveness. Rituals of material sacrifice no longer became necessary when Jesus became the perfect sacrificial lamb, and so even though rituals are historically interesting to us, it still seems a foreign practice. But, what would you do for God if there were no Jesus in your life experience? Can you imagine yourself as an early believer in God who wanted to please Him?

The altar would become the natural element of worship for you. You would want to give something back to God in the form of reverence and respect for Him. We do that with tithing today in our churches. We know that the great commission says to "go into the world and preach the gospel", so we give our monies to missionaries to accomplish this goal. We also give our time and energy teaching Sunday school, visiting the sick, caring for the needs of the poor and sponsoring and designing outreach programs. All of these things are our modern day sacrifices.

I think God used sacrifice at the altar as a way of creating within new believers a sense of His power, strength and protection in their lives. He knew that He must keep them constantly aware of His presence or they would wander away into other pursuits. It was important to give them a head knowledge that would eventually become the heart knowledge of His existence in their lives. Similarly, today we go to church each Sunday and in all the various worship styles of the Christian faith, we keep alive this reverence for God and His son Jesus. Our prayers to God are heightened by the existence of the Holy Spirit as He leads us through our prayers and the study of His Word, but the Israelites didn't have that dimension in their lives.

However, we are not too different from the Israelites in that the Holy Spirit often has to re-order our priorities. We have the Word of God to search and to seek after for the answers to our problems, just as they had the altar, but we can and do get side-tracked. We too should be thanking Him daily for our blessings, but we get lost in the worries of today. God wanted these new believers to dwell on the concept of His presence in their lives until it became a fact of faith. He's working in each of our lives that way today too.

No experience in our lives happens without a purpose. God was setting a framework of experience in the building of that altar in the first tabernacle. Today He builds experiences in our lives that lead our hearts and minds to altars of conscious worship and the awareness of His presence. God still desires to communicate with us daily, just as He wanted to communicate daily with the Israelites. There is not a day or an hour that a believer cannot turn his focus to the things of God, if he chooses to exercise what is available to him. Each step we take toward our God heightens our awareness of Him in our life and our faith can grow in new and precious ways. Our daily experiences are altars that we build to God if we allow Him to be in them. All the altars we build are uniquely fitted for our needs and mark the presence of God in our lives. What is the altar God is allowing you to build today and what are the altars you have been a part of most recently? God wants you to practice your awareness of Him every day.

A BEGINNING PLACE FOR PRAYER TODAY:

Lord, heighten my awareness of You. Point me toward scripture and prayer that communicates what I am to reflect upon so that I am pleasing in Your sight. Open my mind and heart to experiences about me which can cause me to seek Your specific plans for my life. Let me value everything in my life as a gift from You, even when I don't understand it. And please Father, help me to use the time of this day in a way that will honor You and all Your gifts in my life.

DISCUSSION QUESTIONS FOR TODAY:

1. How can I become more in tune with God? What are the things that keep me from letting God be a part of my life?

2. How specific should I be when I pray: What kinds of things does God want to be a part of in my life: Am I limiting God?

DAY 107

ONE THING I HAVE DESIRED OF THE LORD, THAT WILL I SEEK; THAT I MAY DWELL IN THE HOUSE OF THE LORD ALL THE DAYS OF MY LIFE, TO BEHOLD THE BEAUTY OF THE LORD AND TO INQUIRE IN HIS TEMPLE. PSALM 27: 4

READING FOR TODAY– EXODUS 27: 9-19, PSALM 40:3, PROVERBS 18: 10 & ISAIAH 26:3

The courtyard was the gathering place of God for His people. Obviously, with these detailed instructions, it is apparent that God wanted His people in His presence on a regular basis. The dwelling place for the Israelite was the temple, but we as believers are a little different in that the dwelling place of God is within us. We are told by scripture that we are the temple of God and because of the presence of the Holy Spirit we are inhabited by Him. God is always dwelling with us because we are the gathering place; nothing else is needed for us to be in His presence.

The dwelling place of God within us is both active and alive or it is empty and seldom visited. Believers can seek to dwell with God all the days of their lives or upon occasion. I believe that the beauty of the Lord in our lives is in direct relationship to how much time we dwell with Him. It's a necessary place in time of trouble, but is it a necessary place in time of pleasure and ease in our lives?

To keep the light of that temple burning and visited often we need to keep an awareness that all the aspects of life are under the control of God. No matter where our interests lie they are always of interest to God. He wants to offer us a quiet place to sort out the good and evil of the day. He wants us to have a complete understanding of life in His perspective; lives separate from anything the world can imagine because we are not of this world, we are just passing through. Nothing in the world's economy can keep us in perfect peace, only the courtyard of the temple of God provides that perfect peace.

Perfect peace does not depend on life being perfect or peaceful. Perfect peace is our choice to let God reign supreme over everything—even the small details of our lives. Life seen through God's eyes is simple and straight forward, life in the world's eyes is ME in charge of everything. I have learned that "in charge" only works when I understand what is going on.

Upon occasion I do understand the order of things and my part, but there are some things in life that defy logic and are so painful that I cannot be in charge. During these times, I am especially grateful I have a place to hide in, for in His courtyard He will lift up my head above my enemies. No matter what the enemy does, His covering protects me, and He makes me stronger and gives me hope because He has a plan for me. (Jeremiah 29:11)

In His courtyard, He hears my cries and He gives me comfort. When the world hands me worries God hands me mercy. His mercy is an escape to a quiet uncomplicated place where I am loved, forgiven and rejuvenated. Because of His courtyard, I have a strong tower to run to and a counselor to ask questions of, but most importantly He is a counselor with answers to meet all my needs. I will never seek His face and not find Him. My job is just to run to Him and His job is to have everything I need covered and put in perspective—His perspective.

I can sing His praises freely when I have freely allowed Him to dwell in me. There will be wonderful evidence of His Spirit in my life if I dwell in His temple daily. He will always be there for me. He will always keep the storm at bay, while I get warm and rested in His courtyard. Then, I can go back to my responsibilities refreshed and not overwhelmed by them? Have I forgotten where my high tower is because I have not come to dwell in His courtyard lately? Perhaps today is the day I need to run in?

A BEGINNING PLACE FOR PRAYER TODAY:

Lord, You are so remarkable. I cannot begin to fathom how much You love me. Whatever I need, You can supply. Why do I not run to You first before I try to figure it all out? Father, please help me to stay focused on You. I need You in my life every moment of this day. Help me to dwell in Your temple—give me Your perspective. Please help me to keep the world at bay and focus on Your mercy and grace. Thank You for Your love for me. Forgive my anxiety and these silly mind games I play—keep me on Your path today by holding my mind and heart in Your presence. Please raise my awareness, teach my heart to rest and my voice to sing Your praises. Thank You Father, I love You.

FOR THUS SAITH THE LORD GOD, THE HOLY ONE OF ISRAEL; IN RETURNING AND REST SHALL YE BE SAVED; IN QUIETNESS AND IN CONFIDENCE SHALL BE YOUR STRENGTH. Isaiah 30: 15

DISCUSSION QUESTIONS FOR TODAY:

1. Am I running into or away from the courtyard when I need answers to my problems? Who do I run to for answers? Is it working?

2. Why should I desire quietness and confidence in my life?

DAY 108

WHEN THOU GOEST, IT SHALL LEAD THEE; WHEN THOU SLEEPEST, IT SHALL KEEP THEE; AND WHEN THOU AWAKEST, IT SHALL TALK WITH THEE. FOR THE COMMANDMENT IS A LAMP AND THE LAW IS LIGHT; AND REPROOFS OF INSTRUCTION ARE THE WAY OF LIFE. PROVERBS 6:22-23.

READING FOR TODAY– EXODUS 27: 20-21, II TIMOTHY 3: 16 AND II PETER 1: 4

Pure oil was used to keep the lamps of the Tent of Meeting burning all through the night. Darkness causes confusion and God wanted His people to live in light with honesty and without fear. God's presence in our lives produces these two benefits. The light of God is pure and that is His Word in our lives. To become partakers in the divine nature of God we must look to His pure light and that light is provided by the pure oil of His Word.

I think a successful walk with the Lord requires three things: determination, direction and discipline. The determination is our choice to serve the Lord and seek His help in every aspect of our lives. This determination comes into power when we become wholly submitted to Christ and become His servant. From the moment we submit, His power is given to us and also His protection The direction we take to accomplish whatever He has allowed us to be passionate about is then accomplished in us by Him as we study the Word and learn His principles for living. The acting out of those principles becomes our discipline for living. In keeping His Word we are given the promise of being "thoroughly furnished unto all good works".

My Mother recently passed away and as I sought to write a eulogy for her I discovered that she held these three principles all the days of her life. She was a quiet unassuming woman, who served her husband and children diligently, never making statements of what she was about. Quietly, she worked as a servant to all. She was voted Woman of the Year twice by the women of her church and she was never the head of a fellowship or the leader of a Bible study group—she was just always there to do what needed to be done. Her confidence lay in her sense of direction and purpose for living and she did not fear tomorrow because she had upheld God's principles for today.

Discipline is a character element that is required by man to accomplish consistently what God requires of us. Perhaps, in all the areas of our lives this is our major weakness. It is easy to do what must be done when the battle is going well, but it requires great fortitude when life just isn't handing us rewards. We can become discouraged or even give up and that is why the pure oil is so necessary. The pure oil keeps us going through the night of our journey. To be able to open the Bible and see there, first hand, the promises of God becomes the constant reminder to us not to give up and to stay the course and then receive the reward of being thoroughly furnished for all good works.

The simple things of living for a child give him great stability: a Mom and Dad who are there when he needs them, a clean house, warm bed, food on the table, clean clothes and lunches made for school. We often take for granted the simple things of life, but it is important to remember that the small disciplines of life and the accomplishment of them are even more important to our children than our wealth and fame. The pure oil of God requires us to do the simple things first and then surprisingly the big things are also accomplished. When we are disciplined in our nature we will also be trustworthy in the eyes of others. Love is really based on trust and the consistency and safety that it offers. God's love for us never fails; His consistency in His pure oil keeps us thoroughly furnished for all good works. I must never take for granted the opportunity I have here on earth to be vigilant in my pursuit of striving for that mark in this race we call life. I pray one day my God will welcome me with the words: "Well done, good and faithful servant!"

Do you not know that in a race all the runners run, but only one gets the prize? Run in such a way as to get the prize. Everyone who competes in the games goes into strict training. They do it to get a crown that will not last; but we do it to get a crown that will last forever. (I Corinthians 9:24-25) I have fought the good fight, I have finished the race, I have kept the faith. Now there is in store for me the crown of righteousness, which the Lord, the righteous Judge, will award to me on that day (II Timothy 4: 7-8A)

A BEGINNING PLACE FOR PRAYER TODAY:

Dear Father, I thank You for a Mom who taught me Your principles and kept Your principles in the way she lived her life. Let me be an honor to her memory and let me be an honor to Your memory for my children. You have given me pure oil in Your word, please keep me disciplined in my searching of those scriptures so that I do not overlook the small things and in so doing miss the really important things in my life. Thank You, Father that You have taught me that if I stay in Your Word and in fellowship with You I will be "thoroughly furnished for all good works". What a blessing You are to me all the days of my life!

DISCUSSION QUESTIONS FOR TODAY:

1. Have I been taking my responsibilities for granted? Can my children and my husband or wife count on me to be faithful in the little things of life?

2. Have I ever mistakenly given little value to being an excellent parent? If I am not married, how do I value my singleness and my work ethic?

DAY 109

SEE, I HAVE INSCRIBED YOU ON THE PALMS OF MY HANDS; YOUR WALLS ARE CONTINUALLY BEFORE ME. ISAIAH 49: 16

READING FOR TODAY– EXODUS 28: 1-14, PSALM 138 AND PSALM 139: 1-18

One of my very favorite scriptures is Isaiah 49: 16. When life is considerably troubling I recall "I (Jesus, the living God) have inscribed (me) on the palms of My hands." No matter where my life goes or what befalls me He remembers me. Immediately, I do not feel insignificant or alone. When God required of the artisans of Israel to make two engraved stones with the names of the twelve tribes on those stones I could not help but think of that verse.

Our high priest is Christ and He not only bears our names before God as our intercessor before God—He bears them on His hands. The shoulders of a man are strong and he can carry much weight there, but the hands are the personal, loving, touching, and holding part of a man. Can anything be more personal?

As we get older I think we make more lists, so we don't forget what's most important. How precious it is that Jesus looks at His palms and we are there. Like the lists I make so I can continually remember the smaller detail, so God makes a list with Me on it and I am "continually before" Him. Looking at Psalm 139 I see how his hands (verse 5) "are laid upon me" and "Your hand shall lead me, and Your hand shall hold me" (verse 10). When I read this Psalm I am reminded of His love for me, I become more aware that He is not some far away entity, He is real, alive and an active part of my life.

"Your walls are continually before me." Everything that encompasses me—my spouse, my children, my extended family, my job, my friends, all my concerns, my delights and my desires are all me—MY WALLS. He evaluates those continually and He keeps the enemy from coming inside the walls and destroying or causing trouble within those walls. Psalm 138:6 says: "Though the Lord is on high, yet He regards the lowly; yet the proud He knows from afar." It is my job to keep in contact and not become proud. I want Him to be a part of everything; yet if I do not talk to Him He will remain afar.

I desire the works of verse 7 and 8 in Psalm 138 because I don't always know when "my walls" are being attacked and I want that protection for my life and Him constantly working on that protection. Life is so much easier when I take my hands off of the things that concern me and allow God to have "HANDS ON" contact with everything, especially the things I do not understand.

I know it is a great reward to have my name in the Lamb's Book of Life, but I think I treasure just as much that I am also on the palms of His hands. Every day requires so much of me and to know that He is actively apart of this is too wonderful to comprehend, but I like the knowledge of it! My spirit soars because His hands are on me "continually".

A BEGINNING PLACE FOR PRAYER TODAY:

Thank You, Father, for holding me. I do not want a light touch of You in my life. I love the fact that Your hand is "laid upon me". I love that You will protect my walls and all I have to do is allow it. Help me to place all the cares of this day and all the praises of this day at Your feet. Let me not forget who leads me and how personally You will do it because You love me. Thank You that Your thoughts are always with me. All of Your care is too wonderful to comprehend, but Lord with all my heart I want to think on that today and do so every day until I see You face to face. Thank You Father. I love You.

DISCUSSION QUESTIONS FOR TODAY:

1. Do I feel His hands upon me? Can I recall incidences in my life when I really knew He was with me? Record one of those times to share with the group.

2. How can I keep myself from falling into the trap of "feeling" that I am all alone in my troubles? Does scripture play a part in this for me? If so, what scriptures minister to me when I am fearful? Record some of those scriptures.

DAY 110

FINALLY, MY BRETHREN, BE STRONG IN THE LORD AND IN THE POWER OF HIS MIGHT. PUT ON THE WHOLE ARMOR OF GOD, THAT YOU MAY BE ABLE TO STAND AGAINST THE WILES OF THE DEVIL. EPHESIANS 6: 10-11

READING FOR TODAY– EXODUS 28: 15-21, EPHESIANS 6: 11-18 AND JEREMIAH 17:9

In this portion of scripture this morning God instructs Moses to have a breastplate made for Aaron that will be a part of his priestly garment. He refers to it as the breastplate of judgment and on that breastplate He wants the names of the twelve tribes of Israel inscribed. Many beautiful stones adorn this breastplate and I cannot help but speculate that the breastplate must have been heavy as well.

In Ephesians 6 Paul tells us to put on the breast plate of righteousness everyday as our part of service to the Lord. This also is a heavy responsibility, but it must be put on. Aaron, the priest of the Israelites, represents them before God, as Jesus represents us before God. Like Aaron, Jesus wears the breastplate of judgment before God for us and He expects us to wear a breastplate of righteousness before the enemy and in His presence.

Righteousness is the behavior of a man after he has accepted the judgment of God on his life. The breastplate is heavy and it protects his heart. I believe that if God has the heart of a man that he becomes the complete possession of God. Scripture uses the phrase "put on" the breastplate of righteousness and to me that means it is an everyday event and that every day event keeps me safe. When I put His words on my heart each new day, I am protected from all the darts of the enemy for that day. I want my heart of righteousness protected so that my actions will also be righteous in God's sight.

Standing against the enemy is really an everyday event. The truths of God keep us ever ready to stand against evils we will face each new day. God requires me to represent Him in the world and I cannot let my heart be swayed by the sinful nature of the world. The only way I can stand against the enemy is to have my heart pure, covered by His righteousness and then, and only then, can I represent my Lord and Savior well.

Jeremiah 17:9 is a great scripture of warning about the human heart. God's heart is always righteous toward us, but man's heart is deceitful and cannot always be trusted. It is quite possible for our heart to desire something that is not of God. Our own sinful and often subtle interpretation of life can take hold of us if we are not protected by His breastplate.

No matter how intense the battle, God can become my power and strength if I put on His Word each day. I cannot stand against the enemy, I need Jesus everyday to do that for me. I can however, be prepared for the assault, but that is my responsibility. The enemy only gets a foothold when I am not properly prepared for battle. As a wise soldier it is my responsibility to train and store my weapons and have them ready for use because sometimes a battle arrives before I am even aware that I am under siege. It is difficult to fight a battle while you're trying to find your weapons. Constant communication with God is a way of being in constant communication with the general of your own personal war. I do not need the traitor of a deceitful heart in my camp, so I need to keep the camp pure and secured, without God's armor I am defenseless.

A beginning place for prayer today:

Oh, Lord, keep me ever vigilant to be prepared. Don't let me be foolishly relying on my own strength. I need my heart protected. The enemy can come into my heart and cause such confusion and harm. Please help me to settle my spirit with Your Word today so that when the enemy arrives on the scene my heart is already protected with Your righteousness. Thank You that You have given me Your Word so I know what righteousness and evil look like and I am vigilant so that I cannot be easily deceived. And thank You, Father that You forgive me when I am not vigilant. Please make the desire of my heart be to put on Your armor everyday. Thank You, Father, for Your always faithful protection.

Discussion Questions for today:

1. Can I put on the breastplate of God a few times a year and expect to be saved from the enemy's darts? Why is everyday communication with the Lord so important in our lives?

2. What instances can I think of in my own life when evil took me by surprise?

DAY 111

HOWEVER, WHEN HE, THE SPIRIT OF TRUTH, HAS COME, HE WILL GUIDE YOU INTO ALL TRUTH; FOR HE WILL NOT SPEAK ON HIS OWN AUTHORITY, BUT WHATEVER HE HEARS HE WILL SPEAK; AND HE WILL TELL YOU THINGS TO COME. JOHN 16:13

READING FOR TODAY– EXODUS 28:22-30, JOHN 14: 13-18 AND HEBREWS 4: 14-16

Aaron wore a vest which contained two stones, the Urim and Thummin. Wearing these two stones over his heart he went continually before the Lord on behalf of the people of Israel. Today, Jesus is our high priest and He stands on our behalf before God. He is responsible for protecting and directing our lives.

As Christians we are in the unique position of being represented by the Son of God, our Savior, Jesus, and He was once also fully man. He thoroughly understands the nature of man and sits at the right hand of God giving us the light we need, guiding us and ultimately perfecting us so we can one day enter into the presence of God. Without Jesus as our Savior, we would be subject to the judgment of God and this judgment would be void of mercy and grace. Through the Holy Spirit we are given comfort and strength. Jesus and the Holy Spirit work in tandem to promote God's divine intervention in our lives.

The Urim and the Thummin were the medium by which God spoke through the high priest to the tribes of Israel, but we have the Holy Spirit and the scriptures of the Bible to direct us. We no longer need earthly priests or stones to understand what would honor God, the Holy Spirit calls those things into our remembrance whenever we need that direction.

As portable as the tabernacle of God was—so is our Lord. Whenever and for whatever, He is always available to us through the Holy Spirit, but one thing has not changed, we must go to Him to have fellowship with Him. It is important to remember that the time we have for quiet reflection and prayer may be limited, but He is always there for fellowship throughout our day. Jesus is the Spirit who dwells within us and He is always available to us. Anything we ask in His name that will glorify the Father, He will do. (John 14: 13)

The scriptures we have been reading appear to be tedious and repetitive at times, but they are not. They are exact directions for building the Tabernacle of God. He is perfect; His instructions for us are always complete and perfect—He leaves nothing to chance. We could not stand before God on our own, Jesus had to be the perfect sacrifice for us and He guards our place in heaven with the Father.

The Holy Spirit is here to direct us so we can have constant communion with Jesus. God's plan for each of us is tailor made. The perfect pattern for successful living is Jesus as our Savior and the Holy Spirit as our Comforter and Guide—how perfect God is in all the things concerning us!

A BEGINNING PLACE FOR PRAYER TODAY:

Lord, thank You. How can we not succeed with You beside us? Nothing we can plan could ever be as perfect as Your plan for our lives. Open up my heart and let me communicate freely, openly and often with Your Spirit. Please lead me Father; You know where I should go. Give me Your Wisdom for the big and small decisions of this day. Thank You Father that You desire to fellowship with me, not through other people, but through Your Spirit. Help me to remember that I need only call Your name and You will be there. Thank You Father, I love You.

DISCUSSION QUESTIONS FOR TODAY:

1. Why should I check in with God before I make my plans for the day?

2. Why is the Holy Spirit so vital to me?

DAY 112

THERE IS THEREFORE NO CONDEMNATION TO THEM WHICH ARE IN CHRIST JESUS, WHO WALK NOT AFTER THE FLESH, BUT AFTER THE SPIRIT. ROMANS 8:1

READING FOR TODAY– EXODUS 28: 31-35, JOHN 5:24 AND I JOHN 1:9.

Christ's work on the cross is the suit of armor which can never be taken from us once we believe on Him, just as the robe of the priest protected him from the wrath of God and allowed him to seek the face of God as a pure vessel. Jesus is the protection we need before a Holy God when we come to Him at the end of our lives or even in time of need. Our robe is Jesus.

The bells on the hem of the garment sang as the priest went about his work before the altar, but… if they stopped making their song the people knew the priest was dead. Fortunately, we need no bells because condemnation and death are not a part of our relationship with God—our advocate is Christ Jesus. He lives eternally with God and His form of communication with us through the Holy Spirit produces conviction, not condemnation and death.

If I am convicted by the Holy Spirit of a sin in my life I am not condemned. Conviction means that I am convinced of my sin and I must take the step to confess it and ask for forgiveness so that the Lord can do His part to start me off on a new path. This truth is simply stated in the scripture:

IF WE CONFESS OUR SINS, HE IS FAITHFUL AND JUST TO FORGIVE US OUR SINS, AND TO CLEANSE US FROM ALL UNRIGHTEOUSNESS. I JOHN 1:9

Nothing can separate me from the love of God. He made the perfect sacrifice of Jesus to assure I'd be in heaven with Him someday. When I yield myself to God I can become a new instrument of His daily. I do not confess my sins like a lucky charm before God to assure my salvation because my confession of faith in Jesus as my Savior needs only to be done once. However…I do need to get my heart cleaned up everyday just as I bathe every day. And, after that moment in time I need to put on Christ so I can hide in Him for the rest of the day.

The robe is a symbol of what we have as New Testament believers in a living Jesus who now sits at the right hand of God as our covering and protection (Hebrews 12:2). There is great comfort in the fellowship of Jesus through the Holy Spirit. He is not way off somewhere in the by and by. He walks with me every day—guiding, protecting and enlightening me so I can be self-assured that He is in control of my life. Jesus is an active part of me.

A Christian does not have a religion, he has a relationship. An active relationship with Christ is my choice in life. I can also choose to be out in the world unprotected and working on life in my own terms, but doesn't that seem foolish? I like being hidden in Christ and being protected from the evil of this world, how about you?

A beginning place for prayer:

Lord, thank You for covering and protecting every part of my life. Look closely at my heart Father and see if there is any wicked way in me. Father, I want to be a blessing to You. Please help me to bless others by speaking of You often before believers and non-believers alike. Please help me to see the places where I need to give you credit for my blessings and let me boldly share that knowledge with family and friends. I desire to take nothing for granted, for You are the source of all the good things in my life and You are my guarantee of eternal life. Thank You Father for loving me.

Discussion Questions for Today:

1. Read I Peter 1: 3-7. What are the promises I find in this passage?

2. Jesus can only be an active part of my life if I seek Him. Have I noticed any difficulties in this area lately? What part of my life is He being left out of and how can I solve this problem?

DAY 113

BUT THE LORD IS FAITHFUL, WHO SHALL ESTABLISH YOU, AND KEEP YOU FROM EVIL. II THESSALONIANS 3:3

READING FOR TODAY— EXODUS 28: 36-43, ISAIAH 26:3, ROMANS 8:6 AND JOHN 14:27

Interesting, the turban of the priest is marked with a sign that reads "Holiness to the Lord". Everything I think on in this head of mine should be: "Holiness to the Lord". My thoughts cannot be confused or wicked, they must be holy. Perfect peace comes from the mind set on Christ Jesus. If my mind is set on holiness then my heart is not troubled.

No matter how complicated life and people are, my peace lies in my ability to keep my eyes focused on what God has for me today. I cannot control anything—God controls everything. If I fill my head each day with His words and I allow the Holy Spirit to speak to me about what I've read then I can go about my business, being me before Jesus, with peace in my heart. The alternative to peace is confusion and fear. If I am fearful then I lack the wisdom of God. Proverbs 3:5 and 6 reminds me to not lean on my own understanding, but to acknowledge Him and He will direct my path. To get God's wisdom I simply have to ask for it! (James 1: 5)

James 3:16-18 defines wisdom from above as: "pure, peaceable, gentle, and easy to be entreated, full of mercy and good fruits, without partiality and without hypocrisy." When I am unhappy, discouraged or worried I have to search my heart for the root of these emotions, and as I ask God to join me in the search of my heart I can find true wisdom. I need to ask myself: "How am I approaching life today?" Do I dwell on impure thoughts, am I harsh and unbendable in my judgments and so I have no forgiveness and no good works in my life? How much of my thought life is getting in my way because I am partial to my way? How much of my life is lived out doing empty and shallow deeds, but I act as if it is okay and pleasing to God?

In Psalm 139 God says He knows my thoughts. We may be fooling others, but God requires daily, moment by moment housecleaning of the brain so it can function on a holy and spiritual plane. We destroy our lives with inner conversations which are not based on fact. Dialogues can run in our heads over and over again about crazy unsolvable situations like having regrets about the past, something we cannot change, it's done, or fear of the future and we don't even know what the future holds.

Godly wisdom says we are to put our minds toward the tasks of today and put those at the feet of Jesus and let Him take care of them as we do the footwork that seems reasonable and within our abilities to accomplish. If I have the mind of Christ, I respond to life one day at a time, I do not let my mind wander fearfully off into the future nor destructively back to the past to dwell on past mistakes.

I can and am expected to be a good steward of the things in my life, but I need to keep clearly in mind the phrase "if the Lord wills". I need to know in my heart that at any moment my plans for this day or even for my future can change because the Lord wills it to be that way or allows something in my life. Wisely, I am aware that surprising events take place all the time and sometimes I have nothing to do with their conception. I like to think that the best of the surprising events are God guided adventures and the worst of the events are evidence of His comfort and care in my life.

If my mind is set on the acceptance of the control of God in my life then I can be assured that no matter what the event, He will prepare me for the challenge of it. Scripture says He has clothed me properly in His protection and I can therefore put aside my confusion and ask Him to replace it with His wisdom. It is amazing to me how He so perfectly and completely guards my mind and keeps me in His peace when I surrender that mind to Him.

A BEGINNING PLACE FOR PRAYER TODAY:

Thank You Father that You care so much about my mental health. You have thought of everything concerning me and I need not be afraid. I am glad I do not know what the future holds, but I know that You hold the future. I can trust You with everything and let go of everything and You will give me wisdom. Please help me to recognize thoughts that are strictly condemnation from the enemy. Keep me ever aware of negative discussions in my head—they are not of You! You love me and want to prosper my character. Thank You for Your Holy Spirit and the work He performs in me every day. May I be a blessing to You today in everything I do and say.

DISCUSSION QUESTIONS FOR TODAY:

1. What can the Lord accomplish in my life if He is given control and I seek His wisdom concerning all the details of my life?

2. Do I seek God's approval of my plans or do I let God be a part of the plans I have made and am happy to do it my way? How successful have my plans been lately and why do I think the results are what they are?

DAY 114

AND THEY SHALL KNOW THAT I AM THE LORD THEIR GOD WHO BROUGHT THEM UP OUT OF THE LAND OF EGYPT, THAT I MAY DWELL AMONG THEM. I AM THE LORD THEIR GOD. EXODUS 29:46

READING FOR TODAY– EXODUS 29: 1-46

The consecration of Aaron and his sons is very precise, so also is the consecration of the tabernacle. For this time, and until the coming of the Messiah, Israel was to have priests directing the worship of God and making sacrifices on behalf of the people. The Tabernacle was to be the meeting place of God and His Children; His spirit was to dwell there so that He could be their God. They would know where He was and who could approach Him. Through ritual, the priests and the people were made Holy and able to stand before God.

Communion and fellowship for man with God's heart has always been God's desire for His people. Christ was the ultimate and complete instrument of God to provide salvation for His creation and a living advocate for them, but when these scriptures were written this tabernacle and these priests were His only communication with the chosen people. Comfort is always found in a place to go and that comfort and confidence is also bolstered by direct commands of what to do. God accomplishes it here in His directives to Moses.

Seven days a week something was happening to keep the people tuned into God. Today we also need that seven days a week awareness to be strong in our fellowship with Him. One day a week with the teachings of a pastor and the participation of a congregation in praise and worship just isn't enough.

And if it is enough, then I think we can assume we are in charge of our lives and that in itself, to me, is a pretty frightening situation. I cannot and do not wish to make decisions for my life without God's perspective because I want those decisions to honor God's perspective. A pastor has studied for himself the scriptures and his remarks concerning them are simply a jumping off place for each of us. We must never assume the scripture is too hard for us. The Bible is concise and highly profitable and so is God's wisdom for each of us.

ALL SCRIPTURE IS GIVEN BY INSPIRATION OF GOD, AND IT IS PROFITABLE FOR DOCTRINE, FOR REPROOF, FOR CORRECTION, FOR INSTRUCTION IN RIGHTEOUSNESS: THAT THE MAN OF GOD MAY BE PERFECT, THOROUGHLY FURNISHED UNTO ALL GOOD WORKS. II TIMOTHY 3: 16-17

I firmly believe that not a single day should be approached without the comfort of Christ richly dwelling within us. He speaks clearly if we will set aside emotion and settle into His quiet power, when our mind is given to Him, He is faithful to meet us. Quiet places don't always happen and yet with God, even in a moment of pain or suffering, He can be there ministering while even chaos and potential harm loom close at hand. He has no limits in time or space for being where we are when we need His attention—He is highly available and convenient. Physical locations have no way of limiting His access to us—that's why we can pray with our eyes wide open, standing, seated or walking about. Communication with God is always a "seek and ye shall find" situation.

SO SHALL THEY FEAR THE NAME OF THE LORD FROM THE WEST, AND HIS GLORY FROM THE RISING OF THE SUN. WHEN THE ENEMY SHALL COME IN LIKE A FLOOD, THE SPIRIT OF THE LORD SHALL LIFT UP A STANDARD AGAINST HIM. ISAIAH 59:19

A BEGINNING PLACE FOR PRAYER TODAY:

Lord, please be in the middle of this day. Mark each difficult moment with Your presence and help me not to handle things in my own wisdom. Please give me new and fresh scripture so that I might have insight into Your plan for me and for those in my care. Help me to make You pleased in what I say and do today. Let my life be a blessing for You and Your children as I meet them and let me remember there are no strangers when I encounter believers along the way.

Thank You for the blessings of this day—please keep my heart quiet before You and speak to me clearly about that which concerns me today. Thank You Father for just being there for me, You never disappoint me and You always amaze me in Your loving care and concern for me and those I love. Thank You Father.

DISCUSSION QUESTIONS FOR TODAY:

1. Have I ever been so frustrated or confused by something that I have forgotten to ask God for His help? How do I think this happens in my life?

2. Do I have quiet time with the Lord daily? How formal does that encounter have to be? Have I been unable to read the Bible or spend time in prayer because my expectations are too rigorous? What changes can I make to assure myself that each day I will get something of the Lord in my life?

DAY 115

AND WHATSOEVER WE ASK, WE RECEIVE OF HIM, BECAUSE WE KEEP HIS COMMANDMENTS, AND DO THOSE THINGS WHICH ARE PLEASING IN HIS SIGHT. I JOHN 3:22

READING FOR TODAY– EXODUS 30: 1-8, ROMANS 12:1-2 AND I TIMOTHY 2:1,3,8.

The incense of the altar represents the prayer and the praise of the priests on behalf of the Israelites. As New Testament believers in Christ I believe we have become that altar to God built up as living stones to be our own priests.(I Peter 2:5,9) Our incense is praise and prayer—constant communication with our God and this is good and acceptable in the sight of God as it says in I Timothy. Without this constant communication we are running the risk of being out of fellowship with God.

When we praise God for His blessings it says: THANK YOU GOD. When we pray it says: I WANT TO SHARE MY LIFE WITH YOU FATHER. Praising Him keeps me mentally healthy and positively aware of all of life's blessings through Christ. I can't get too down, when I feel so loved, and I rehearse to myself the constant concrete evidence of His provision for me daily. My goal is that nothing gets taken for granted. I want no one but God to get the credit and the glory for my blessings from Him. Daily I must let it be my responsibility to let others hear me say that I am thankful because God has done such wonderful things in my life.

When I pray I keep an open dialogue with God. Long quiet times or short quick prayers—the success of these prayers lies not in their length, but in the phrase "perpetual incense." What got me through yesterday, does not give me the same support or the reinforcement of that support in my life for this new day. I can't take a day off mentally from God and expect to stay on the same level of fellowship with Him. It is too humanly possible that I will take charge of my life when I don't sacrifice it to Him daily. "HE IS THE REWARDER OF THEM THAT DILIGENTLY SEEK HIM." Hebrews 1: 6

The concerns of my life are God's concerns. He can give me peace concerning all of the things I do not understand, but that does not always mean He will answer my prayers with "Yes" or even on my time table. But…little by little He will give me peace about His plans when He turns down my plans and my expectations. Confidently, I remind myself that I am not in charge—thank goodness—and He will do what is in my best interest because He knows the big picture of all I cannot see in the future. Letting go of my life is the most freeing step I can take.

Praise keeps us ever aware that He keeps blessing me even when I haven't asked. Prayer loses all the uncomfortableness of "saying the right words" when I remember God just says "talk to Me, tell Me everything, ask and let Me decide what will be most valuable for you to experience." I have learned that even the worst experiences of life are bearable as seen through the eyes of Christ. My eyes are wide open to what He has for me when I pray and my strength is reaffirmed every day as I let Him sustain me with His wisdom, power and might.

A BEGINNING PLACE FOR PRAYER TODAY:

Thank You Lord for all Your blessings. You have worked mightily in my life and I expect you will continue to do so if I'll just "let go". Help me Lord to lay before You all the concerns of this day and help me to leave those concerns at Your throne. I don't get the full picture of what it is that You are doing in my life and I don't want to know the whys or hows of it. Please keep me in the palm of Your hand—just resting and waiting on You, Father. Only You Father, are worthy of praise and can calm my spirit. Thank You Father for Your perfect commitment to me, I value Your power and strength in my life—nothing else can sustain me. Thank You, Father, I love You.

DISCUSSION QUESTIONS FOR TODAY:

1. Do I have a constant dialogue going with the Lord? Why not?

2. Name the things the Lord isn't interested in hearing me say thank you for and the conversation topics the Lord doesn't want to be a part of in my life? What have I learned from thinking about this question?

DAY 116

BLESSED IS HE WHOSE TRANSGRESSION IS FORGIVEN, WHOSE SINS ARE COVERED. BLESSED IS THE MAN WHOSE SIN THE LORD DOES NOT COUNT AGAINST HIM AND IN WHOSE SPIRIT IS NO DECEIT. PSALM 32:1-2

READING FOR TODAY– EXODUS 30: 9-16, EPHESIANS 1:6-7, ISAIAH 55:7 AND COLOSSIANS 2:13

Jesus Christ is our atonement for our sins, but the Israelite of Exodus had only the law to follow for atonement. Perhaps the law had to be there first so that man would have moral boundaries and guidelines that he would constantly struggle to maintain so that the unrelenting failure to live up to that law would then give man an understanding of Christ's sacrifice on the cross. How could I feel blessed unless I knew what I was being saved from?

To come once a year to the temple to make a blood offering for my sins and to give my half a shekel seems like such a small requirement. The rich could not give more nor could the poor give less. Sin is equal in every man and the payment is also equal. Jesus was that equal payment for all of us. He was and is no respecter of persons. God alone knows the heart of man, we cannot judge that. We only see the fruit of a persons' faith, but we do not know him as Jesus knows him.

The scriptural reference of continual incense is to me a symbol of the Israelites constant awareness of God. In our case, our constant awareness is our fellowship and communion with God through prayer and scripture. Through the scriptures we are pointed toward Jesus as our Savior and our goal is to please Him by letting His Holy Spirit work within us. Our atonement comes daily, hourly and even moment by moment at times, when we open ourselves up to the Lord's scrutiny. It is hard to be angry or disappointed with other people when we view the things we do that should surely anger and disappoint Jesus.

Why ask every day for forgiveness? Weren't our sins forgiven once and for all on the cross? Yes, but…we are in transition before our Lord. He works in us every day to make us into His own image. In Philippians 1:6 it says that He began a good work in us, it does not say He has completed that good work. When we confess our sins He is faithful to forgive them, but our acknowledgement of those sins puts up on a path to clear that sin out of our lives with His power and strength having free reign in us.

Sin harms us either emotionally, spiritually or physically. Nothing the Lord tells us to stay away from is good for us. He doesn't limit our life; He expands it so we suffer from nothing unnecessary in our lives. Guilt, shame and unhappiness are the end result of all sin. God does not want us experiencing those emotions, so He provided Jesus for us as a perfect sacrifice for our sins—we are more than forgiven, we are constantly being washed by the blood of Jesus. God does not see our sin, because Jesus washes us daily.

Just as the Israelites had the responsibility of coming to the temple for atonement, so we have the responsibility of communion with Jesus. Our job is to do what Jesus cannot do for us—that is to choose to add to our life that which will make us truly in fellowship with God. We can hear His voice, we can respond to His voice and because we take everything to Him we can expect His fellowship to direct us. Choices are always up to us. God prescribes in His scriptures the path of life, but we still get to choose whether we heed His words or go our own way. Whose path are we following today?

A BEGINNING PLACE FOR PRAYER TODAY:

Thank You Father for Your cleansing blood. Each day You wash me clean. Please help me to see the areas in my life that I need to lay at Your feet. Help me to hear Your voice clearly, Father, over my own foolish desires. Please keep my life focused on the concerns of this day. Help me to see You clearly and to keep my choices ever before You. Let me know that I am ultimately responsible for my choices and that You choose life for me and all I must do is be in agreement with You. Dear Father, thank You that You always know what is good for me. Thank You Father for this day.

DISCUSSION QUESTIONS FOR TODAY:

1. Do I forget to ask God to cleanse me from all of my sins daily? Am I so perfect that I do not have to ask for His forgiveness daily? Have I "arrived" simply because I am a believer?

2. Why do I think the Bible constantly talks about sin?

DAY 117

NOT BY WORKS OF RIGHTEOUSNESS WHICH WE HAVE DONE, BUT ACCORDING TO HIS MERCY HE SAVED US, BY THE WASHING OF REGENERATION, AND THE RENEWING OF THE HOLY GHOST. TITUS 3:5

READING FOR TODAY– EXODUS 30: 17-21, I JOHN 1:9 AND I CORINTHIANS 6:9-11

The washing of the hands and feet of the priests was a symbol of purification before the Lord. We were washed in the blood of the Lamb when Jesus was crucified on the cross. He seeks to regenerate us each day by washing us with His word. The renewing of our minds, the washing of our minds daily, is the only way we can cast away the dirt and the confusion of the world.

Soaking in the Word keeps us from becoming brittle and dry and then broken by the world. Have you noticed that things seem to cling to us and weigh us down if we do not wash them off? The condemnation of the enemy sticks to us if we do not let the water of the Word bathe us. It is all too easy to forget that God has His perspective. We need to look into His perspective when the world has made us afraid. Lost in a sea of confusion is not God's choice for us—only God can wash away that confusion.

The priests were not washed once so that forever they would be clean. Every time worship began they washed. This was a daily responsibility of the priest and as believers this is our daily responsibility too. Just as each day is new, so the responsibility is new to wash away the dirt of the day before. Renewing is washing my mind so that I count my blessings instead of my sorrows, focus on the good and put off the bad, and look to the present of this new day and put away the hurts of yesterday.

Our lives are lived out by what we believe. As Christians our hope is in Christ for His power, protection and blessing and that translates into a walk of faith. The prescription, God's prescription, for a life of joy and peace is the daily renewing or re-energizing of us. If we were vacuum cleaners we would be of little value if we were not plugged into the socket. The Holy Spirit is that socket of energy in our lives. We cannot store up power; we must get it one day at a time. The needs of each day are different and every day we need God's fresh source of power for that unique and complicated span of time.

Maturity tells us that we store up the knowledge of God's past power in our lives, but the power we need for each day must be new. There is nothing I cannot face or even survive when I operate on the power of God. He keeps me in the today of my life. If I foolishly dwell in the past I can become sad or never experience the newness of today. If I choose to look exclusively to the unknown of the future, I can become anxious, but I also will not experience the blessings of today. Each day is a new chapter in the book of our lives; it opens and closes never to be experienced again.

When we lose something special to us we always wish we could recapture it. The trick to living is to live as God says: one day at a time. We must know that it will never come again and we must experience each day knowing full well that we will never be able to recapture it. The "things" of this day are of little consequence, but the people of this day are the source of growth in my life and the blessing of the Lord. When all is said and done in this day, the real treasure of today will lie in the time I spend with the people in my life. The people in my life are helping to transform me into the image of Christ even when I am not fully aware of it.

A BEGINNING PLACE FOR PRAYER TODAY:

Lord, thank You for this new day. Help me to set aside the things and stuff of this day and focus on You. Let me look carefully at the people of this day? Who are they Lord? What are their needs? How can I be a blessing this day? Thank You that You have taken away the negative of this day and renewed my mind to think of the possibilities and the excitement of this new day. Please let me be a blessing to You Lord. Help me to share Your love in Your name with all the people and events of this day. Thank You Father for Your infinite love and care for me; I cannot even begin to comprehend Your love for me, but I want to embrace and accept it fully into my life.

DISCUSSION QUESTIONS FOR TODAY:

1. How is my power source today? Am I weak because I have not taken the time to be rejuvenated by the Lord? What do I need to do to insure His power in my life?

2. Has my power run down and so I find myself in negative places today? Is this what God wants for me? What is my best source of rejuvenation?

DAY 118

He who pursues righteousness and love finds life, prosperity and honor.
Proverbs 21: 21

Reading for today– Exodus 30: 22-33, Matthew 28: 18-20, Galatians 5: 22-23 & Proverbs 22:11

If our lives are not different from the unbeliever's life then we are not fully anointed. Without the love of Jesus actively working in us and reaching out to other people we cannot be "the light on a hill" that draws others to salvation in Jesus Christ. As Jesus is the anointed Son of God so are we the anointed chosen of God just as the priests are identified in our scripture today. Ideally, we will no longer walk in our own ways but we will follow the scriptures of God and be separate and obedient to serve all of God's children.

Our very countenance—our smile—is the best invitation to Jesus that we can offer. We should always be approachable. A smile makes us approachable and no matter how uncomfortable or lonely we may feel inside, a smile covers it. Smiles are interesting because they're usually the only body language other people cannot ignore. I have discovered that when a smile is in place, an attitude of openness and generosity moves in and life gets easier. If I look like I've been baptized in lemon juice I don't attract many people.

Missionaries to foreign countries are wonderful examples of the visibly different appearing in a foreign place. But, for the majority of us there will never be a foreign land for us, yet all about us are foreigners—those who do not have a personal relationship with God. The light we shine is a beacon of one of the gifts of the Holy Spirit working in us. Our job is to keep our eyes on Jesus and serve Him. Whether we like it or not, the eyes of non-believers are constantly on us. Carefully they will look at us and judge us. The big question will always be there: IS THIS JESUS BUSINESS FOR REAL?

Our great commission is to share the gospel. Credibility plays a big part in our effectiveness in doing this successfully. The Bible never promises us an easy life— tribulation falls on the believer and the non-believer alike. The light we are is actually often the evidence of God making something good out of the tribulation in our lives before the eyes of the unbeliever. We are constantly being evaluated by family, friends and strangers. Quite often others are drawn to Jesus simply because they see one of the gifts of the Spirit working in us and they desire it.

Our anointing grows as we practice the quality of thankfulness in our lives. Thankfulness gives us a lighter heart, but more importantly it makes us more generous. While you choose to count your blessings the awareness of others who are in need grows and you develop an affinity for generosity. Our appointment by God to be His anointed was never meant to be a selfish gesture to be hoarded—it was meant to be shared outside the body of the church, across denominational lines and with non-believers. We can practice on other believers but we need to move out daily and perfect it on unbelievers so we can comfort them with the comfort only God can give through His salvation.

Life becomes quite exciting when we expect the unexpected blessings of non-believers in our lives. The anointing has been given to us so we can pass it on. Who will I smile at today: a grumpy husband or my child, a frustrated anxious friend or a stranger who needs help at the super market? Life can be a wonderful adventure when we keep our eyes off of ourselves and on the children of God who need Him and His Holy Spirit this day.

A BEGINNING PLACE FOR PRAYER TODAY:

Please make me a willing servant Lord. Help me to keep my eyes open. I have simple gifts and talents I can use for Your glory. Help me to do that this day. I need You in the middle of my life; always under Your control is where I want to be. Please help me to count my blessings and become more generous for You. My desire is to let everything I am reflect You in my life. Help me to see the needs of other people so I can take the focus off of myself and magnify You before man. Thank You for this exciting new day and all it will hold. I look forward to all Your miracles today!

DISCUSSION QUESTIONS FOR TODAY:

1. Do I have an open or closed countenance for strangers? Have I ever thought of the importance of a smile as a ministry tool?

2. What does being thankful do for my countenance and am I magnifying His blessings before strangers and non-believers?

DAY 119

FOR WE ARE TO GOD THE AROMA OF CHRIST AMONG THOSE WHO ARE BEING SAVED AND THOSE WHO ARE PERISHING. II CORINTHIANS 2:15

READING FOR TODAY– EXODUS 30: 34-38, II CORINTHIANS 2: 14-17 AND PSALM 31

We are the incense of the tabernacle of God. Our responsibility is to attract people to the living God. Attracting people to God is not the same as being popular. Popularity is not what we seek, but rather purity and not purity for ourselves, but for the service we are before man as God's witness to man. All our goodness is to point to Jesus the author of all mercy, grace and goodness.

When God is honored our lives produce a fragrance which others experience. If we're the only one blessed by what we do in life, then there is no fragrance of Christ in our lives. Selfishness is a fragrance for myself, honoring myself and meeting my needs. Generosity of spirit is a fragrance which shares itself and does not expect anything back for it serves the growth of the kingdom.

Pride is a dangerous fragrance. It is the sin which comes before a fall. When I do what I do simply to be honored I lose the fragrance of Christ. I am capable or bright or creative and successful because God has allowed these characteristics in my life. And…positive gifts don't come to us all the time. Sometimes the most negative events of our lives produce the most lasting fruit—when I am weak, He is strong. God can use even my failures for good if His fragrance is attached to them. But, pride will limit my success because I've always got my eyes on myself and not on God.

The fragrance of service is to be constantly coveted. Ordinarily, we are not given to service. We like reward for service. Service without constant reward has to be supernatural and that supernatural characteristic has to be given to us as a daily prayer request. There will be a reward someday, but for today our reward is the fragrance of joy—not a crown for men to see here on earth. For example, a man who works hard, takes care of his family, and takes seriously the role of husband and father is blessed by God. But, if he takes his responsibilities seriously for his own selfish nature, he will not be a fragrance, which is loving, kind or compassionate. Chances are a man who serves himself will become bitter when things don't go his way. His demands for respect will supersede his kindness and his insatiable desire to gain materially will make him anything but compassionate. He could begin to seek perfection in everything and everyone who serves him—wife and children included. He loses his fragrance and becomes a stench to all he encounters.

We are to be a fragrance for those who are perishing. Perishing in the Christian terminology means someone who will die the ultimate death and go to hell rather than heaven. Now we're talking serious, aren't we? This concept of being a fragrance for Christ is a sobering responsibility. "IF YOU HAVE DONE IT TO THE LEAST OF THESE, YOU HAVE DONE IT TO ME!" People are dying all about me. I have the gift of life to share if I am a fragrance for Christ and not for myself. My words will be words "spoken before God with sincerity, like a man sent from God" for those people who "are being saved and those who are perishing."

A BEGINNING PLACE FOR PRAYER TODAY:

Lord, whether I am a fragrance for those being saved or for those perishing, help me to speak clearly and to act with wisdom. I know I do not know who I will affect for You today. Please help me to not discourage Your children from getting to know You and the salvation You offer. Help me to be responsible and deliberate in choosing You today and please take away any fragrance that will cause people to turn away from You. Thank You for the potential I have to be a fragrance for You, please let me be a blessing to You, Father, today.

DISCUSSION QUESTIONS FOR TODAY:

1. Have I ever thought of myself as the fragrance of Christ? How do I feel about this responsibility?

2. How do good intentions turn to pride and how do they affect the people I love and those I do not even know? What are some of the danger signs in my life that might make me a stench rather than a fragrance?

DAY 120

YOU ARE MY LAMP, O LORD; THE LORD TURNS MY DARKNESS INTO LIGHT. WITH YOUR HELP I CAN ADVANCE AGAINST A TROOP; WITH MY GOD I CAN SCALE A WALL. II SAMUEL 22: 29-30

READING FOR TODAY– EXODUS 31: 1-11, II SAMUEL 22: 26-37, DEUTERONOMY 31:6 AND HEBREWS 13: 5-6

When God calls us to a foreign place in our lives He equips us for that place beforehand. The planning and building of the tabernacle is precise for it represents God's vision and that vision has exact measurements and materials, even its use is predetermined. It is a huge undertaking for His people, but God is faithful. He does not call them to something they cannot handle. He gives them Bezalel "with skill, ability and knowledge" in all kinds of crafts and Oholiab "to help him". Then He goes further and says: "Also I have given skill to all the craftsmen to make everything I have commanded you."

Life seems to me to be a constant set of walls to scale. If it were not for God and His faithfulness this statement would be depressing. Life is a challenge, but service for the Lord is a wonderfully intriguing adventure when looked at through the eyes of a believer in our Lord Jesus. Nothing He allows to come my way will He not empower me to endure or conquer. No matter what the situation, I believe it will produce something good in my life.

Times of extreme sadness and anxiety befall all of us and we wonder: "Lord, what are You doing to me?' Fear, frustration, disappointment—we have known them all, even if we've lived a short time as an adult. But, the good news is: "You are my lamp, O Lord; the Lord turns my darkness into light. With your help I can advance against a troop; with my God I can scale a wall." Have you looked at "the walls" in your life this way—walls God has allowed you to scale?

He is a shield "for all who take refuge in Him" if we pray and ask for His peace. Peace in times of turmoil can only come from God. His word is "flawless" and "His way perfect". On my knees in prayer is the only way I can sort out the emotional arrows of the enemy and find the path of God's logic. Accepting what I cannot control only becomes possible when Jesus comes alongside with the Holy Spirit and moves me one step, one day at a time down a path I could never have imagined surviving, much less traveling through victoriously.

One of the benefits of having walked with the Lord a few years is having the historical perspective of His past help, knowing that "He will never leave me or forsake me". If it's an operation for me or a loved one, the prospect of divorce, the loss of a job, the death of a loved one or an unbelievably painful event in my family—He is always there. When God is the master over everything in my life, then "joy comes in the morning."

Obedience is the key element to letting me get over the wall. If I try to figure out everything I will fail—for some things there are no answers. Emotions can be stirred so strongly by the enemy that despair becomes overwhelming. But, if I get on my knees immediately (even mentally) nothing can over-rule my peace with Jesus. Fearful, accusing and devastating thoughts can all fall under the blood of Christ and immediately I can stand and face the crisis for: "It is God who arms me with strength and makes my way perfect."

A BEGINNING PLACE FOR PRAYER TODAY:

Lord, you have been with me through the big and little trials of my life. Please continue to stand with me. Let me not forget to commit everything to You today—even the small things. Help me to let go of my vision and put on Your perspective. You bless me every day. Help me to review the walls You have conquered for me, the growth You have made in my character through all my trials. Thank You God that You turn all tribulation into triumph when I use Your eyes to see the blessings of all my "walls". Thank You Father for Your constant presence in my life.

DISCUSSION QUESTIONS FOR TODAY:

1. Have I taken for granted the "walls" God has allowed me to leap over in His strength? Have I even asked Him to help me leap those walls in my life that have now surrounded me and have prevented me from moving forward in my Christian walk?

2. Is there a wall right now in my life and have I given up because it is just too hard for me?

DAY 121

HE BROUGHT ME OUT INTO A SPACIOUS PLACE; HE RESCUED ME BECAUSE HE DELIGHTED IN ME. II SAMUEL 22:20

READING FOR TODAY– EXODUS 31: 12-18, II SAMUEL 22: 17-21 AND PHILIPPIANS 1:6

"I am the Lord, who makes you holy. For it is God who works in you to will and to act according to His good purposes." (Philippians 2:13) Being holy is being set apart by God. We choose to serve God by first admitting that we are sinners, then by believing Jesus is the son of God and then lastly by confessing our faith in Jesus Christ as our Savior and Lord. When that confession is made then the Holy Spirit moves in and He makes me holy. Going to church on Sunday does not make me holy.

Attending church is only an outward sign of my commitment to God by keeping the Sabbath holy. Church is actually wherever I am throughout the whole week when I invite the Lord to be a part of my day. When the Holy Spirit works in me, He works seven days a week. There's a lot to be done in each of us. It is an ongoing work of construction that God has taken on. Maturity works slowly in our lives and completion will never come until we see Him in heaven.

Our works show us to be believers, but the source of the desire to make progress and be holy, or set apart in our lives for God, is the gift that God gives us through Jesus and the Holy Spirit. Our responses to life and our attitude about accepting life are what make us holy. Church is a great place to gather once a week and worship God, fellowship with our brothers and sisters in Christ and be fed by the pastor of our small flock—but it is not what makes us holy. A Sunday service is a formal setting that sets us apart from the world for a morning. In this special time we can begin to be refreshed and washed of the past week's dirt and our eyes can be placed on God rather than the world.

Obedience is the fruit of an every Sunday commitment. If we are not faithful with the simple commandment—GO TO CHURCH—how will we be faithful with the harder commandments: READ MY WORD and PRAY? The Lord's plans for all of us start from our obedience to follow His commands in our lives. Every Christian walk is different. Who we are, what God wants us to be and how and where He will use us is always unique to us. He will make us holy, but we must first start by attending church and honoring Him by setting aside that time.

In fact, I believe that if we're real comfortable in church and the pastor never makes us uncomfortable; then our heart is in the wrong place. God seeks to make us holy by making us uncomfortable and aware of our sin. The more we are aware of our weaknesses the stronger God will be able to make us. I can't get holy by being in church, I can only get holy by being convicted that I am a sinner, in other words: a "me centered" person who needs to be a "God-centered" person.

Asking God to work in me on Sundays will allow me to gratefully sing those hymns of praise and give me insight and understanding in the words I sing. I need to ask

Him to make me generous and loving for my family's sake. I need to see if He has anything He needs me to work on this week—personally or community wise. I must thank Him for all He has done this past week and have Him search my heart for the things I have been overlooking. It is important to look carefully at the believers about me, hear their prayer requests with my heart, and pray with them and for them in my own pew. When I observe the older and the younger believer—I can see more clearly what they can teach me? "I am the Lord, who makes you holy" means in a small part—come to church and get a full perspective of what God has for you as a place to begin your walk for this week with the Holy Spirit. Remember: He needs to speak to us to make us holy.

A BEGINNING PLACE FOR PRAYER TODAY:

Lord, all my works will not make me holy—You alone hold the keys to everlasting life. Forgive me please for taking church attendance for granted. Help me to make it a celebration of You in my life instead of a ritual I do "because I am a Christian". Please open my eyes to You in my life—I want You on the throne of my life. Help me Father to take one day a week and commit it to hearing You speak to me. I talk too much, let me listen, please Father, help me to hear Your voice. Thank You Father for keeping me under construction, I love You Lord.

DISCUSSION QUESTIONS FOR TODAY:

1. What have I discovered about my attitude when I attend church? Am I pleased with my heart or do I need to make some adjustments?

2. Do I listen to other people's needs and pray for them? Why do I need to focus on the needs of other believers in my church? Will I profit from this endeavor? How?

DAY 122

TEACH US TO NUMBER OUR DAYS ARIGHT, THAT WE MAY GAIN A HEART OF WISDOM.
PSALM 90:12

READING FOR TODAY– EXODUS 32:1-6, PSALM 89:30-34, PSALM 91:14-16 AND PSALM 30

Life can be very discouraging. We lose our patience; some days we question why we even try to honor God and we find ourselves asking: "What good is all this?" Before we can go on our sanity must return and we must answer the alternative question: "Who else would I choose to serve and what will be my reward for serving that god?"

When the thoughts of the enemy are pushed away by the Holy Spirit, I remember the real reason why I have decided to serve my God: I serve the one true God who loves me unconditionally and offers me refuge and shelter and eventually the reward of heaven. This is a God I can trust. When I fail Him, He waits patiently for my return to sanity. He put His Son on a cross to die for me because He knew I needed the perfect sacrifice for all my sins against Him. Without His sacrifice I would never be able to fellowship with Him nor would I ever be able to return home to Him.

Patience seems to be the hardest thing for us to deal with for we don't see immediate answers or things take too long and we lose our patience. Patience is one quality that we should desire above all else. I have found that the most complete and satisfying experiences of life are usually the culmination of hard work and time spent earnestly pursuing their completion.

I am sure God looks at us that way too. He will patiently pursue our best interests and let all the elements of life have their perfect work in us, no matter how painful, until He is satisfied with the development of our character. We are foolish, yet very human to wish to see the evil things of our days pass away without ever having to fully learn the lessons which only those days can teach us. The experience of trials in our lives creates in us wisdom and in that wisdom comes the knowledge of the presence of God in our lives. Without tribulation I will not and cannot grow spiritually.

He doesn't give up on me. He does not take His love from me nor does He ever betray His faithfulness to me. Consequences may be mine if I violate His decrees and fail to keep His commandments, but even in receiving the fruits of my bad deeds there is security. Security is what God offers me. When we are secure in the righteousness of God, even our own unrighteous acts or those of others upon us become bearable because we know "joy comes in the morning." He always judges fairly and He can provide a good outcome for the worst of our behaviors.

We can give up, but He never gives up. His patience will outlast our frail egos and our conscious efforts to stray down a slippery slope of self-pity because He has appointed us as His for eternity. Momentary lapses or long trips down terrible roads of personal destruction can all be turned around to His glory if we repent. The enemy can paint us into black and fearful days when he is allowed to rule in our minds, but our God can turn that darkness of fear into light if we repent and reject that darkness. There are really two questions to answer: How much darkness will I allow in my mind? How much fear, confusion and frustration will I allow to cloud my view of today? If I turn immediately and praise His safety and security, my disposition will change my countenance from darkness into light and He can again take over my life. Being a free-will being I have the ability to choose to trust God and let Him increase my patience while I learn to smile and count my blessings; even the ones I haven't yet received. His work is not only perfect in me; it is complete because He loves me with a love I cannot even comprehend.

A BEGINNING PLACE FOR PRAYER TODAY:

Father, forgive my lack of trust in Your timing and in Your plans for my life. The longer I know You the more I see how much I need to learn about You and how much You love me. Your concerns are always toward me. If I ask, You are in the middle of things, helping me to sort them out, without fear or anxiety. Forgive me that I get angry with You because I think You have failed or forgotten me.

Please help me to keep the enemy from clouding my mind, I know in my heart that You love me, but my sinful brain is so easily overtaken by the enemy. Please forgive my foolishness and put me on a new path of confidence in You. Thank You Father that You love me so much that I can even admit these wicked thoughts to You and You remain faithful in Your love for me. You are too much for me to comprehend, but I love the knowledge of Your love for me.

DISCUSSION QUESTIONS FOR TODAY:

1. Have I ever been mad at God? What was the outcome of my rage? If I have never experienced these emotions can I understand how this can happen?

2. What steps in my life must I take so that I can stay away from anger with God? Who do I think is the ultimate worker of anger in my life? Why does he desire me to be at odds with my God?

DAY 123

THE KINGS WRATH IS LIKE THE ROARING OF A LION, BUT HIS IS FAVOR IS LIKE DEW ON THE GRASS. PROVERBS 19:12

READING FOR TODAY– EXODUS 32:7-14, PSALM 116:1-2, 12-14 AND PSALM 117

Notice how Moses stands before God and pleads for the lives of his "stiff necked" tribe and God relents from doing them harm. Jesus carried the message of love and salvation to "a stiff necked generation" and God granted His blessing on those that heard and received Him. How God could have wanted to destroy them all when they did not receive His Son, but He sacrificed His Son for the few that did believe on Him and set His heart on those who would come after. Now that Son sits at His right hand to make amends for us. God put His Son in charge of us, just as He put Moses in charge of those "stiffed-necked" Israelites.

Jesus knows us. He is "acquainted" with our sins and our sorrows and nothing we do takes Him by surprise. We are His. He suffered at the hands of people as He walked this earth. He felt human sorrow and pain. He knows this is a hard place to live in, but He allows us His forgiveness as He trains us to be the people He needs us to be. Jesus prayed constantly to the Father for wisdom. We need that kind of wisdom too. Stiff-necked people are not happy people; we need God's forgiveness and His wisdom. Jesus is the supplier of all our needs if we will but pray and ask.

For that time in history Moses stood between the wrath of God and His people, but Jesus now stands for eternity in that position. From the time that Adam and Eve sinned in the garden until this very moment in time God knew who He would be dealing with—we are weak. He is a holy God and only Jesus can present us without spot or wrinkle when our time comes for judgment. How foolish man is when he sees himself as acceptable to God. Man has often said, "Why should I accept Jesus: I am a good man—I am better than so and so!" God's standards are high, but because of Jesus we are all acceptable in the sight of God. If we believe Jesus to be the sacrifice for our sins and Him to be the Son of God who we worship we will not experience the wrath of God.

We are not different from the Israelites. Today we mumble and grumble when life doesn't go our way. On occasion we even bargain mentally with God to try and get Him to go our way. We are fearful, anxious, impatient and we still don't get how much we are loved. For this moment in time, we must remind ourselves of what we often forget: we have "inherited the land", we are a blessed people. We have a leader, Jesus, who loves us, protects us, guides us, comforts us and is always with us. No harm can come to us because we are His.

The disappointments and sorrows of this day, are just that: "for this day!" We have a reward greater than we can comprehend when our days on earth are over and tomorrow will be a new day. It is time we praise the living God and all His blessings and stop serving the gods of temporary pleasure and momentary comfort. All that God promises, He delivers and all that God says He will do He does. And…He never turns

His wrath on us, He never gives up on the believer; He "just" forgives us when we repent. We serve an awesome God!

FOR I WILL BE MERCIFUL TO THEIR UNRIGHTEOUSNESS, AND THEIR SINS AND THEIR INIQUITIES WILL I REMEMBER NO MORE. HEBREWS 8:12

A BEGINNING PLACE FOR PRAYER TODAY:

Lord, please let the words of my mouth be a blessing to Your ears. Help me to see You daily. Help me to praise You in all the ways You bless me and let me put my wants aside as I dwell on all the needs of my life that You have so abundantly satisfied. Thank You for this day let it be a blessing to You. Make my path a joy for You to observe. Thank You Father for loving me.

DISCUSSION QUESTIONS FOR TODAY:

1. How thankful am I? Do I need an attitude adjustment today?

2. Can things get out of perspective for me? How do I keep things in God's perspective and make that perspective mine?

DAY 124

The crucible for silver and the furnace for gold, the Lord tests the heart.
Proverbs 17:3

Reading for today– Exodus 32:15-24, Psalm 97 and I Corinthians 1:18-2:1-5

I think man's worst enemy is his need to be in charge of his life. God calls us to a new wisdom when He says through Paul:

> *For I resolved to know nothing while I was with you except Jesus Christ and Him crucified. I came to you in weakness and fear, and with much trembling. My message and my preaching were not with wise and persuasive words, but with the demonstration of the Spirit's power so that your faith might not rest on man's wisdom, but on God's power* I Corinthians 2:2-5

Paul is the "every man" of the Bible. What he says to us about himself is what we can easily see in ourselves. To "know Jesus Christ crucified" is all we need. When we look at Jesus the world grows dim about us. Our focus becomes a desire to serve Him. This single mindedness is foolish to the world, but to us, it is the order and protection of our lives. This single mindedness gives us peace and ultimately joy.

We cannot understand God's ways except by faith as we pursue God's ways. Experience and history proclaim God's truths of righteousness always triumphing over man's wisdom. God's power is what we need in our lives and Christ crucified for us as our center of focus is how we gain the faith we need to pursue a life without fear.

Fear is the enemy's tool and when Jesus is not our focus we try to be in charge or look to someone who can lead us so we can overcome our fear. Nothing has changed in the nature of man; when we lack faith the Israelites are us at our worst. We quickly try to find an answer to our problems when we lack patience in God's plan for our lives. If building an idol will work, we build it! Bank accounts, doctors for the body or doctors for the spirit, quick fixes for our problems, that's what we need! We throw down the tablets which are engraved by God in stone. Madly we begin searching for answers instead of the power of God. If we would just submit to His ways we could experience Him through the Holy Spirit—but that is too simple for us!

Psalm 97 says we will experience His guardianship and joy if we worship the living God rather than images which have no power. God is the power of the believer, not the believer's works, wisdom or his possessions. Man is nothing, but God's power is everything. The crucible of life is God's power working through our impurities to make us strong and pure, a vessel worthy to serve because it is focused on Jesus Christ crucified for us. When fear comes we can either build idols or seek the power of God and His righteousness. We have a choice and there in the choice lies our power—the power of the Holy Spirit. "The mountains melt like wax" before our God. So our fears will melt like wax if the living God is who we choose over our own power or the wisdom of this world.

But He knows the way that I take; when He has tested me, I will come forth as gold. Job 23:10

A beginning place for prayer today:

Forgive me Father, it is so easy for me to become fearful. Put me in Your Word daily. Shore up this heart of fear with Your power and Your strength. Let me focus on Jesus. Let me feel Your love for me when I am fearful. Help me to walk a straight purposeful path instead of looking for quick shortcuts. You are my solutions to life. You have chosen to put me in Your crucible, to burn away my weaknesses, let them become the folly of the enemy as I stand strong in You. Thank You Father for who You are in my life.

Discussion Questions for today:

1. Where do I run when trouble hits? Have I started erecting some idols to solve my problems? Why is this so easy to do?

2. Is the crucible of God a good place to be in? Why?

DAY 125

The fear of the Lord is wisdom, and to shun evil is understanding. Job 28:28

Reading for today– Exodus 32: 25-35 and Psalm 77

Fear is only good when it is the fear of the Lord. This fear is the ultimate respect we have for God. We submit to Him because we fully understand the power of God. Job knew the power of God, he feared the power of God, but he knew in his heart that he loved God and God did not intend to harm him, but to build him up and love him. When Moses says, "Whoever is for the Lord, come to me" and when "all the Levites rallied to him." Moses stood with the righteous to cleanse the people of God.

God can be quick and decisive in His judgment and when we see it we are afraid, but God does not mean for us to learn fear, He intends for us to learn respect for righteousness. Nothing prospers in sin, only purging creates purity. God is always producing purity in us. Righteousness is purity. There are no shades of gray—there is black and there is white in God's economy. The black, or the unrighteousness, was purged among Moses' people quickly in the killing of the three thousand.

When God purges us of a sin, it is most memorable for us and most valuable when it costs us something. Choosing the right thing to do against the face of the world's view might seem harsh or even cruel, but it is necessary. God's perceived cruelty in our lives always produces fruit. He alone chooses the time and place to harden His heart and for our own good sometimes punishes us. I have come to believe that we should not always intercede for others where lessons need to be learned. Every man has lessons to be learned and consequences to face. God chooses those lessons and those consequences because He wants us to have a healthy fear of Him. That fear produces comfort and strength in us and at the same time allows us to seek righteousness so we can stand before a holy God.

We serve a holy God and He expects us to pursue holiness. Our choices in life before we came to Christ were always "me centered choices". When the Holy Spirit came along and inhabited us, our choices began to be God centered. Our rationalizing became: WHAT WOULD JESUS DO? This rationalization becomes evidence that the Holy Spirit has changed our lives. I know what sin looks like and through scripture I can learn all about it and what I should flee from, but this wisdom grows and continues to grow within me and will never be complete until the Lord takes me home. I must never forget that I am a work under construction and I am not a completed work because I have accepted Jesus as my Savior.

Sometimes we are the victims of other people's sin, but God can use that to make us strong and create wisdom in us. God's wisdom should allow us to stand firm in the knowledge that all sin is equal and all sin is injurious and we need to flee from it. Sin for those who do not know the Lord is a blinding experience. We must pray for those who do not know God and therefore do not choose to flee sin, our only tool for the non-believer's blindness is prayer! When we pray for non-believers we stand in the gap for them until they themselves meet our Lord and learn to fear Him. Actually, standing in the gap is what we do with our children until they come to a saving knowledge of Christ. It is a privilege that we are allowed to stand this vigil.

A BEGINNING PLACE FOR PRAYER TODAY:

Thank You, Father, that You are my protection and my standard for living. Keep me ever vigilant—please don't let my sin grow. Help me to seek you daily for the purging I need. Please create in me a right spirit. I am truly sinful in nature and I require Your loving touch each new day. Please help me to turn my loved ones over to You, to allow You to purge them so they too can fall under Your protection. You are my strength and You alone light my path. Thank You Father.

DISCUSSION QUESTIONS FOR TODAY:

1. When God deals with us about a sin in our life, do we necessarily expect it to be a painless experience? What does this tell us about disciplining our children?

2. Have I ever tried to save someone from the consequences of their sin and then discovered they were bent on doing the sin at a later date? Can our actions sometimes prevent God from doing a complete work sooner?

DAY 126

IF YE BE WILLING AND OBEDIENT, YE SHALL EAT THE GOOD OF THE LAND: BUT IF YE REFUSE AND REBEL, YE SHALL BE DEVOURED WITH THE SWORD; FOR THE MOUTH OF THE LORD HAS SPOKEN IT. ISAIAH 1: 19-20

READING FOR TODAY– EXODUS 33: 1-6, ISAIAH 55: 8-13 AND ROMANS 13:14

How long does it take me to see my sin and ask for forgiveness? The Israelites were beginning to understand that God was in charge. I am no different today than they were then. The quicker I come to a realization of my sin the quicker God can work with me. He could have great plans for me, but if I keep fighting Him because I don't have the complete vision for the thing He is trying to accomplish, it will surely be a longer and more difficult process.

Our commitment to God really becomes valuable when others can see and feel it in their presence. Our job is to let the Holy Spirit point the way through us to Christ. Submission to Christ is power and strength under control. Quiet strength in Christ is the powerful garment we can put on.

We all have ornaments we wear that keep us from coming to know God and submitting to Him. Some ornaments we hide behind, some keep us blinded, some we wear because we are afraid to be seen by other men because we know we can't face our insecurities. Whatever the reason for hiding behind our ornaments—nothing happens until we take them off and put on Christ. When I put on Christ I wear a garment of complete protection. The Israelites are beginning to get that picture in this passage of scripture.

Being stiff- necked is really a dangerous way to live. God is a gentleman, He waits to be invited into our lives, but a constant stiff-necked approach to God could someday garner from God the response: "I never knew you." We can get real busy making ourselves Christians and leave Christ completely out of the equation. He becomes a consultant rather than the head of our heart. We don't respond to God's plan because we never even bother to check in. We just make plans and travel farther and farther away from His plan for our lives. God deserves a responsible heart in His people. He cannot lead if we will not follow and He does not make us follow Him, He allows us to follow Him if we choose to do so. Now the question is: How stiff is my neck?

God says to the Israelites: You can go into the promise land, but I won't go with you! The thought of going in a direction that God does not want to be a part of is a scary proposition to me. When God is not in the middle of something, it is a sure sign it will fail and cause me a lot of heart ache. When I am considering anything new, I pray about it and let it rest for a while until I am peaceful about what I have chosen. If that peace doesn't come and doors start closing, I walk away. It has been my experience that when God is in favor of something in my life it goes relatively easy and it is not a major struggle to accomplish what God has purposed. When bumps in the plan come, God smoothes out the way to accomplish His plans. It is important to note though that things that are morally correct can be difficult to stand against the enemy and the world with, but over time God becomes victorious because the Word supports your position because it is His position. Whatever I choose to do, it always goes better if I discuss it with Him first and let Him have the final say before I proceed.

A BEGINNING PLACE FOR PRAYER TODAY:

Please forgive my stiff-necked attitudes Lord. It is selfish behavior that keeps me from being the servant You desire. Help me to have a love for others that transcends my need to have my way at the expense of other's happiness. Take away the ornaments of life and present me faultless before Your throne. I desire Your peace and Your mercy in my life. Please help me to let go of the unnecessary trappings of life. Thank You, Father for Your mercy upon me.

FOR THE MOUNTAINS SHALL DEPART AND THE HILLS BE REMOVED BUT MY KINDNESS SHALL NOT DEPART FROM YOU, NOR SHALL MY COVENANT OF PEACE BE REMOVED, SAYS THE LORD WHO HAS MERCY ON YOU. ISAIAH 54:10

DISCUSSION QUESTIONS FOR TODAY:

1. What ornaments do I hide behind upon occasion? Are there some ornaments I need to be rid of completely so God can really use me?

2. Have I ever been stiff-necked before the Lord? What was the outcome? Am I still that way today and is it time to give in to God's way?

DAY 127

I WILL DWELL IN THEM AND WALK AMONG THEM. I WILL BE THEIR GOD; AND THEY SHALL BE MY PEOPLE. COME OUT FROM AMONG THEM AND BE SEPARATE, SAYS THE LORD. II CORINTHIANS 6: 16B-17.

READING FOR TODAY– EXODUS 33: 7-11, PHILIPPIANS 4: 6-7 AND PSALM 34

Fellowship with God must be a deliberate discipline for the fullness of that fellowship to occur. Chance meetings do not produce deep fellowship with the Lord. To pursue that fellowship we need to set aside a place for that encounter. Prayer is first obedience and then time set aside for that obedience.

When Moses needs complete focus, what does he do? The scripture tells us that he has a tent away from the camp. We're not much different today. In order to have fellowship with God we have to get away from the daily interruptions of life—family, friends, phones, televisions, books, newspapers, work; whatever your passion or area of distraction you have to get away from it. Moses needed a quiet place, so the tabernacle was set up. The Israelites who needed fellowship with the Lord also went out to that tabernacle of meeting.

Setting aside time to seek the Lord occurred whenever Moses left the camp and went to the tent. The pillar of cloud descended at the door when Moses and God were fellowshipping. God set this example before the people because He was training them up to be His people. We are expected to do the very same thing, but the Holy Spirit is our guide, not a pillar of clouds. The responsibility of fellowship falls completely on the shoulders of the believer. God has given His perfect sacrifice in His Son and the Holy Spirit is willing and able to communicate with us, but the choice of fellowship is up to us.

The scriptures say, "the Lord spoke to Moses face to face, as a man speaks to a friend." Friendship with God is the best friendship man can have. Through it we receive joy, comfort, peace, love, forgiveness and direction for our lives. If I am to be on the path God has for me, it has to be discussed with God on a daily basis. Everyday is new; so my responses to the good and bad challenges of this day must be new and fresh. I cannot rely on "old news", "old bulletins", I need up to the minute reports from God.

My attitude is the first thing God checks when I begin to talk with Him. An attitude adjustment is probably first because He can't really expect me to have an accepting heart if something is keeping me from Him. When He adjusts my attitude, He gives me the mind of Christ. I can face anything if I have the mind of Christ. I can't be anxious or fearful, I can't be grumpy or selfish, I can't be stubborn—my attitude must be opened up and made pliable in the hands of God. When my attitude is pliable, God can work with me and use me. Joshua stayed even after Moses left the tabernacle. He sought after God a little longer than Moses because he wanted to hear God's heart for himself. Moses had experience on His side, but Joshua felt he needed a little more and because he came away to be separate with God, God considered him a righteous man. God's ears were open to hear Joshua and He knew his voice when he called.

I want God to know my voice and to respond to me. Perhaps it is not an audible response, but He responds in scripture to me and He definitely adjusts my attitude when I take time to come away with Him. I have tested and seen that He is good and He alone has made my life change and grow. God is the friend I seek because He alone can deliver me from all my fears—yes, troubles sometime remain, but the strength I need to abide and grow strong in Him allows me to see through the trouble. Nothing that comes my way will ever be greater than the fellowship I have with God in prayer.

A BEGINNING PLACE FOR PRAYER TODAY:

Lord, please help me to come away with You every day. Help me to set aside time for Your scriptures. I am weak when I do not have the strength of Your Spirit and Your scripture within me. Nothing I can think up can meet the solutions of my daily dilemmas, let alone give me peace, like Your scriptures. Please help me to seek Your scriptures and learn Your ways so I can be approved by You. Only Your opinion matters to me Lord.

DISCUSSION QUESTIONS FOR TODAY:

1. How successful am I at getting away with the Lord? What are some of the times of the day that work best for me and have I chosen a time or am I running on empty?

2. Time is the most precious thing we have to give God, next to our hearts. I need to ask myself what am I spending time on that is taking precious time away from God?

DAY 128

THE RIGHTEOUS CRY AND THE LORD HEARETH, AND DELIVERETH THEM OUT OF ALL THEIR TROUBLES. PSALM 34: 17

READING FOR TODAY– EXODUS 33: 12-16, ISAIAH 43: 2, ISAIAH 41: 10 AND I PETER 5:6-7

Moses wants a bigger picture of what God has for him. He obviously does not trust his own judgment and he does not have a vision for what God is doing in his life or in the lives of the people he is leading. Asking God to consider his nation, he pleads with God: "but You have not let me know whom You will send with me. If I have found grace in Your sight, show me now Your way that I may know You and I may find grace in Your sight."

So often this is our dilemma today. We ask: "Am I doing what You want me to do Lord? What is happening here in my life? I do not feel secure because nothing seems to be clear to me. Am I pursuing the right things in life?" Our God is a hands-on God. He wants us to interact with Him. He gives us lots of options for our lives, but how do we find the best for ourselves and those we love?

Faith is letting God take the lead. Here are my needs Lord and what can I do to get them accomplished? There in lies the problem—we present our needs and we need the faith to let Him accomplish them. Our faithfulness to pursue honor for Him in what we do is important, but I believe it's more important that we allow Him to work out the details. We need ears to hear Him and hearts that accept His decisions.

God says to Moses, "My presence will go with you and I will give you rest." Today the Holy Spirit goes with us and He alone can give us rest. Lost jobs, prodigal children, illness within our family, our own illness, the economy, wars among nations, terrorism—there is so much that only God's peace and rest can cover. If I stay up all night worrying it does no good, because all it accomplishes is that I am exhausted for the coming day.

I need to take God at His word: "I will go with you, I know you by name, and I will give you rest." We cannot solve anything. God works out the details and our job is to be faithful to do the things we can do about a situation and then wait for God to accomplish the rest. Moses says: "If Your presence does not go with us, do not bring us up from here." In other words, "I will stay in this place—idleness, joblessness, poverty, whatever it is—until You see fit to move me forward." Like Moses I know there are some problems I cannot solve. I have tried to solve problems, but often I needed a new vision, acknowledging that until it came I too would stay put at His feet, determining in my spirit that He would move me forward when He saw fit. I have learned that where He is I am safe and at rest.

Time is such a stumbling block for us. Answers to the most serious prayer requests usually take time. We measure our mood by: "How long Lord?" It would be easier on us if we were able to say: "However long it takes Lord, my times are in Your hands. I do not want this problem in my hands, because I cannot see a solution." Faith is the sum of things not seen to have solutions, but the peace to know that God is in control and if I will stay close to Him, He will show me another path to take when His timing is right.

A BEGINNING PLACE FOR PRAYER TODAY:

Dear Father, help me to not be discouraged by my woes. Let me feel Your presence. Things stay on my mind Lord, way too long. You alone have the answers to all things. Help me to allow You to work and take rest in the knowledge that I have done what is humanly possible, now the rest is up to You. Please take away my discouragement and replace it with hope. Let me learn well the lessons of this dilemma and make Your work perfect in me so I can hear You say to my heart: "I know you by name and you have also found grace in My sight." Thank You Father for so carefully watching over me.

DISCUSSION QUESTIONS FOR TODAY:

1. Where does my confidence lie? Have I been experiencing peace and rest? If not, what do I think might be the problem?

2. Is time a stumbling block for me as I try to wait on the Lord?

DAY 129

BETTER IS THE END OF A THING THAN THE BEGINNING THEREOF; AND THE PATIENT IN SPIRIT IS BETTER THAN THE PROUD IN SPIRIT. ECCLESIASTES 7:8

READING FOR TODAY– EXODUS 33: 17-23, PSALM 89: 1-2, 6-7, 11-18 AND ISAIAH 55: 8-9

"Please show me Your glory." Can God do this and still be in control of our lives and even the very spinning of the world? He is all powerful and all knowing, but we are not. Simply put: man is too weak to know all God has for him. "We shall know in part", I Corinthians 13: 9-12, is all that we are really capable of handling. God is our refuge and our protection as He puts our lives in order. Not everything He allows in our lives will seem profitable at the time it unfolds.

Patience and trust are the gifts encompassed in the word faith. God clearly states: "No man shall see me and live." This means in part that we are not wise enough to understand His will for us nor strong enough to choose the events of our lives. A heart that seeks to be open to God will have the assurance that all things work together for good—even when things appear to spin out of our control. God is in control. He alone will choose whom He will be gracious to and have compassion on.

God's comfort and support are offered in the scripture: "Here is a place by Me, and you shall stand in the rock." In standing "by God" we have chosen a place which God offers for our emotional and physical safety to separate us from the things of this world.

The rock we stand on is Jesus Christ and the Father's gift of the Holy Spirit is within us. Jesus left His Comforter behind so that each of us who has accepted Christ will have the strength to make it through whatever life offers us.

"So it shall be, while my glory passes by, that I will put you in the cleft of the rock, and will cover you with My hand while I pass by." God will move in our lives as He needs to in order to perfect us into His image. When He does this He does it as gently as He can, but He is like a surgeon cutting away the infected parts of our lives. His anesthetic is to put us under His care ("in the cleft of the rock") while He works on the things we have not chosen; i.e. job loss, prodigal children, divorce, illness or anything that hurts us and we would obviously like to avoid. "I will cover you with My hand while I pass by." No matter what comes our way, He puts us in the cleft of the rock and covers us with His hand of protection. Nothing God allows in our lives can destroy us, He will put it to good use and we will be honed like a diamond to one day sparkle in His crown.

"Then I will take away My hand and you shall see My back." When the dilemma, the hurt, the incident is over I will look at it, at its' completion for good in my life and then I will see what God has accomplished. God has walked and is presently walking through my life, but only upon occasion do I get to see the full impact of His handiwork upon my life and those for whom I have prayed. Marvelously and miraculously He works miracles and blessings every day I do not fully see until He has passed through my life and I then only see His back as He exits--His work completed.

A BEGINNING PLACE FOR PRAYER TODAY:

Thank You for the miracles of protection You have worked in my life. Lord, I need to allow You to work without my permission on so many things in my life. Thank You that You take the time to do that very thing. Thank You that You do Your will in my life without giving me a reason or a complete vision. I need You, Father, because I am so very weak and You are strong enough for every detail of my life. Thank You for everything You are allowing in my life for those people I have been praying for and including my prayer partners. You love me so much Father, please let me always remember that and not let the world frighten me.

DISCUSSION QUESTIONS FOR TODAY:

1. Have I experienced God's putting me "in the cleft of the rock" as He walked through my life. Have I slipped out of the cleft temporarily and maybe need to run back in?

2. What would it be like to know everything about the future events of my life? How would I honestly feel about this kind of knowledge?

DAY 130

The Lord has established His throne in Heaven, and His Kingdom rules over all. Psalm 103:9

READING FOR TODAY– EXODUS 34:1-8 AND PSALM 103

Sometimes we take for granted the character of God. These verses remind us of what we often forget. For Moses, it is a reiteration of who God is in relationship to His children: "The Lord, the Lord God, merciful and gracious, longsuffering and abounding in graciousness and truth" Exodus 34:6.

We experience our positional place in Christ when we truly understand His title— He is master over us; we are His charge and He governs us. Then He says, "the Lord God", He is our master but we must also remember that He is the creator of the universe. The God we serve is extremely powerful, He controls everything and surprisingly He has particular concern for His people and because I am His He has control over me.

God's character toward us is "merciful, gracious and longsuffering". This is a promise as well as being a truth for my life. No matter what I do He will be merciful and gracious to me—unmerited kindness and love flow toward me because I am His. But, most importantly He is longsuffering toward me. Moses had broken the tablet in his fit of anger with the people and God has put aside the sins of man, once again He is preparing to write the commandments on stone.

God is longsuffering beyond all we know, understand or have experienced. He has no concept of time, He waits on us as we grow and we are expected in turn to wait on Him as He works His will in our lives. Thankfully, we see that He "abounds in goodness and mercy" toward us because we have to rely on that goodness, that never ending goodness and mercy for Him to continually forgive us. He constantly picks us up and dusts us off and gives us a new day.

Fortunately for us, God "abounds in truth." Confusion is an easy state of mind for man to get into, but God is in charge, and because He deals in truth we see less confusion in our lives. Truth is our comfort zone so we can make decisions that will give us confidence and hope while at the same time those decisions can be an honor to God. For every situation He gives us His truth so we can stand against the things which would otherwise defeat us.

The enemy is kept away from us and cannot harm us as long as we are constantly turning toward God's truths which we find in His scripture. The world likes to twist truth and even reason its' way out of truth, but God's people are constantly given truth to discern between good and evil. His truths are without end for those who fear Him. Truth is not just the laws of man handed down by God to man, truth is the very basis of order— emotionally, physically and spiritually. Truth and its order balances man and sets him apart from all the other creatures on the earth.

The forgiveness of God is the next character of God mentioned. He gives us forgiveness simply because He loves us with unmerited mercy and grace. The enemy would like us to forget His forgiveness. Without a firm grip on how forgiving God is the enemy can make us miserable with guilt, anxiety and frustration. God can forgive us if we seek His forgiveness, for nothing stands between my Lord and His abundant forgiveness toward me.

In the scripture you read this morning, there was a warning: sin can by no means go unpunished. It can be forgiven, but there will always remain consequences. We are warned of sin because it has a ripple affect—that ripple affect can even be passed down to our children and our children's children. Sin causes things to happen which we have no control over. Other people are harmed by our sin. Sometimes the sins of man are felt for generations—war, epidemic disease, family disputes, child abuse or wife beating—these can all have generational affects. Forgiveness is the comfort of God toward us for our sin—it is the stopping point of that sin and God's acceptance of us back onto the path He has for us—but that sin can still have far reaching consequences.

Moses sets the perfect example for us here in this portion of scripture. After Moses hears about God's character from God, his response is to be in awe of His authority and to bend his knee and bow his head before God. To worship God and give Him complete authority shows a mature response to God's authority and power in our lives.

A BEGINNING PLACE FOR PRAYER TODAY:

Heavenly Father, You alone are worthy of my worship. You alone are the one I love and call Lord of my life. You are in charge of everything in my life and I give you all my love. I thank You for Your constant abounding grace to me—You forgive me when I can barely lift my head up to ask for it. You are always with me, generously giving me Your truth and fulfilling all Your promises to me. Thank You, Father, You are too wonderful for me to even comprehend.

DISCUSSION QUESTIONS FOR TODAY:

1. Is truth always the easiest thing to deal with? When the truth is difficult to bear does that give us an excuse to find an easier way around the truth and not face it squarely? What is generally the outcome of finding a way around doing the hard, but right things in life?

2. What to me is the most serious consequence of sin in my life?

DAY 131

BUT THE LORD IS FAITHFUL, WHO SHALL ESTABLISH YOU, AND KEEP YOU FROM EVIL. II THESSALONIANS 3:3

READING FOR TODAY—EXODUS 34: 9-17, PSALM 37:18-24, I PETER 1: 3-5 AND JOHN 10: 27-30

Blessings cannot flow to us from God if we are not His. Verbally, audibly, we must confess we are His and then we can receive His inheritance. Christianity is a two way street, I must make steps toward and choose to have Him in my life and then God can honor that request and accept me as His. In the first verse of this text in Exodus Moses does just that—he confesses that he and his people are sinners and asks God to forgive and accept them.

Blessings come everyday to everyone because God is generous to everyone, but...there are limits to what God can do if He is not the center of someone's life. I must be born again to see heaven. All people can come to God, but not every person will choose to do that. Our being good and earning the respect and love of other people is not a passport to heaven. Only my full belief in and acceptance of His Son, Jesus, will guarantee heaven for me. Even though I do not fully comprehend heaven, I know that it will be my precious gift from Him and I can look forward to spending eternity with Him.

The "awesome work I will do with you" has always been such a marvel to me. He began working in me the minute I accepted Him. I could feel His presence and I wanted to hear Him speak to me. I wanted Him to guide my life and the Holy Spirit immediately came alongside of me and began to do just that. I was raised in a church from the time I was an infant, it wasn't until I was thirty that He took over my life because I gave it to Him.

I was the proverbial "good person", I had no great testimony of my glaring sinful life and my conversion was simply that I asked Him into my life. Little by little He began to show Himself in me and I was a changed and inhabited person. It has been an amazing adventure with Him. The scriptures I had heard as a child became real to me and the verses of the hymns I had learned to sing before I had a personal relationship with Him were now not just words.

I will always have to make a conscious choice to follow Him. Evil thoughts and situations can still come my way. The Holy Spirit will divert that evil if I continue my fellowship with Him, but I need to be aware that I can be tempted so I must walk circumspectly every day. My desire allows God to bless me abundantly. He promises I will be with Him in heaven if I truly believe, but the paths I take can either be hard or easy because of the truths I choose to believe in. Trouble will come my way because I live in a fallen world, but because of God I will be strengthened and made wiser with each event instead of beaten down and defeated. My joy is in the Lord for now and for eternity.

Like the Israelites, I must seek to destroy the altars of evil all about me, but I don't do it on my own. God's Spirit walks with me daily to show me the evil about me and sometimes the evil in me that He needs to purify. Through His Word I know more about what can cause me harm or give me joy. If I pursue Him, He will call me His child, but even when I don't honor Him, He is that longsuffering God who waits for me to respond to the Spirit He has put in me. Responding to His Spirit allows me to come to my senses so "I will not make a covenant with the inhabitants of this land" (the world).

It is all too easy to fashion gods to worship. Today I must set aside time and worship the one true and living God. Praise God, He is real and alive and He desires my full attention. Marvel of all marvels, He simply desires my attention so He can bless me with His fellowship. His love toward me is constant and unchanging. My desire is that I love Him in the same way.

A BEGINNING PLACE FOR PRAYER TODAY:

Dear Father, thank You for Your infinite love toward me. Help me to open my eyes to You and also my heart. Please let me not be caught up in this world and in myself. Help me to serve You everyday with a pure heart and mind. Words are empty things, please help me to show Your love through my actions. Lord, help me o bear fruit which is an honor to you all the days of my life. Thank You, Father, for Your constant and unchanging love toward me.

DISCUSSION QUESTIONS FOR TODAY:

1. What are the things I can "make a covenant with" that are "the inhabitants of this land"?

2. Why is it necessary to confess my faith in Jesus Christ? Can't I just be a good person and please God that way? What role does submission play in the confession of my faith?

DAY 132

HE WHO HAS MY COMMANDMENTS, AND KEEPS THEM, IT IS HE THAT LOVES ME. AND HE WHO LOVES ME SHALL BE LOVED BY MY FATHER, AND I WILL LOVE HIM, AND MANIFEST MYSELF TO HIM. JOHN 14: 21

READING FOR TODAY– EXODUS 34: 18-28, EPHESIANS 5: 1-2 AND TITUS 3:5

Sometimes we read scripture in the Old Testament and it seems far removed from us. We are not Jewish, we do not follow Jewish law and all the details of sacrifice and feast days seem irrelevant to us, however, a closer look reveals the lessons that are to be learned within these scriptures. Through religious practices God is creating order in the lives of His children. By having them practice these religious rituals He is creating a personal relationship between Himself and the believer.

God functions in order and He expects us to be persons of order. He does not function in chaos and confusion of mind. When God is in charge of our lives there is order and purpose. He is the provider of all things and He is the power who decides and allows us to move through life in our own unique way. Scripture says He is a "jealous God"; He desires our full attention. If our focus is on Him, we will not be distracted by other things and turn to worshipping the things of this world: money, power, material goods or seeking worship for ourselves. In infinite wisdom He established strict boundaries and guidelines for the Jews.

Boundaries represent safety. Laws create order. God's laws show us the type of moral character we are to desire. Our moral character is both private and public. I believe the two should always be the same. God doesn't require us to be holy for Sunday, He requires us to be holy all week, even when no one else but God knows or sees our behavior. Outward obedience to God does not make us holy.

We become living sacrifices to God by walking in love and by being imitators of Jesus, because God gave us, once and for all time, the perfect sacrifice of His Son Jesus as our Savior and He is to be the model we follow. The Jews did not have His sacrifice at this time in their history, so they were obediently working their way to God through good works and ritual. Even today, many are still trying to be holy, but it is impossible because we are human and therefore prone to our sinful natures.

The work of the Holy Spirit washes and renews our spirit. This is accomplished through His daily watchfulness over us and the prodding of our heart toward our Father so that we will do His will and seek His forgiveness for our sins. Jesus sits at the right hand of God making petition for us. I believe He says: "This is my child, I love him and he loves me. I am a covering for this child's sins." God sees no sin in us because Jesus is our covering before His eyes. We are not able to do anything of ourselves except choose Jesus as our Lord and Savior. The rituals we are to practice are prayer and scripture reading. We are encouraged to do these two things and by them we can keep in fellowship with our personal and interested God. We are His and He loves us. Is that too simple? Well, that is the wisdom of God, He confounds the wise!

A BEGINNING PLACE FOR PRAYER TODAY:

You alone have the words of life, Father. Please keep me focused on You. There are no short cuts in living for You. You require that I deny myself and do Your will. You bless me even when I fall short and disappoint You. Please Father, make clear the things I should be about today. I want to be a blessing for You. Help me to have ears to hear and feet that walk in the direction of Your leading. Let me follow Your path without question or doubt. I desire to be Your obedient servant this day. Thank You Father for this new day.

DISCUSSION QUESTIONS FOR TODAY:

1. Have I ever thought of Jesus as my covering before the eyes of God? Why is this a necessity?

2. What rituals are important to me on a daily basis? Do I have a priority list for the day's events and is God a part of that list? Why not?

DAY 133

Peace I leave with you, My peace I give unto you; not as the world giveth, give I unto you. Let not your heart be troubled, neither let it be afraid. John 14: 27

Reading for today– Exodus 34: 29-35, II Timothy 1: 7 and Psalm 91: 4-7

Am I afraid of the will of God in my life today? Has there ever been a time when I was afraid of God's will? The Israelites were afraid; Moses was not. By the time we see Moses in Chapter 34 of Exodus we see him talking with God and letting Him direct his life. The trusting of God's goodness, for Moses, was as natural as breathing for him. This kind of trust takes time to grow and mature. Moses is certainly a much different man than the one God appeared to in the burning bush. We can expect God to work in us the same way. If we lack faith in the perpetual, unrelenting goodness of God toward us, we can experience the exact same fears of the Israelites in this chapter.

Fear is the acceptance of evil in our lives; we get too comfortable in our fears and this is a sinful behavior. It is easy to trust God and accept his ways when life is going well. But what about the times when things are terribly confusing or painful? What about when we wonder: Where is God in all of this? Does He really care about all of this?" Or, what about: "What will He take away from me next?" No matter what the evidence of the past, fear is a very successful tool of the enemy when I allow it to be played out in my mind. If fear is allowed to crowd out the truths of God our fellowship with Him suffers and therefore we suffer. Fear can even block out of our minds how much we are loved and cherished by God

In a state of fear, we move to irrational thoughts like: "Well, maybe my LUCK has run out. Maybe I'll stay forever in this pit!" His promise: I WILL NEVER LEAVE YOU OR FORSAKE YOU can even ring empty when we have allowed fear to consume us. I personally do not think we are much different from the Israelites. So often we stop coming to God with a problem because He has not answered it the way we have petitioned Him to answer it. God is not Santa Claus—He makes the decisions about what is best for us and He gives them to us in His perfect timing. When we stop communicating with God, we lose the peace and joy found only in God's comfort. Coming to God with childlike faith is the hardest thing most adults have to do, but as they mature in their faith it becomes their survival tool. I don't know who said it, but I like the notion "that God is not a crutch for the weak, He is a stretcher!"

God does not choose for us to be afraid of His decisions. He purposefully gave us a picture of Himself in the character of Jesus. Then He gave us the Holy Spirit to dwell inside of us. It is hard to comprehend, but scripture says the Holy Spirit prays for us and intercedes for us (Romans 8:26) and I believe He does this even when we are walking away from communication with God.

Fear is not uncommon in Christians, yet it is the most harmful tool that the enemy has in his arsenal when it comes to destroying a peaceful relationship with God. I believe that fear must be identified immediately in our lives then the Holy Spirit has to be invited in to clean house as soon as possible. When the Holy Spirit is set free, He can invade our everyday thoughts and flood us with the light of God. Searching and reading scriptures can dispel the lies of the enemy in our minds. When our minds are delivered from the lies of the enemy our hearts are open to the truth of God. Scripture reading or the reciting of scripture to ourselves is a daily must! How is it we can become so afraid of life? We are not permanently stuck in any life event because God refashions and refines our lives daily. Fear is a wall we can get over. God is constantly turning evil to our benefit if we allow it. He can make in the insurmountable a pathway to a new place—a place better than we could ever have imagined!

Jesus is the veil that stands between man and God. On the earthly side, the Holy Spirit works so we can see the sin in our lives and ask for forgiveness. He brings into focus what He wants us to work on and the things we must release to God through our Savior. We are only responsible for the things we have control over. It is our job to choose to turn from fear and then to turn everything that makes us afraid over to God. God responds to our obedience by setting us free to live a life without constant fear as our companion.

A BEGINNING PLACE FOR PRAYER TODAY:

Lord, I can be so miserable when I do not let go of fear. Help me today to see You as You are: Omnipotent in all the details of my life, loving me more than I will ever be able to comprehend. Please forgive my foolish and destructive thoughts. In Jesus name, curb the enemy; keep him away from my peace with You. Help me to see irrational fear, give me Your words to cover his words. Thank You Father for the Holy Spirit who inhabits me, I free Him now to do His work in my mind and in my heart. Let me see others who are suffering needlessly with fear and let me speak boldly of Your love. Thank You Father for this day. I love You.

DISCUSSION QUESTIONS FOR TODAY:

1. What am I afraid of today?

2. Does fear rob me of certain spiritual blessings? What are the blessings I lose when fear rules my life?

DAY 134

OH LORD, I KNOW THE WAY OF MAN IS NOT HIMSELF; IT IS NOT IN MAN WHO WALKS TO DIRECT HIS OWN STEPS. JEREMIAH 10:23

READING FOR TODAY—EXODUS 35: 1-19, JEREMIAH 29: 11, LUKE 12: 16-21 AND PROVERBS 16: 1-3

Fear can be overcome in our lives when we begin to understand that God is in charge of who we are to become and everything that is in our lives. Our potential is released and our joy increased only when we submit to God and He is given the power to produce the best fruit in us. Our hearts desire to use a gift that God has given us is unique to us and God can orchestrate the use of it better than we can ever think or imagine. If my plans are to succeed they must be blessed by God first.

Planning for anything and everything is necessary. It's okay to plan, but the plans must be presented to God first with a heart that says: "If the Lord wills we shall live or do this or that", which is found in James 4:15. God wants our talents to further His kingdom, but before He allows your talents to be used, He needs your submitted heart. When He asks the Israelites to "not kindle even a fire in their homes on the Sabbath" He is in essence asking for their full attention. It is as if He says: "Put aside your household chores (your plans) and clear your minds of your worries—Come listen to Me!"

Once He has the Israelites' attention, He gives them His work list. These are the things they must do for the Tabernacle. Where will all these things come from? They will come by the willing hearts of the Israelites through their labors for the Lord. "All who are gifted artisans" will submit their talents to the Lord and He will use them to glorify Himself as the God of Israel—the Great I Am. These men and women are called, as we are today, to come together to have a plan and a purpose for their lives that honors God.

The Sabbath is a great day to plan and to reflect on the past weeks' events. It is even a good time to present your plans for the coming week. But….it is also the time we need to just listen. God plants in us the desires of our heart and He also clears insurmountable pathways for us when we just LISTEN and sit before Him quietly.

Make no mistake; whatever your talents God can use them. Aren't we the happiest when we use what we know best and are confident in? His only requirement is that we use those talents to honor Him. He is saying: "Show the world Who you honor, use your talents for Me!" If you want real blessings in life, you will make detailed plans with the Lord and You will allow Him to close down old dreams and create better dreams.

Sometimes He creates dreams we could never have dreamt possible. And sadly, sometimes, because we are so limited in perceiving what He has for us, we settle for small dreams. God has a plan for us that is for our own good and not for evil; He has a plan for us that is a hope for our future. Surprisingly, we are usually the only ones who limit God's work in our lives, because we are not submissive nor are we obedient in following His leading. When we replace the questioning heart with a willing heart we receive a trusting heart.

All of God's Word is a personal love letter to us. These are not empty commandments. These are the requests of God that make us the person He intended us to be. We need to honor these commandments because they honor Him. Wherever there is peace, we will find God's will in operation. Wherever there is confusion and striving we will find a Christian working his own plan in his own strength.

We can even get into the unfortunate habit of giving God our plans only for His approval, long after we have moved out in our own strength. Only expecting God's approval, limits God. This attitude puts us in charge and we are really quite taken aback when the doors close on those plans. The only plans that succeed are God's plans—so why waste our time always having doors close on our plans?

A BEGINNING PLACE FOR PRAYER TODAY:

Lord, thank You for all Your blessings in my life. Please show me what it is that I need to do to bless you before man. Help me to step aside, Father, and let You take over this day. Please forgive me for my lack of trust I know that all You require of me is to just let it all go and let You take care of everything. There has been too much planning on my part, so help me, please, to consult You and expect You to open and close doors.

DISCUSSION QUESTIONS FOR TODAY:

1. Why do I think God's plans are better for me than my plans?

2. Have I been experiencing a lot of "door closing" recently? Where do I think the problem lies in my lack of success?

DAY 135

FOR THE LORD DOES NOT SEE AS MAN SEES; FOR MAN LOOKS AT THE OUTWARD APPEARANCE, BUT THE LORD LOOKS AT THE HEART. I SAMUEL 16: 7

READING FOR TODAY– EXODUS 35: 20-29, PSALM 112 AND ECCLESIASTES 12:13

"A willing heart" and "everyone whose spirit is willing", these are the people who serve the Lord and please Him. For our work to be pleasing to the Lord it must be done with a willing heart and a spirit of willingness. There is power and strength and even divine purpose in all our works when they are committed to the Lord.

It is not, therefore, what we do that pleases God; it is the WHY of what we do that honors and pleases Him. If we look about our world we will observe that the truly happy people in this life get the most joy out of life when their labors provide or produce joy in other people. God's great commandment is "to love God and others as yourself." It is important I think to remember that love is a verb, it is an action word, and when there is action there is fruit for God's kingdom.

The simplest task can become burdensome if we do not do it for the right understanding of God's faithful blessings to us. It is important first, I think, to take the ability to do something as a blessing. I have my health, for example, the simplest task could not be performed without that health--thank You Lord for my health. The fact that I can think through a task and accomplish it is a blessing. Thank You Lord for the intellect you have given me. I can do the task with special skill—that is another blessing because you have taught these hands to be capable for the doing of this task. The most joyful way of doing a task is always about thanking the Lord for His blessings, even for the mundane in appearance.

God needs all kinds of laborers in this life to build His kingdom, so no one is of more value than the next. There should never be a time when we say: "I am only". No one is "only", they are "all" that God has called them to and the completion of that task is both their labor in service for the Lord and their reward from the Lord. I think real joy comes in knowing that you have fulfilled your responsibilities in life well.

The verse from I Samuel 16 at the top of this study is taken from the story of David and his selection by Samuel to be king. David was faithful over the little things of life; he was a shepherd. God knew the heart of David and David was God's choice as a leader. No matter what the task, God could count on David to seek His face and try to do it God's way. David grew to be the man God needed to him to be because his heart was turned toward God and the task at hand.

In these scriptures today, we see the people of God stepping forward to do the tasks needed for the Tabernacle. They are filled with the joy of the Lord because they are each working at what they do best. The sum of all their gifts and talents will produce a beautiful work that will honor the Lord and at the same time will bless each of them with a sense of joy and accomplishment. I have learned that a willing heart, for whatever the job at hand, always produces joy and a sense of accomplishment.

A BEGINNING PLACE FOR PRAYER TODAY:

Lord, I need your forgiveness. I get weary in doing because my eyes are on the task and not on You. Please forgive my failure to thank You for the simple joy of doing. I really need this heart of mine cleaned up. I need You to set me on a path of joyful, conscious doing in Your name.

Please help me to take my name off my accomplishments and put Your name on them. Thank you that I have the ability to do what You call me to today. Please help me to quickly give You praise for everything You allow in this day and the strength I will need to perform these tasks. Thank You, Father, for this day. I want to serve You and bless You all day long.

DISCUSSION QUESTIONS FOR TODAY:

1. If the Lord were to examine my heart for doing the mundane today, what would He find?

2. Do I have a willing heart to serve? If my heart has become weary in well-doing, what can I do to correct that?

DAY 136

BUT SEEK FIRST THE KINGDOM OF GOD AND ALL THESE THINGS SHALL BE ADDED TO YOU. THEREFORE DO NOT WORRY ABOUT TOMORROW, FOR TOMORROW WILL WORRY ABOUT ITS OWN THINGS. SUFFICIENT FOR THE DAY IS ITS OWN TROUBLE. MATTHEW 6: 33-34

READING FOR TODAY–EXODUS 35: 30-35, EXODUS 36: 1, PSALM 90: 16-17 AND PROVERBS 2:10-12

God has called His people to a task and for that task He gives them "the Spirit of God in wisdom and understanding, in knowledge and all manner of workmanship." "Artistic workmanship" is the gift of God to His people. They have chosen to work for Him and now He will bless them as they labor.

Living in this world often takes artistic workmanship. With God's help we can approach each day as new and fresh rather than feeling the stress or dread of it. When the attitude of the heart is "service for God" we can set aside the worries of this day and focus on the tasks for today. Staying in today and not projecting out into the future can also keep us from being worriers. Planning this day's activities only and not too much more allows us to rest in God's provision for today.

Not every day is a day we can enjoy, but every day is a day in which we can rest in the Lord. Resting in the Lord, to me, is really saying: "I am confident in the Lord." Whatever the work of the day or the events of this day, I know He will get me through them. His Holy Spirit will speak to me all day long, if I will call upon Him. He alone will give me wisdom and order. I cannot plan what I do not know. Piece by piece He assembles the day and the people in it for me.

The beauty of the Lord is upon us when we work as unto the Lord. Prideful problems and interests can be set aside and pure wisdom and the discernment of making a project come together and move to completion through the help of the Lord adds simple joy to living. Things for me are less complicated and far less stressful when I have His presence in my day. A peaceful positive countenance is an attractive thing to a non-believer. We become really good witnesses for God when His peace rests upon us. The confidence we have in the Lord speaks volumes to others when our labors are completed in His strength and not our own.

Evil is always about us and with it comes the influence to try and move us to negative thoughts about tomorrow, but dealing with only one day at a time allows us to focus our energies on the things at hand. God's wisdom and understanding as we go about the day through the power of the Holy Spirit gives us discretion in how we will respond to the challenges of the day. When God is in charge, He is the one opening and closing doors, life is positive and uplifting to our souls. "It (the day) is pleasant to your soul" and according to scripture, "you are delivered from the way of evil." Anger, frustration and fear are the ways of evil and these can be managed and minimized by the Holy Spirit because we are confident in the Lord.

We are like the children of Israel; God still sets the tasks, he still gives wisdom and understanding and He still requires us to work only one day at a time knowing confidently that He is in charge. Nothing we do can be done peaceably or in order without His divine hand upon our lives.

A BEGINNING PLACE FOR PRAYER TODAY:

Please forgive me, Father for worrying about the total picture of my life? I desperately need You to restore peace and rest in me. Let me enter into Your rest each day before I begin my day. You will accomplish what is best for me if I can just let go long enough to let it ALL be Yours to deal with. Please take my hands off this day. Let me be confident that whatever You accomplish through my diligence is exactly what You require and nothing more! Let me praise you for Your faithfulness and let me share Your peace with others. Thank You for the tasks of this day.

DISCUSSION QUESTIONS FOR TODAY:

1. What is God working on in my life today?

2. What is my source of confidence for today's agenda?

DAY 137

BRETHREN, I DO NOT COUNT MYSELF TO HAVE APPRHENDED; BUT ONE THING I DO, FORGETTING THOSE THINGS WHICH ARE BEHIND AND REACHING FORWARD TO THOSE THINGS WHICH ARE AHEAD, I PRESS TOWARD THE GOAL FOR THE PRIZE OF THE UPWARD CALL OF GOD IN CHRIST JESUS. PHILIPPIANS 3: 13

READING FOR TODAY– EXODUS 36: 2-7, PSALM 143: 10, DEUTERONOMY 5: 1, 32, 33 AND COLOSSIANS 3: 22-24

The demands of God upon our lives are usually not for an eternity, they are usually for a season. The materials for the tabernacle mounted very quickly as the children of Israel brought the requested materials every morning. Soon everyone was "restrained from bringing materials" because not only was there "sufficient material", "indeed too much" had been offered by the "willing hearts" of the people.

Willing hearts accomplish much, but we need good leadership within our bodies of believers and in our own hearts to know when a job is complete or when the laborers need to be given a rest. Building projects have beginning and ending places, but lives of service need to be monitored very carefully. God knows when a commitment has come to an end and a new one needs to begin. It is important to listen to the voice God as He speaks to our spirits concerning the ministries we have taken on.

Martyrdom is never the place we need to go when serving the Lord. Pressing toward a goal for the Lord is a heart attitude. It has nothing to do with pride. The turning over of a ministry to someone else is healthy for a ministry. We are not storing up treasures here on earth—especially not in quantities of pride or self-esteem. Sufficient materials are gathered and then it is time to call a halt to the gifts. Joy becomes "the sufficient material" when a job is done to satisfaction and then it is time to begin a new work.

Moses listened to his artisans and he knew the materials were now store housed. The children of Israel worked hard and the Lord honored their labors and let them build their own lives with the fruits of their labors. As it says in Deuteronomy 5:33, they had walked in the ways of the Lord every morning, with their gifts and then they were allowed to live well. We can never out give God. He blesses us continually as we "do heartily, as unto the Lord."

The raising of children, the art of a beautiful marriage, and the committed heart to anything that honors the Lord is valued by God. In the world's eyes, children, marriage, and a committed heart for the Lord are really small achievements, but in God's eyes they are highly valued accomplishments. As Christians we strive to inherit the kingdom of God and so we are not men pleasers, we are God pleasers. Our service to God is always in the end a service to man. The priority of anything we do is first to serve God so we might increase His kingdom here on earth: "We press for the goal which is the upward calling of God in our life." God honors our labors with peace and the rest we need if we are faithful not to get too carried away with anything. When there is a lack of peace in something we are doing for the Lord or we are so tired we cannot see straight, then it is safe to assume we are working on our desires and in our own strength and not God's. We always need to remember that we can be replaced by another saint; our work is our work only as long as God desires us to do it—no one is irreplaceable but God!

A BEGINNING PLACE FOR PRAYER TODAY:

Lord, Thank You for this new day. I desire to serve You where you see fit. Keep my eyes on You and not the task. Give me a light touch toward all my possessions and all my talents. Everything I have or am should serve You and You alone. Let me step aside as I allow You to determine my value to each task. Give me a joyful heart even in the mundane tasks of life. Do not let me be weary in well doing. Please give me a joyful and willing heart to serve You today. Thank You, Father, please forgive my short sighted approach to life—You alone know the beginning and then end of a commitment. Please keep me faithful to You, Father.

II CORINTHIANS 9: 8: AND GOD IS ABLE TO MAKE ALL GRACE ABOUND TOWARD YOU; THAT YE, ALWAYS HAVING ALL SUFFICIENCY IN ALL THINGS, MAY ABOUND TO EVERY GOOD WORK.

DISCUSSION QUESTIONS FOR TODAY:

1. Is there a ministry that I am experiencing burn-out in? What might the Lord be trying to tell me about that ministry?

2. Why is peace a good measuring stick for whether I should be involved in a ministry?

DAY 138

Through wisdom a house is built, and by understanding it is established. By knowledge the rooms are filled with precious and pleasant riches. Proverbs 24: 3-4

Reading for today– Exodus 36: 8-38, Ephesians 1:3, Philippians 4: 19 and Proverbs 8:14

The tabernacle was built to be portable, but its quality, design and function were perfect because God designed the blueprint. Exodus says that the artisans who built the tabernacle where full of understanding and knowledge and that when it was completed it would be filled with "precious and pleasant riches." Like the temple of God our faith is portable and the design of it is constantly being fashioned by God so as a functioning Christian we will be full of the knowledge of God's ways in our life.

God is the master builder, we are not. His blueprint for our lives is revealed piece by piece. It's never quite like we planned and yet is meets our needs perfectly. Knowledge of the Word of God and a willing heart to allow God to do the building of our faith insures us that our lives will stand for something of value in God's eyes—which usually translates that our faith will also bless others.

Sometimes things happen in our lives which defy our limited knowledge to see the value of them and there are times when we question the "preciousness" of them. It is often through hind sight that we see that what the world meant for evil God has turned to our good. Pleasant riches are not what we first encounter as we experience some of the ways God forms our walls. In fact we often second guess the fasteners of the wall, but God knows the metal we need.

No where in the Word of God are we promised a life free from tribulation, but we are promised that we are blessed "in heavenly realms with every spiritual blessing in Christ." (Ephesians 1:3) Also we are told that "God will meet all our needs according to his glorious riches in Christ Jesus." (Philippians 4: 19) The metals God uses as fasteners to faith in Him are overseen by our living Savior, Jesus. Therefore, we can be assured that in time what we experience will be turned into a blessing for us and for those we love.

Spiritual knowledge is an ongoing process and we experience the "counsel and sound judgment of God" as we search His scriptures and pray. God has the "understanding and the power" to control all the facets of our lives. The rooms of the temple of our faith are filled day by day with His blessings. What I have discovered is that my life experiences become my own personal "precious and pleasant riches" and they are the foundation of my faith even when the world looks at some of those experiences as tragedies. I have experienced the growth and the wonder of these tragedies and I now count them as precious and pleasant riches.

A wonderful pastor in my life used to use the phrase: "It's the WORST BEST DAY of your life" when you came to him for counseling after something bad had befallen you. God shuts doors as He wills, but He also opens them as He wills, knowing what we need and how He can prosper us spiritually and emotionally. Spiritual blessings are not monetary or material in nature; they are the things on which our eternal character is established. Little by little, it is our job to let go of the things we hold dear and to commit wholly unto God everything we possess and that requires complete obedience to the will of God. Life changes so quickly that each day produces a new set of circumstances and emotions that only God can fashion into our personal temple of faith. So far the best advice I can offer anyone is: Let Go and Let God Handle It, All of It!

A BEGINNING PLACE FOR PRAYER TODAY:

Father, please forgive me for holding on to things I need to let You take care of. Deliver me from manipulation and replace it with trust in You. You must be my source of sound judgment—especially when I don't even know where to turn. Please help me Father to count the "pleasant and rich blessings" You have already provided. Check my heart for me—draw up the unclean things and purify me with Your Spirit. Thank You Father, I love You, please help me to love You more and be a blessing to You.

DISCUSSION QUESTIONS FOR TODAY:

1. Why do I think obedience to God's Word is important?

2. Can I recall "A Worst Best Day" in your life?

DAY 139

FOR THE WORD OF GOD IS QUICK, AND POWERFUL, AND SHARPER THAN ANY TWO EDGED SWORD, PIERCING EVEN TO THE DIVIDING ASUNDER OF SOUL AND SPIRIT, AND OF THE JOINTS AND MARROW, AND IS THE DISCERNER OF THE THOUGHTS AND THE INTENTS OF THE HEART. HEBREW 4:12

READING FOR TODAY– EXODUS 37: 1-9, PSALM 145, I PETER 1: 23 AND PROVERBS 30:5

The ark is the chest which houses the holy commandments of God. In my Bible sub-notes it says that it "symbolized the throne of the Lord, the great king, who chose to dwell among his people." (Exodus 25:10) From the chest God communicated with Moses and the cherubim marked the seat of the ark as the place of atonement—the act of grace where God made man reconciled to Him because He desired to be one with man.

Real communication with God is possible only for Christians. Many will call on His name, but only the ones who accept His Son as their Savior will experience the Holy Spirits' leading on a daily basis. Sharing with God on a daily basis allows us to experience His comfort and His direction. He is the "discerner of the thoughts and intents of the heart" of every believer who approaches His mercy seat. The ark is the symbol of that throne. That throne is with us every day, wherever we are, in whatever situation we find ourselves and it is wise to go to that seat every morning and every evening to determine what God has for us.

The audible voice of God resounds to us in His word. No matter what the question, He will speak to us in scripture and provide our needs for the day. "The Lord is near to all who call on Him…..He fulfills the desires of those who fear Him….He hears their cry and saves them." (Psalm 145: 18 and 19) According to scripture "the word of God is flawless."(Proverbs 30:5) and it says what it must to us, it should never be watered down or twisted, for it is then that we can become comfortable in our sins.

God is interested in everything we think about. He desires us to prosper and be taken care of spiritually. The prosperity He deals with is spiritual in nature. If our spiritual discernments are focused on God's commandments then our soul and body needs will be met. I believe God wants us to be reliant solely on Him, but at the same time confident to take steps toward our needs because we trust Him. Reliant and confident are two words which can only be the same in God's economy—they are opposites in the world's economy. In God's economy our confidence is based on the fact that we can rely on God's righteousness.

My soul, to me, is my own personality, right or wrong, it is the way I think, act and portray emotion. These are the unique God given character traits that make me who I am. My spirit is the energy or the vitality that I pursue life with—that quality will either be of God or reflect how the enemy has managed to alter momentarily my vitality. When I allow the spirit of God to flow through me, He can control my soul and I can praise Him for "His greatness (which) no one can fathom." When I choose to honor the negative side of my personality—the enemy has His way with me. The ongoing power of the

Holy Spirit in my life to apprehend my thoughts and emotions is proof that God knew I needed more than just an earthly visit from God in the form of Jesus; I needed His Spirit within me. In His infinite wisdom God gave me a permanent part of Himself and because of that Spirit His word speaks to me daily. It is my responsibility to go to the ARK daily and open the pages of His Word.

A BEGINNING PLACE FOR PRAYER TODAY:

Dear Father, thank You for Your Word and Your Spirit. Thank You that You decided to reconcile me to You through Your precious Son. You comprehend and apprehend all my thoughts and prayer and I thank You that You care for me so personally and completely. Please fill me with Your Holy Spirit so that You can speak to me and help me discern the good from the fruitless thoughts of my day. Thank You, Father that you are always ready to instruct me and make me the person that You desire me to be.

DISCUSSION QUESTIONS FOR TODAY:

1. How real have I allowed the Holy Spirit to be in my life? Have I been missing out on using His power in my life? What can I do about that?

2. What do I think in my life limits my fellowship with God?

DAY 140

FOR A LITTLE WHILE YOUR PEOPLE POSSESSED YOUR HOLY PLACE, BUT NOW OUR ENEMIES HAVE TRAMPLED DOWN YOUR SANCTUARY. ISAIAH 63: 18

READING FOR TODAY– EXODUS 37: 10 -16, ISAIAH 63: 7 – 9 AND 64: 4 – 5A

The table of the tabernacle was set with the showbread or the bread which represented the presence of God Himself. There were twelve loaves of bread, each representing one of the tribes of Israel and these loaves declared that Israel was consecrated to God and all the fruits of her labor would be consecrated to God perpetually.

Consecration is the act of setting apart something for God. God has consecrated us through His Son, Jesus. We are set apart for His special attention. Every day He offers us protection and power, not to mention the fruits of His Spirit: love, joy peace, patience, kindness, goodness, faithfulness, gentleness and self-control. These gifts can be forgotten about if we do not purposefully set a table for Him in the sanctuary of our hearts.

Enemies can "trample down" our sanctuary if we are not careful to dedicate ourselves to Him. These enemies are subtle and they all fall within the schedule of the day—TIME. It is important that we set time aside. We schedule all the things we love to do and of course, the things we must do. Why is it that praise and thankfulness are so hard to schedule?

Perpetual or "at all times" is the key phrase to keeping the consecration of our lives in the present tense. God is perpetual in His presence with us and so whether we acknowledge it or not God is always personally present with each of us. Acknowledging His perpetual presence is an attitude of choice. I can choose to thank Him all day for everything that comes along or I can choose to get caught up in the schedule of the day and never put a thought to Him. I really need to be aware of the little things of life: Do I thank him for my health, my talents, my family, my friends, the roof over my head, the food on the table, my transportation to work, my job, the four seasons of the year? What do I thank Him for? How often do I thank Him becomes a really important question if I truly want to have fellowship and direction from Him.

I have found over the years that the easiest way to deal with fear and anxiety is to have a perpetual and well exercised dialogue of praise with the Lord. No matter how simple the experience or even how miraculous some things are—they need to be addressed before the Lord. When we start the day wondering how we'll make it through—do we thank Him at the end of the day that He got us through? Do we thank Him in the middle of the day: How often do we call upon His name? "I will tell of the kindnesses of the Lord, the deeds for which He is to be praised according to all the Lord has done for us"(Isaiah 63:7) is a perpetual consecration of my life, as well as, an acknowledgement of God's care and provision for me.

It has been my experience that the end result of perpetual praise is perpetual blessing by God. The fruits of the Spirit are never mine to enjoy if I let the enemy, Time, become the ruler of my life. Some days I look up and suddenly realize I'm getting it all done, but I'm not enjoying it. Whatever it is that I choose to put my energies into should be a joy to my soul at the end of the day if I can thank God that He has accomplished it. When something has gone to completion and I experience His joy in doing it then I know that it is something He wants me to be about. The table of my heart, like the table in the tabernacle, should always be set with perpetual praise, but if it is not, then it is necessary for me to ask God to make it the desire of my heart.

A BEGINNING PLACE FOR PRAYER TODAY:

Forgive my schedule Lord—how absurd that I do not constantly praise you! Please open my eyes Lord to see You in my life. My desire is that You open my ears to hear Your cries to me, so I can respond to the situations of life at hand.

Please help me to be willing to put hands to the tasks that I don't especially like and at the same time be thankful that I have Your gift of health and talent to pursue and accomplish them. Open my mouth to speak—out loud daily—to all who will listen about much You bless me. Thank You for this new day to begin again and broaden and build my praises to You as a perpetual offering because it is You who have chosen me to be Your consecrated servant. Please let me be a blessing to You, Father. I love You, Father.

DISCUSSION QUESTIONS FOR TODAY:

1. Give some reasons why it is important to be in an attitude of perpetual praise.

2. What does God's consecration in our lives insure in our own personal blessings?

DAY 141

YOU ARE THE LIGHT OF THE WORLD. A CITY ON A HILL CANNOT BE HIDDEN. MATTHEW 5: 14

READING FOR TODAY— EXODUS 37: 17-23, EPHESIANS 5: 8 AND MATTHEW 5: 14-16

Am I a lamp stand? Do I go about life reflecting the light that is God's light in my life? Remember the song: This Little Light of Mine? It's a simple little ditty, but it is really what life with Christ should be like. Life should be the very reflection of God's glory. Other people want my Jesus in their lives when He is reflected in my life in all His glory and majesty.

Once the revelation of God's love for us is real to us; it becomes clear how special we are, as are all His creations. I am complete because God is with me. I need not search for anything more in my life except to be the reflection of Christ's love for me. To me, the oil I have is the sum of all the talents and gifts God has given to me in the very creation of my life. The light which shines from me is the Spirit of God working with me to produce His will in my life so that others may come to know His light in their lives.

Scripture speaks constantly of His light in my life: "He is (the) light unto my path", "the Lord is my light and my salvation", "the Lord will be your everlasting light", "the light shines in the darkness" and "so put on the armor of light." Isn't it interesting that all about us is darkness in this world, but because we know the Lord we have light to share?

When the darkness of 911 over shadowed this nation, the light of God was shed abroad. People came from all walks of life to seek the light from God. Instinctively man knows God is in charge, even the atheists wanted to know why God could let this happen. No one stood on the side of darkness, every man wanted light. Light is more than warmth. It is truth and knowledge and comfort because it is constant and unchanging. Change is the thing we fear the most—the unknown. But, to know God is to know constancy. His righteousness and mercy never change no matter how the world tries to distort righteousness.

I think it is important to remember that even from the task of raising a child to the awesome task of running a nation; God's light always meets the challenge. As Christians, even though we do not understand all things, we are confident that God does. Living life appears to me to be a set of circumstances which continually change and continually need the light of God shed upon them. When I ask for His light, He generously gives it to me and He withholds no good thing from me when I seek to share His light with others.

"And whatsoever we ask, we receive of Him, because we keep His commandments and do those things that are pleasing in His sight." I John 3: 22

A beginning place for prayer today:

Father, please forgive me for not shinning forth. Please take the light from under my bowl and help me set it on the table for all to see. Let me put others first. Who shall I share Your love with today? How can I be of help so others will not be locked in despair? Teach me to see the needs of others first. I have You, I am complete—now where would You have me begin this day? Who is on your list: Please open these eyes and expand my vision. I desire Your vision for my life. Thank You for this new day; this fresh new slate to write upon. I love You, Father.

Discussion Questions for today:

1. How am I sharing the love of the Lord in my life? Am I making a conscious effort?

2. Why is light such a powerful tool in this dark world?

DAY 142

BE IMITATORS OF GOD, THEREFORE, AS DEARLY LOVED CHILDREN AND LIVE A LIFE OF LOVE, JUST AS CHRIST LOVED US AND GAVE HIMSELF UP FOR US AS A FRAGRANT OFFERING AND SACRIFICE TO GOD. EPHESIANS 5: 1-2

READING FOR TODAY– EXODUS 37:25-29, II CORINTHIANS 2: 14-17 AND I CORINTHIANS 13: 4-8A

Every word and action that proceeds from me should be evidence of Christ at work in me. The evidence speaks loudly that God has done a good work in me in some areas and that He's still at work in other areas. It would be marvelous to be that "triumphal procession in Christ" and be that "fragrance of the knowledge of Him" that is spread everywhere—but it is an ongoing process and I must expect it to take time. Some days I'm more successful than others, but I should always be hopeful that I will not let Him down today.

Every day we encounter the saved and the unsaved. The basic desire is to be "the fragrance of life" and not "the smell of death." Being an "imitator of God" requires us to practice love and be in constant prayer. It's one thing to say "I wish I were..." and then another thing to choose the actions of putting that wish into operation. What are the steps I'll need to take that will start "the procession"? Self-awareness serves no purpose, except to identify the sin in our lives. It is the doing something about it that makes the procession begin to move toward my becoming "the imitation of God" for good in other peoples' lives.

Forgiveness and acceptance are the two powerful fragrances of Christ that I need to cultivate. If I can forgive I not only can move on with my life, I can learn to let God forgive me and let God love me just as I am. If I can accept weakness in others, see it for the harm it creates in their lives, then I can be compassionate to those who are trapped in sin. My personal goal in life is to value everyone because I know God values them. To me there is no one person more valuable than the next and I desire to exhibit that fragrance for Christ.

Be it family, friend or acquaintance, I want people to be comfortable in my presence. Granted there are some I have a hard time with, but it's my choice to make the effort. I cannot change people, I can only change myself. An open spirit, a smile, is the first prerequisite to becoming the fragrance of Christ. Then there must come a spirit of giving. Words, a listening ear, generous actions; these are the characteristics of Christ. These are the characteristics I need to foster.

We are "peddling" the love of God if we are not truly loving toward others. No matter what we say our actions will always overshadow our words if we do not enter into tough situations, by choice sometimes, and deal with the tough people in our lives with God's love. Unfortunately, Christianity is viewed as hypocritical more than genuine these days. You can blame it on the TV evangelist peddler, but I think we ought to look first at ourselves. How real is my God in my life when that relationship is seen and heard daily by others? If I am to be the fragrance of God to those who "are being saved" and to "those who are perishing" my words and actions need to be visible and constant in my daily life. Walking God's way is always our choice and that choice becomes our fragrance

A BEGINNING PLACE FOR PRAYER TODAY:

Dear Father, please forgive me for not being Your fragrance. Push me, prod me, keep me moving to becoming a person with an open spirit for You. Everyone needs You. Help me to share You today. Be in the middle of all my energies. Help me to put aside the less fruitful things of life. I need you to oversee and help me make choices. Please don't let me waste this day. Someone close at hand needs Your love, show me. Someone who is a stranger may need that love too, show me Lord. Open these eyes and pierce this hard heart. Please help me to forgive and move on to greater love. Thank You Father that Your Son, Jesus, has set the perfect example for us all.

DISCUSSION QUESTIONS FOR TODAY:

1. Read Proverbs 31: 8-9. How does this scripture speak to me personally?

2. Read II Corinthians 3:1-4. Am I a good fragrance for Christianity or am I professing one thing and saying and doing things that make me anything but a fragrance for Christ?

DAY 143

BLESSED BE THE LORD ACCORDING TO ALL THAT HE PROMISED; NOT ONE WORD HAS FAILED FOR ALL HIS GOOD PROMISE..." I KINGS 8:56

READING FOR TODAY– EXODUS 38: 1-7, PSALM 91: 1, ROMANS 11: 33 AND ROMANS 8: 16

I have come to believe that the best burnt offerings are the sins which God has allowed me to set on His altar and the burnt offerings of evil circumstances that God has triumphed over in my life. This is the part of my faith that proves to me every day that I AM because GOD IS in my life. Nothing ministers more to my soul than the successes God has made in my life, regardless of the gravity of my failures.

In truth, I believe that if it were not for these burnt offerings I would be shallow and of little value to God. No one wants to be around "the perfect Christian", we are usually more comfortable with a "changed servant of God" who has wisdom to share because he or she has "been there"! Survival is a precious commodity when it comes to living life. Everywhere about us people are perishing with the problems of this world: lost love, lost future, lost jobs, lost fortune, and even loss of self. How refreshing we become when we share the fragrance of Christ in the things He has overcome and then accomplished in us and through us.

To be real is the fragrance of the burnt offering. I am most valuable to God when I am not sharing pie in the sky, Pollyanna stuff; I need to share the hard, cold fact of a life changed. It doesn't require that my testimony be a life of drug addition, prostitution, theft or murder. It requires a life that is lived successfully from day to day because my God has made and is making changes in me for His service. It's the doing and the accomplishing of good over adversity that gives us hope for the future because God honors us with His presence in the middle of the things we seem powerless to alter, let alone change for good instead of evil.

How big is our God? Some think too small—think BIG! Think bigger than we can even possibly image and perhaps that is only one one-hundredth of His true size. The burnt offerings of our lives can become outrageous bond fires if we begin to think in terms of the warmth they have offered our souls. When I look back I cannot believe the things He has accomplished nor the circumstances He has used. But…He has blazed a trail through those things like the Lone Ranger, making good where evil could have triumphed. It is good that I rehearse these events aloud because in them is the truth that NO ONE LOVES ME LIKE GOD. I have evidence; I need to share that evidence whenever possible.

My God is an awesome God. He deserves to be spoken of that way. Do a word search. What words describe God? What words do we use to describe Him? My suggestion is that we expand our God vocabulary and then begin to put faith in those characteristics. I know that our burnt offerings can become sweetness to everyone we share them with when we have an expanded God vocabulary and the faith He has produced in us.

A BEGINNING PLACE FOR PRAYER TODAY:

What have I forgotten or taken for granted? Please quicken my heart to the things You have accomplished. Help me not to be afraid to minister to those who are in sorrow or distress. Help me to share how You have helped me. I desire that you give me Your wisdom. Lord, make my life a bond fire of all my sins and all Your triumphs. Teach me to praise You every day. Out of our terrible circumstances You have made miracles. Help me Father to be a better witness for You. Open my mouth so I may praise You this day and for forever. Thank You, Father, for this new day.

DISCUSSION QUESTIONS FOR TODAY:

1. What words do we use to describe God to others and to ourselves? What kind of adjectives are used in the Psalms?

2. Are perfect Christians a reality? What is the best we can hope for in our personal walk with the Lord?

DAY 144

ANYONE WHO LISTENS TO THE WORD BUT DOES NOT DO WHAT IT SAYS IS LIKE A MAN WHO LOOKS AT HIS FACE IN A MIRROR AND, AFTER LOOKING AT HIMSELF, GOES AWAY AND IMMEDIATELY FORGETS WHAT HE LOOKS LIKE. JAMES 1: 23-24

READING FOR TODAY– EXODUS 38:8, ECCLESIASTES 12: 13-14 AND TITUS 3: 3-7

Even though the bronze of the mirrors were used to make the laver, I could not help but think that maybe a mirror would be a good adornment for any church entry. It would not be for the purpose of straightening our tie or checking our make-up, but for looking at ourselves as God would see us. If the church is a place of communion with God; then it should be a place of reflection (NO PUN INTENDED). How carefully do I view myself?

Fortunately, God looks at the heart of man. But, He requires us to look at our own hearts too. There are outward signs of our goodness and of our sins which others see and it is up to us to check those character traits on a regular basis. We can look deeply into the reflection of our heart motives or we can look quickly, making hasty repairs and them moving on without looking too closely or asking God to make changes in that heart that will be permanent.

Once we've seen the dirt in our life it requires action to clean it up—hence the basin! The "washing of the Word" is a powerful tool when applied to the reflection of the mirror of our soul. So often, the root of our problem lies within us and yet we look other places for answers. The mirror can reflect the root of the problem and the basin can clean it out if the reflection is taken seriously.

Peter knew he didn't need just his feet washed—he said he needed "not just my feet but my hands and my head as well". (John 13:9) The basin can wash away the sins of each day, one day at a time, if we choose to use it that way. The mirror of heart reflection for us needs to be a daily process. Repentance is a cleansing process like no other. It is for us a perfect and complete separation from the sin that besets us. God freely washes sin away—but…we have to look squarely into the mirror and ask for His forgiveness.

Sometimes, a mate or a friend is a mirror. Often what I am doing I see reflected in the response of my mate or a friend. To be honest, life circumstances, I think, are in general a reflection of the state of our hearts. How we respond to the sin in our lives is usually a reflection of how committed we are to obeying God's Word. A committed heart bears all things and believes all things to be God's will for their life. I think it is important, therefore, to keep a light touch on the things of this world and at the same time keep checking our heart to see that we are tuned into God's perspective.

Checking my responses to circumstances and to personal relationships, to see if they are a blessing to God is extremely important to my spiritual well-being. Sin will be a part of my life if I am not careful and do not look deeply at things that are buried or seem to be unseen. I believe we need a mirror and a basin to be certain that we are the servants of God that are an honor and a blessing to Him.

A BEGINNING PLACE FOR PRAYER TODAY:

Father, please help me to stay ever vigilant about my motives in life. Help me to look squarely and not only take the blame for things, but do what is right in Your eyes to solve the problem. Please keep me continually searching this heart. I deceive myself so easily. Self-pity and dissatisfaction are the enemy's tools. Please help me to set myself aside and be real—even if the truth hurts. Then, let me act on what I see, never accepting just the sin and allowing it to stay with me. Let me be so uncomfortable with my sin that I will continually scrub away at it with new choices that will honor You. Thank You, Father, that You love me so much that You provide a mirror and a basin which is so conveniently near by, if I will but choose to use them.

DISCUSSION QUESTIONS FOR TODAY:

1. Why is a mirror and a basin needed on a daily basis?

2. What are the things which might keep me from using the mirror and the basin?

DAY 145

BETTER IS ONE DAY IN YOUR COURTS THAN A THOUSAND ELSEWHERE; I WOULD RATHER BE A DOORKEEPER IN THE HOUSE OF MY GOD THAN DWELL IN THE TENTS OF THE WICKED. PSALM 84:10

READING FOR TODAY– EXODUS 38: 9-20 AND PSALM 92

God's courtyard is always open to us. Because of His Son, Jesus, no curtain stands between us and God. He desires our presence in His house and we are foolish children when we try and hide from uncomfortable truths in our lives or rush off to important places before we seek Him. Peace and safety are found in His courts and no man has the wisdom of God, but God.

Life's successes and problems are all up for discussion with the Lord. The alternative is to keep them to ourselves and be limited by our own understanding. In His courtyard there is always wisdom for us. Through Him we can each discern all that is relevant to us. I think a mark of spiritual maturity is demonstrated when I finally understand that all I have, or am, is dependent on His plan for my life. How foolish I must appear to God as I fret and stew: "How long", He must wonder, "will it take before she finally gives it over and relinquishes her perception and analysis?"

His courtyard is a private phone booth with a direct line to His throne room. The walls of His courtyard are mercy and grace and the fasteners of His courtyard are patience and understanding. No matter how many times I cry out, He hears and responds as if it were the first, and not the hundredth (or thousandth) time I've let an emotion drag me away.

The tapestry of my life is displayed on the walls of His courtyard. When I come within His walls I see the woven events of my life more clearly and upon occasion He even lets me move to future visions of who I can become. I prefer that He knows the patterns of my life and that I get to see the pattern piece by piece as it unfolds. What appear to be knots sometime in the weaving are really the places where the pattern is not yet completed. I know I must wait for the knot to be absorbed into the pattern and then in due time the pattern will return and I will understand better the plan God has woven.

It is important that I learn to wait in His courtyard. His time tables are much different from mine—even the order of my needs is not always in tune with what He knows I need to address. The privacy and separateness from the world allows me to settle comfortably within the arms of His shelter. I cannot hear Him nearly as well outside of His courtyard. In fact, the enemy can keep the noise and the confusion of my life to such a degree that I can be without the courtyard experience completely. I must step through His door immediately upon need and then know, that if I wait, His peace will settle over me.

If I want to flourish like a palm or a cedar I must stay planted in the courts of my God as it says in Psalm 92. His promise to me is that I will bear fruit and even in old age will I stay fresh and green. Life can make us cynical and we can dry up if we stay in the world's negative and selfish environment, but in the courts of the Lord my focus can be on praising Him for all His blessings to me and to those I love. I will not give up on the next generation nor will I fear the plans of the world because He will give me His perspective. I love that I am separated by Him from this world and because of that separation I have a very special audience with Him whenever I choose. God will always make my heart glad when I take time to consider His wonderful deeds.

A BEGINNING PLACE FOR PRAYER TODAY:

Dear Father, I need to be in Your presence. Help me to set aside the time daily to sit at Your feet. I can be so easily filled with the dry dust of the world. It is refreshing to my soul to take a drink of You, You are my pure fountain of life. Please go before me today and let me follow after You with praises in my mouth for all to hear. Let me linger in Your presence to hear Your voice and be refreshed. Thank You Father that You always have time for a conversation with me.

DISCUSSION QUESTIONS FOR TODAY:

1. Why do I think a courtyard is an appropriate description for a time of prayer?

2. Why and how do courtyard experiences with the Lord elude us?

DAY 146

But thanks be to God, who always leads us in triumphal procession in Christ and through us spreads everywhere the fragrance of the knowledge of Him. For we are to God the aroma of Christ among those who are being saved and those who are perishing. II Corinthians 4:14 and 15

Reading for today– Exodus 38: 21-31 and II Corinthians 4: 7-18

The furnishings of the tabernacle were made with three elements: gold, silver and bronze. Gold was the most valuable material and was also the softest and most refined. Silver was stronger than the gold and was used as an overlay for many of the objects in the tabernacle. Bronze was a combination of elements and it was used for the rougher more sturdy needs of the tabernacle. Symbolically, I believe, as Christians we are made up of each of the elements used in the tabernacle, because we are the temple of God.

Our basic understanding of God begins in the bronze of our life. We see God as a practical supplier of our needs. The strength He needs in us He builds as the element of bronze and day by day He begins to inhabit us; the result is that we are beginning to appear righteous or good in the sight of other men. Our lives are uniquely fashioned by the events God allows in our lives. Modern science has proven that our DNA is uniquely different from any other person God has ever made. We have the basic needs and basic functions that God has created in all of us and yet each of us has special strengths that God can use for His service and ministry needs. I believe He develops in us a heart that says, "I have strength because You have made my life practical and valuable for service and I am uniquely made for that service."

The silver of my life is the use of the practical brought up to an attractive level that will cause the world to notice me as a servant of God. I am practical and serviceable, but I have special areas that I shine in for the Lord. These are my ministry tools, my gifts; they are faithfulness, kindness and patience. It is my job to polish them, so they shine and are never allowed to tarnish with a lack of use. Some non-believers will be attracted to the Lord because I have the bronze strength of God in my life, but my special gifts can draw them unto God when they are used to meet His needs for them.

The gold of my life is really the softest and the finest points of my spirit. These aspects of my life have taken time and sometimes traumatic purification to make me worthy of service. Refining is a process that burns away what God considers the natural sin nature of man. My sin nature is constantly being refined away so that I can move into a place of service that only life experience has given me—it is called personal wisdom from God. Personal wisdom comes only from the personal exposure of tough things in my life. In it are found the active elements of mercy and forgiveness, long suffering and self-control. These things work together to become the gentleness of Christ living in me. We are fit to serve when we have been refined. God's wisdom is used through us to minister to other people because we have simply "been there, done that and got the tee-shirt"! Whatever befalls us is always stored away as gold. The refining of life's circumstances when filtered through the love of God makes each of us unique and fit for service as it says in II Corinthians 1: 3-4.

The lengths of my days are known only by God, but in that knowledge He is working through the bronze, silver and gold elements of my life to make me who He intended me to be for His service. Even as a new Christian gold is being stored up in me, but is of little value unless the bronze and silver are also present in my life. I never need to strive after the three elements—God is at work in me to produce all three so I can be an attractive aroma for Him.

A BEGINNING PLACE FOR PRAYER TODAY:

Dear Father, there are days when I question the metal I am made of—please forgive me. Help me to use the gifts You have given me and not to be afraid or question the use of them. Let me just come alongside those You present to me with a willing heart to serve You. I know You will provide the words and the timing so I can be a blessing. Please open my eyes to the people around me. Let me see what You would have me see and use it wisely for Your service. Thank You for this day Lord. May I be a blessing to You.

DISCUSSION QUESTIONS FOR TODAY:

1. Why are silver and bronze necessary in my life?

2. Can we name some of the gold experiences to ourselves and then ponder their value? Can I share with the group just one of these and its impact on my life?

DAY 147

LET US PUT ASIDE THE DEEDS OF DARKNESS AND PUT ON THE ARMOR OF LIGHT ... CLOTHE YOURSELF WITH THE LORD JESUS CHRIST. ROMANS 13:12B AND 14A

READING FOR TODAY– EXODUS 39: 1-7, ROMANS 13: 11-14 AND PROVERBS 31: 10-31

Aaron was dressed by God in a very particular way for his service in the tabernacle. Dressing to be a Christian requires that we put on Jesus every day. He is our protection as we are instructed in Ephesians 6: 10-17, but most importantly how we are perceived as Christians is how He is perceived by others who come in contact with us. We must put on Christ daily.

The actions of our day are who we are in Christ. To put on Jesus means to be fully covered by Him daily in the reading of His Word and being fully prayed up in our communication with Him. We are only in danger when we step out of Christ. In Christ we have righteous inward character and outward personality. Our personality and inward character in Christ are love, joy, peace, patience, kindness, goodness, faithfulness, gentleness and self-control. These are the gifts of the Holy Spirit, but they must be purposely put on and sought after every day and all day long. The sin nature of man assures us that we will fail in some areas of our lives every day, but the assurance of Christ, as we mature in Christ, is that we will know it quickly and seek forgiveness immediately when we do fail.

Our character as a Christian is righteousness. Without clothing ourselves in Christ we run the risk of being unrighteous. Our personalities are assaulted daily by the world. We have people and situations in life to face that are often unexpected and sometimes troubling to us just because they can get us to step out of the character of Christ and expose our basic sin nature. No matter how hard we try—we always fail in our own strength to be without sin. Out of our mouths can come the very words we don't want to hear in the tone that is the least of what we want to express. Our patience can be tested simply because we are too selfish to wait or are being too inconvenienced. When tasks get hard and frustrating we can lose patience and self-control. We cannot afford to face the world not clothed in Christ.

For our personal actions to approach righteousness we must slip into the covering of Christ and refresh our memories, sometimes hourly, so that He stands between us and the situations of life. We are at our best when we are in Christ; our success rate in relationships and life situations is a lot higher when we do not work in our own strength. There is a choice to be made each new day. The clothing of us in Christ is not a one time experience, done once and then never done again. It is an "every new day choice" to put Him on through the reading of His scripture and the communion of prayer with Him. If we are to expect our inward character and our outward personalities to grow in a more Christ-like fashion it must be an everyday commitment.

It is important to keep short leashes on things that can quickly get away from us if we choose to overlook them. If my sin nature appears I can step back quickly behind the covering of Christ and expect to see Him adjust it. Not taking the time to be in fellowship with Christ daily causes me to lose the opportunity to gain ground in the perfecting of my faith and in my own personal peace.

Proverbs 31: 10-31 is the model for the admirable Christian woman. It doesn't hurt any of us to review her characteristics. She is fully clothed in the attributes of Christ and these attributes are shown in this portion of scripture in practical everyday application. Note in verse 15 that she gets up early to provide food for her family and her servants. I have always interpreted this as getting spiritual food—the covering of Christ for the day—before she faces the day she hides herself in Christ. Each of us has a different time of day that allows us to spend time with the Lord—for Moms it may only be at night when the house settles down or even in bed before she drifts off to sleep. There is no set time to go about getting my covering, but I do believe, with all my heart, that each day there must be time for me to hide myself in Him. My commitment to Him daily keeps me safe in His care and gives me peace beyond all understanding in all things.

A BEGINNING PLACE FOR PRAYER TODAY:

Dear Father, please forgive me that I get ahead of You and do not always manage to set aside time with You daily. As I reflect on my days, I realize the really successful ones were accomplished with Your presence in them. Foolishly, I think I can handle the day and I do not even check in, until I am in distress. When Father will I learn to slow down and let You go before me? I want to be completely hidden in You, so that all people see is Your love in my life. Thank You, that You bless me daily despite my lack of communication—but don't let me be foolish, please keep my attention focused on You. Place me in Your Word and bless me with Your wisdom—I desire to be clothed in You.

DISCUSSION QUESTIONS FOR TODAY:

1. What steps can I take to insure that I check in with God each day?

2. What is my best time for communion with God? Do I need to be flexible about the time each day or is this a trap to not having the fellowship I need with God?

DAY 148

BLESSED IS THE MAN WHO FINDS WISDOM, THE MAN WHO GAINS UNDERSTANDING, FOR SHE IS MORE PROFITABLE THAN SILVER AND YIELDS BETTER RETURNS THAN GOLD. PROVERBS 3: 13

READING FOR TODAY– EXODUS 39: 8-31, PROVERBS 2: 1-5 AND PROVERBS 3: 13-20

The breastplate was the covering over the heart of the priest and on that breastplate were the stones which were engraved with the twelve tribes of the sons of Israel. In the breastplate Aaron carried the Urim and the Thummin stones. Whenever Aaron entered into the presence of the Lord, these stones helped him to make decisions for the Israelites.

Moses and Aaron both sought the wisdom of God through prayer for themselves and for their people; the Bible instructs us to do likewise. Our breastplate as a Christian is often prayer. Prayer is the covering sometimes over our heart that allows us to pursue wisdom from God. Prayer for us should be as natural and constant for us as breathing. It needs to be the very air we breathe. We of course do not cast the Urim and the Thummin because the knowledge we base our decisions on comes from the Bible. I believe that a daily encounter with the scriptures and sound teaching by our pastors based on the Bible can give us a storehouse of knowledge which when we pray can become the heart of Christ in us. Wisdom for making decisions requires that we pray and get God's leading on those scriptures.

Thanks to the Bible, man today, has a storehouse of knowledge at his finger tips. No matter how wise or accomplished man is in the sciences, or in any of the disciplines, he is never able to fill all the needs in his life—that is the void that only God can fill. If I want the wisdom of life to be mine I must first accept Christ in my life. Through Him I fill that void and with that filling comes the direction of the Holy Spirit in my prayer life and in my scripture reading. God's wisdom promises man that "long life is in her right hand; in her left hand are riches and honor. Her ways are pleasant ways and all her paths are peace. She is the tree of life to those who embrace her (God's wisdom); those who lay hold of her will be blessed." Proverbs 3: 16-18

Wisdom is the understanding of knowledge. All the facts in the Bible will be of little value unless we seek the heart of God to allow Him to tailor the perfect answers for our needs. Intimate fellowship with God is attained in prayer—without that fellowship there is no wisdom. Through intimate fellowship with God I think we begin to experience the knowledge that He is the covering over our hearts that allows us to be protected and perfected by Him for His purposes.

God asks that we "preserve sound judgment and discernment" and that we "do not let them out of (our) sight." He further says that sound judgment and discernment "will be life for (us), an ornament to grace (our) neck. (Proverbs 3: 21-23) Without God's wisdom we are lost in all our ways and we will never find satisfaction—and according to scripture God's wisdom will be visible to others like an ornament around our necks.

God's desire, I believe, is that the unbeliever will first notice and then desire the riches and honor of God's wisdom. In us the unbeliever will see the riches of God's wisdom: love, joy, peace, patience, kindness, goodness, faithfulness, gentleness and self-control. The honor of the wisdom God gives us becomes the trust of others in our judgment.

Our job as Christians is to always point others to the source of our riches and honor—Jesus. We are not given the precious gift of wisdom so that we alone are to be prospered. Our gift of wisdom is to be shared with our mates, our children, our extended family, friends and the world so that they may come to know Christ as their own personal source of wisdom. Jesus is the only way man will have life and that "more abundantly", more abundantly than man can ever even imagine, and we as believers hold that wisdom to share with mankind.

A BEGINNING PLACE FOR PRAYER TODAY:

Dear Father, please forgive me that I let Your Word sit idle on my nightstand sometimes. Forgive me, for the world can consume me and my time and that my prayers are always there before You, but my time in Your Word can get shortened. I need Your wisdom everyday and yet I rely on stored wisdom. Quicken my heart, Holy Spirit, and make me accountable to get fresh manna everyday from You. Please Father create in me a desire to learn something new and precious from You so I will know the source of my life and be able to share those rich blessings with others.

My decisions in life are critical to the well being of so many in my life and I never know when I will need Your perspective before I speak—keep me ever mindful of the difference between Your powerful life sustaining wisdom and my limited knowledge which I sometimes mistake as wisdom and regretfully pass on to others. Thank You for how available to me You are and how faithful You remain to me when sometimes I only think of me. Thank You Father, I love You and ask for Your continued patience with me—I truly desire not to disappoint You or make You ashamed of me.

DISCUSSION QUESTIONS FOR TODAY:

1. Why is it important that I read the Word everyday? What will it hurt if I just skip it for a few days and work on stored knowledge?

2. What, if anything, do I put as more important than setting aside the time to read the Word. Am I consumed with life instead of being consumed with God?

DAY 149

But we request of you, brethren, that you appreciate those who diligently labor among you, and have charge over you in the Lord and give you instruction, and that you esteem them highly in love because of their work. Live in peace with one another. I Thessalonians 5:12-13

Reading for today– Exodus 39: 32-43 and I Thessalonians 5: 9-24

The Exodus passage closes with: "And Moses examined all the work and behold, they had done it; just as the Lord had commanded, this they had done. So Moses blessed them." Man often speaks for God. Fellow Christians are often used by God to bless the body and to exhort one another in the good and the bad times of life. Here we see Moses letting the people know how pleased God is with them in their obedience to His directions and the workmanship of their hands. For this moment in time, God uses Moses as his flesh and blood embodiment to make His people feel His love for them.

Once there was a little boy who was afraid of the dark and his parents told him not to be afraid because "Jesus is always with you." The child's response was something to the effect: "Yes, I know, but it sure would be nice to have someone with skin on to be with me!" And, quite frankly, we humans sometime need the physical touch of Christ through our brothers and sisters. We often need the physical touch and encouragement of a brother or sister in Christ to allow us to keep going or not be weary. "An out loud compliment" by another is sometimes all we need. If life is tough it feels good to have that phone call, letter or hands on prayer with another believer to feel the assurance of God's love and presence in our life

I Thessalonians tells us to "encourage one another, and build up one another." God knows our weakness for needing "someone with skin on." At the same time He knows our sin nature and He doesn't want jealousy or self-pity to alter our dedication to righteousness when life just gets too hard. He knows we need to tell others that we appreciate their work or their attitude in times of hardship and this allows us to say "thank you" to them for God. Jealousy and strife often happen in a church family when we purposefully do not say thank you to one another. Thank you is an interesting phrase because the one who receives it feels good and the one who says it also feels good. We just need to remember to use it generously for even the smallest things and not withhold it until something really big is done for us. "To esteem one highly in love" is the best character building attribute we can share with one another.

Working and living together also requires honesty. So God calls us to "admonish the unruly, encourage the faint hearted, help the weak, and be patient with all men." To me, this part of living together seems to be the hardest—it requires Christ-like qualities to be extended daily to everyone, even when we are dealing with the unruly and the unlovable. Constant self-evaluation is a necessary tool for us, because we have to always remember that we also are not always lovable and we can easily become unruly when the enemy gets momentary inroads into our basic sin nature. This Christ-like personality is only arrived at through constant and often moment by moment prayer on our part—maybe that is why "pray without ceasing" is so opportunely placed as an exhortation in verses 14 and 15. Prayer is the only answer when personal attitude adjustment is needed. We can't change other people, God does that, but we can request of God to change us so that we can meet the challenges of living together in peace. "Faithful is He who calls you, and He also will bring it to pass" is a great reminder that He equips us for everything we need to become His servant, if we will but ask! With the responsibility for living a Christ-like life placed on the shoulders of God daily, we assure for ourselves that we will have a much lighter load to carry all the days of our lives. Thank You Jesus!

A BEGINNING PLACE FOR PRAYER TODAY:

Lord help me to generously use the phrase "Thank You". Let me first of all say it to You over and over again daily—for moment by moment You bless me with Your presence—Thank You. Please help me to have a thankful heart toward others and the role they play in my life. My life is made so much easier by the talents and love and support of others and they need to know I know that fact.

Please open my mouth and let my thankfulness flow out to those who serve me, even when they don't expect it from me. Help me to give hugs with words and actions and to never be afraid to also confront in love those people I do love and want to succeed in your kingdom—especially my children. Father I need Your courage to speak boldly to others and then also to ask for forgiveness when I have been offensive. Please wash me with Your love and work in me this day—Thank You Father!

DISCUSSION QUESTIONS FOR TODAY:

1. Am I good at saying thank you or do I take other people for granted? How can I work on the skill of having a thankful heart and also a heart that exhorts others to good deeds?

2. Father, is there someone in my life that I need to admonish and speak frankly with? How do I know when it is You putting me in the position of admonishing and not just a prideful adventure on my part? What are some of Your righteous clues to me and where do I find those clues?

DAY 150

LIFT UP YOUR HEADS, O GATES, AND BE LIFTED UP, O ANCIENT DOORS, THAT THE KING OF GLORY MAY COME IN! PSALM 24:7

READING FOR TODAY– EXODUS 40:1-38, I CHRONICLES 16: 22-31 AND PSALM 24

The day has arrived, the tabernacle is complete and it is installed and so is this devotional study of Exodus. Moses and all his people have now been exposed to the constant fellowship of God. God wanted fellowship and a personal relationship with them and His work for this season in time is complete. At the close of Exodus He stands as their God and His glory, "the glory of the Lord", fills the temple.

Today as Christians the glory of the Lords fills us, not as a cloud, but manifested fully in His Holy Spirit. He leads us from the inside, something no worldly man can see or understand unless He accepts Jesus Christ as his savior. With His spirit He protects us from everything that would come against us. We are like the Israelites in that every day is a new day and we must seek His direction. Scripture and prayer are the outward signs of our life hid in Christ just as the cloud was the outward sign that God was with the Israelites. I think it is important that we check in with God daily to find out if we should move on or stay within the issues of our lives until He has given us the direction to make those necessary changes. As foolish as it would have been for the Israelites to ignore the cloud, so it is with us, a foolishness to ignore the promptings of the Holy Spirit.

When Exodus began it showed us a people who needed God in their lives. It has progressed with the miraculous moving out of Egypt by this captive people and an incredible journey into the wilderness of life with God as their source of strength. Each of us has come to know the Lord because we have had that same kind of need and we needed to meet Him and have Him become alive in our lives. We have confessed Jesus as our Savior and we have chosen to travel out of the bondage of this world into the pathways of His choice. Our perspective on life has changed, our approach to life and its' circumstances are now viewed through the eyes of Christ. He has become our glory, strength and honor before the world.

Exodus has been a relevant text to us for in it we have seen ourselves and in it we have identified how Christ has worked in our lives. But this, as with all scripture, is not the end of a personal odyssey for us—it is the beginning of the building up of our spirits' alignment with the Holy Spirit so that we can experience His fellowship in our lives for the rest of lives here on earth. Each day we are to move out on the constant journey of seeking those who do not know Him and of being about the business of sharing Him with others. As the years pass we have gotten to know Him better, but we know with each new day there is still much to be discovered about Him.

Our walk with Christ is an extraordinary adventure. We know He loves us, He pursues us and He keeps us safe. We must always remember that we are a constant work in progress for it says in Philippians 1:6: "that He who began a good work in you will perfect it until the day of Christ Jesus". I must never consider myself to "have arrived" at the perfect place, but neither am I to be dismayed that I keep finding sin in my life.

My life in Christ is to be pursued consciously every day. Every day is new and in it will be the Lord's will for my life. If I am faithful to pursue His scripture, pray about what I need and am willing to listen to His voice, He will give me an abundant life. I need not fear tomorrow for He holds that for me—I must let Him lead me through life one day at a time. When anxiety and fear overwhelm me I need to pray. It is my job to continually pray for the peace that momentarily can slip away from me and I must request it back, sometimes daily and sometimes more than once depending on the day. It has been my experience that He is always faithful to bring that peace back to me.

I have learned that if I will try to "regard nothing from selfishness or empty conceit, but with humility of mind regard" each person that I encounter without preconceived judgments, I will find them to be "more important" than myself. I have also found that this supernatural love enhanced by the Holy Spirit removes the all consuming "me" from my daily life. It is important, I think, to remind myself daily that life is not things, it is people and the blessings of my contributions to them and them to me by God's hand that will make each day a day of purpose for the Lord.

For me to grow, I believe it is important that God be ever before me. My prayer life is my fellowship with God. I do not need a prayer closet to speak to Him nor do I need to build an altar. My words need not be eloquent, just honest. When I bow my knee (even figuratively) He is there in an instant. Nothing is too small for Him to consider and nothing is too big for Him to handle. My job is to go to the throne and place my praise and petitions at His feet and leave them there. He is the cloud of glory that will direct me all the days of my life! Thank You Lord.

A BEGINNING PLACE FOR PRAYER TODAY:

Thank you for this day Father. It is another day of my journey here on earth. It is a new day, a new adventure, designed specifically for my growth in You. I need not be eloquent in my prayers, I need to be honest. Please Father, keep this heart clean. Forgive me of my sins and then give me Your wisdom. Without it, I can do nothing of value. Oh, Father, I desire to do things of "value" for You today. Please keep my journey moving toward You. I do not know the length of my journey here on earth but I desire with all my heart that it be a glory and an honor to You. Thank you, Father for this new day – this blank slate, which You can write on. Make of me what You will. I ask these things in Jesus' name.

DISCUSSION QUESTIONS FOR TODAY:

1. What has Exodus taught me?

2. Am I excited about my journey with Christ? Why, or why not?

SHARON WOOD'S BIOGRAPHY

I am a transplanted native of Southern California and am now living in the San Juan Islands off the coast of Washington. My husband, Dick and I have lived on Orcas Island since 1998. We have been married for 47 years and have been born again believers for over thirty years. Our immediate family consists of three grown children and two grandchildren. We are active members of the Orcas Island Community Church. Every step of my walk as a born again believer has been blessed by encountering and sitting under amazing pastors and lay teachers who have simply allowed the Holy Spirit to lead them in their teaching of the Bible.

Our church represents a combined congregation of no less than 41 different denominations. Our first ten years here on Orcas we were masterfully led by Pastor Dave Van Boven—through his and God's patient weaving of traditional and contemporary worship styles he created this uniquely intertwined fellowship of believers. Dick Staub has been our pastor for the last three years. He is a retired nationally syndicated Christian radio talk show host and author. His energy and enthusiasm have greatly expanded our knowledge of the Bible and our goal of becoming a church of service in our community. These years on Orcas Island have been a filling place for me of new wine in the Word of God.

Over the years I have always written my prayers as I have studied small portions of scripture each day. Journaling my prayers has kept me focused and free from distractions in my daily time with the Lord. Before retiring I worked with my pastor's wife, Karyn Johnson, at Calvary Chapel of Downey adapting materials and creating Bible studies for our weekly 250 member women's Bible study. With a BA degree in English and a life-time teaching credential from the state of California I was also blessed to fill a need in the satellite college campus at Downey for The School of the Word. For a semester I served as an English grammar teacher helping our curriculum be accredited by the state. It was my joy during that season of time to teach aspiring pastors to organize their thoughts for sermons and other written documents.

I am confident that all my wonderful experiences in life have been at the hand of God's leading. I am sure you as a Christian would find the same to be true of your life if you sat at this computer trying to explain who you are and what qualifies you to do what you love. I can honestly say that I did not sit down to write a devotional study for others. What began as a personal Bible study for me as we traveled, with a few adaptations, has become in this book a shared experience with others and even a group study if the format is followed that way. I have always believed that God speaks to me through His scripture. My prayer is that this book will be an encouragement that He wishes to speak to you too if you will be faithful to pursue Him daily.